Spain & Portugal by Rail

Spain & Portugal by Rail

Norman Renouf

BRADT PUBLICATIONS
THE GLOBE PEQUOT PRESS

First published in 1994 by Bradt Publications, 41 Nortoft Road, Chalfont St Peter, Bucks SL9 0LA, England and The Globe Pequot Press, Inc, 6 Business Park Rd, PO Box 833, Old Saybrook, Connecticut 06475-0833, USA.

British Library Cataloguing in Publication data
A catalogue record for this book is available from the British Library
ISBN 0 9469 83 60 7

Library of Congress Cataloging in Publication data
A catalogue record for this book is available from the Library of Congress
USISBN 1-56440-553-2

The author and publishers have made every effort to ensure the accuracy of the information in this book at the time of going to press. However, they cannot accept any responsibility for any loss, injury or inconvenience resulting from the use of information contained in this guide.

Maps by Patti Taylor
Cover photo: The Image Bank
Typeset from the author's disc by Patti Taylor, London NW10 1JR
Printed and bound in Great Britain by
The Guernsey Press Co. Ltd, Guernsey, Channel Islands

TABLE OF CONTENTS

For Kathy:

My absent friend who **ALWAYS** travels with me; everywhere.

INTRODUCTION

Hundreds of thousands of people travel through Spain and Portugal by train each year, most armed with a Eurail or Inter-rail pass, but with only the most basic knowledge of the cities they are to visit, and even less of the Spanish and Portuguese railway networks. It is for these travellers that this book is written.

Until now, few details of the Spanish railway network have been available outside Spain. Even there — apart from timetables and a plan of the network with some helpful hints — such information is not readily available. Recognising these facts, I had discussions with senior executives of Red Nacional de los Ferrocarriles Españoles — universally known as RENFE, the organisation that runs the Spanish railway — and they agreed to both sponsor and co-operate with me in the writing of a new, definitive guide in order to provide all the necessary information to travellers before they leave home. The routes mentioned are those run by the state railways, RENFE and CP, which are of particular interest to the tourist. They are by no means exhaustive, and the traveller will of necessity need to consult a current timetable.

Every large railway network has its own idiosyncrasies and RENFE is no exception. There is therefore a chapter detailing the important things a traveller needs to know about the system, together with information about the network and national and international services and trains, and a glossary of terms. Although much of this information is relevant to rail travel in both Spain and Portugal, those planning to visit Portugal will find information specific to the Portuguese railway network, Caminhos de Ferro Portugueses (CP), in Part Three, *Portugal*.

Each large city and town has its own section. With the interests of the Inter-rail or Eurail traveller in mind, only the most important cities have been covered, with a view to giving all the relevant information needed for those arriving in a city by train for a limited stay. Those that have been included, with the exception of Algeciras, the main ferry port for services to North Africa, all have places of exceptional historic or cultural interest. Information is broken down as follows:

The city

Basic facts about each city. For those cities with a long and complicated history the most important dates, and their respective events, are highlighted first.

Places of interest

Since some places of interest are more important than others, this section is usually sub-divided to help those on tight schedules:

Must see   Should not be missed under any circumstances.
By choice   Many of these places are certainly of interest but are of secondary importance.
Museums   Included here are all the museums not listed in the other categories.

Each place has the address, telephone number, days and hours of opening, entrance price and details of concessionary prices for students, etc, as well as a description of its historical background and what to expect to see. Inevitably, however, prices can only be a guide, and opening times may change, so try to remain flexible wherever possible.

A word of warning here! Many places are closed on Sunday afternoons and Mondays. Be careful to check your travelling schedules against the opening hours of places in the towns you are going to visit. Nothing is more frustrating than going out of your way to see something special and finding it closed for the day.

With the exception of most of the museums in Madrid and Barcelona, and a few other places so noted, I have personally visited all the places described in this guide. I am most grateful to Albert Padrol for his help in checking the Barcelona chapter.

Station/location/transport to city centre

This concentrates on the railway station(s), giving name, address, telephone number and location in the city, as well as the following information:

Layout   A diagram of the station showing the location of each facility.
Key   Details of each facility shown in the layout.
Train station to city centre Details methods of reaching the city centre, **by bus**, **on foot** or **by taxi**, etc. The format of this section is different for Madrid and Barcelona due to the number of stations involved.

Train services

This section details the types of trains (refer back to the RENFE and CP chapters for more details) that run on different routes from each city to other cities detailed in this guide. Approximate journey times are given, to the nearest quarter hour. The exact timetables are not given as these change three times a year.

The Metro

This section will appear in the Barcelona and Madrid chapters.

Accommodation

Accommodation has been carefully selected to meet everyone's requirements, and I have visited almost all establishments personally, though not necessarily the rooms. As many people will be travelling on limited budgets, the majority of the places listed are at the lower or middle end of the market, and have been chosen both for their price and location (but note that prices will almost certainly rise during the life of the guide). In Spain, minimum standards are set by central government, with a complex star rating system applicable to different types of accommodation. Generally, room prices do not include breakfast, and they are subject to 6% VAT.

For those who want places of a higher, and consistent standard I would recommend hotels in the *Grupo Husa* chain. These are located in Barcelona, Burgos, Cádiz, Córdoba, Madrid, Málaga (Mijas), Santiago de Compostela, Sevilla, Valencia and Zaragoza, as well as many other cities in Spain. Reservations can be made, and information obtained in Spain on the following toll free number: 900 10 12 25.

Ferry services

Many travellers will be taking the ferry from Algeciras to Ceuta, or from Málaga to Melilla, the Spanish protectorates in North Africa, or direct to Tangier from Algeciras. This section, in the chapters for Algeciras and Málaga, covers Trasmediterranea's services.

General information

This section gives details of other things and places which travellers might need to know about, eg: telephone codes and tourist information.

Portugal

Travellers visiting Lisbon and Porto will find chapters on Caminhos de Ferro Portugueses (CP), the state railway, and on Lisbon and Porto. Many thanks to Pilar Perila at the Portuguese National Tourist Office in London for her help.

Beware when changing travellers cheques in Portugal. Since summer 1993 the banks have imposed a minimum charge of 2,000$00 plus 0.9% tax on every transaction, no matter how small.

Getting there

Often people using this guide will be travelling to or from the UK and/or through France. This is more complicated than it appears and the final part, *Getting There*, has been compiled with the assistance of BR International, European Passenger Services (EPS), Hoverspeed, P&O European Ferries, Brittany Ferries, Rail Europe (Eurorail Pass), Stena Sealink Line and French Railways, representatives of the Société Nationale des Chemins de Fer Français (SNCF) in Great Britain and Ireland.

Part One

Spain

REGIONS AND PROVINCES
Introduction
Since Franco's death the political structure of Spain has evolved into one of a central government and seventeen autonomous regions *comunidades autónomas*. The latter have two levels of autonomy which are dependent, amongst other matters, upon population, economic power and historical implications.

The central government's principal responsibilities are those of international affairs, security and taxation, whilst the regions have control of most other matters including, for example, local policing.

Autonomous Regions and Provinces	Capital	Tel Code
ANDALUCÍA:	Sevilla	
Almería		951
Cádiz and Ceuta		956
Córdoba		957
Granada		958
Huelva		955
Jaén		953
Málaga and Melilla		95
Sevilla		95
ARAGÓN:	Zaragoza	
Huesca		974
Teruel		974
Zaragoza		976
ASTURIAS:	Oviedo	985
BALEARES:	Palma de Mallorca	971
CANARIAS:	Las Palmas	
Las Palmas		928
Santa Cruz de Tenerife		922
CANTABRIA:	Santander	942

Autonomous Regions and Provinces	Capital	Tel Code
CASTILLA-LA MANCHA:	Toledo	
Albacete		967
Ciudad Real		926
Cuenca		966
Guadalajara		911
Toledo		925
CASTILLA Y LEÓN:	León	
Ávila		918
Burgos		947
León		987
Palencia		988
Salamanca		923
Segovia		911
Soria		975
Valladolid		983
Zamora		988
CATALUÑA:	Barcelona	
Barcelona		93
Gerona		972
Lérida		973
Tarragona		977
COMUNIDAD VALENCIA:	Valencia	
Alicante		96
Castellón		964
Valencia		96
EXTREMADURA:	Mérida	
Badajoz		924
Cáceres		927
GALICIA:	La Coruña	
La Coruña		981
Lugo		982
Orense		988
Pontevedra		986
LA RIOJA:	Logroño	941

Autonomous Regions and Provinces	Capital	Tel Code
MADRID:	Madrid	91
MURCIA:	Murcia	968
NAVARRA:	Pamplona	948
PAÍS VASCO:	Vitoria	
Alava (Vitoria)		945
Guipúzoca (San Sebastián)	943	49
Vizcaya (Bilbao)		94

Note: Provincial capitals of the provinces are cities with the same name, except for País Vasco where they are shown in brackets.

THE LANGUAGES AND DIALECTS OF SPAIN

It will come as a surprise to many visitors that Spain is a multilingual country; in fact over 40% of the population live in regions that are bilingual. Under Franco regional languages were less than encouraged and *Castilian*, the Spanish foreigners are taught, was the official language. However, with the advent of the autonomous regions, cultural differences, including language, began to flourish. The most unusual of these is the Basque (*Euskara*) language, its frequent use of Xs and Zs making it almost unpronounceable for foreigners.

This can cause confusion for tourists as in some regions the local language can be almost dominant and is used for street names, etc. In others there is a mix and, for example, street and station signs can be in both languages. One of the most obvious examples is the word for street; in *Castilian* it is *Calle*, in *Catalan* it is *Carrer* and in the northwest of Spain, close to Portugal, *Rúa* is used.

To confuse matters even more there are the regional dialects of *Castilian*. Perhaps the most difficult of these, for foreigners, is found in Andalucía and is known as *Andaluz*. The most common variation in this is that all Ss, except at the beginning of a word, are dropped. For example *buenos días* becomes *bueno día*, *adiós* becomes *adió* and *agustín* becomes *agutín*.

In fact I have a house in a traditional mountain village in the remote *La Alpujarra* region of the province of Granada. Life there, especially for the older generation, has varied little for centuries and elderly people very rarely even leave the village. One of my neighbours, a little old lady, invariably comes by every morning with her goat and likes to have a conversation. Unfortunately, this becomes very one way as her *Andaluz* accent is so strong that, in four years, I have not understood one word she has said!

RED NACIONAL DE LOS FERROCARRILES ESPAÑOLES (RENFE)

The Network and Services

RENFE has an extensive network throughout Spain that, with the principal exceptions of coastal regions in the north (Atlantic side) and the far south, has direct connections between most major cities. There are several junctions, otherwise rather obscure places, but located at strategic points in the network, of which travellers should be aware, as there may be long stops whilst waiting for ongoing connections, or for trains to be joined together, or you may have to change trains. The most important, in alphabetical order, are Bobadilla, Espeluy, Medina del Campo, Monforte and Venta de Baños. Of these, most travellers will encounter Bobadilla as it connects Algeciras, Cádiz, Córdoba, Granada, Málaga and Sevilla. My first experience of Bobadilla was many years ago, when taking a train from Sevilla to Algeciras; when I got off at the end I found I was in Granada! Not an altogether unpleasant experience, but much better when planned.

The rationale behind the services is rather complicated, but nevertheless logical, and is as follows:

Núcleo de Madrid

These are services originating from, and returning to, Madrid and whose destinations are every other important city in the country (see diagram A).

Núcleo de Barcelona

These are services originating from, and returning to, Barcelona and whose destinations are many other important cities throughout the country (see diagram B).

Núcleo de País Vasco

These are services originating from, and returning to, the País Vasco region and whose destinations are, with the exception of Valencia, Alicante and Andalucía, cities in the north of the country (see diagram C).

Líneas del Grupos

These are services between cities and regions that are grouped geographically; in 1992 there were three of these. Diagram D completes the network, with the exception of Cercanías, and shows that the *líneas del grupos* connect cities already served by the above *Núcleos*, as well as many others.

Cercanías
These are local trains that operate only from the following stations or areas: Asturias, Barcelona, Bilbao, Cádiz, Madrid, Málaga, Murcia, San Sebastián, Santander, Sevilla and Valencia.

The Trains
There are many different train types with a variety of facilities and different names. As with the services there is a logic to it and the first thing to understand is that the trains fall within the following four categories:

Alta Velocidad Española — AVE
These very high speed trains, inaugurated in April 1992, run on specially built track between Madrid, Ciudad Real, Puertollano, Córdoba and Sevilla, with the minimum journey time being only 2½ hours between Madrid and Sevilla.

Trains have their own system of classification and services throughout the day are divided into four types, but only the following three will be of interest to most travellers. *Tren punta* run at times of the day when most people are likely to be travelling, *Tren valle* run at times of the day when fewest people are likely to be travelling, and *Tren Llano* run at times between the two.

There are three different classes: *Turista*, *Preferente* and *Club*, in ascending order, and the pricing schedule is such that the more popular the train classification, the higher the fare. The facilities on these trains are excellent; for all classes there is a bar/cafeteria, telephone, drinks machine, seats for babies and games, as well as audio/visual entertainment. In *Preferente* and *Club*, food is served to your seat, with a free drink in *Club*, and free daily newspapers are also distributed.

Largo Recorrido (Long-distance) Trains
These trains are further sub-divided depending upon whether they run during the day or at night.

There are three types of daytime trains (*diurnos*)
Talgo (red and white trains) and *Talgo pendular* (blue and white trains) These offer the highest level of service on the longest, and

most important, of the daytime routes. They have first and second class seats, restaurant and cafeteria, air-conditioning, audio/visual entertainment, and stewardesses and free daily newspapers in first class. It is planned that they leave either in the morning and early afternoon, and sometimes both. Although faster than the *diurnos* they are not, with the exception of those using the new AVE tracks, actually that fast.

Diurnos These also operate on the longest of the daytime routes and it is planned so that they leave in the morning and arrive at their destination in the evening. They are much slower than the *talgos*, offer a lower level of service and the trains are not so comfortable.

InterCity — IC These are different from the other trains. They are very fast, generally only have three coaches — one first and two second class — and do not operate on that many routes. The level of service is also high: cafeteria/bar, air-conditioning and audio/visual entertainment in all classes with stewardesses and free daily newspapers in first class.

There are three types of night trains (*nocturnos*):

Tren-Hotel These are of the very highest standard and operate solely within Spain on the most important routes. The *gran clase* cabins have their own individual telephones, toilets, washbasins and showers with towels, soap and shampoo included. You even get a morning call allowing you time to shower and breakfast before reaching your destination. There are also single, double and four-bed compartments but the latter are 'single-sex' except when booked by a family group. These also have a restaurant and a bar.

Talgo camas These are the same as the *tren-hotel* but without the *gran clase* facilities and they operate on more routes.

Estrellas Literally 'Stars', these are the night-time equivalent of the *diurnos*, offering beds (first and second class), couchettes (second class only) and regular seating. There are few facilities, generally only a restaurant, cafeteria or bar — depending upon departure time. Also they are very slow; the departure time is often early evening and the planned arrival is usually around 0800 the next day.

Regional Trains

There are three types of these and their rationale is to connect, over medium distances, capitals or urban centres of administrative, commercial or academic importance.

Regional expres These have fewer stops, first and second class seating, are air-conditioned and usually have an automatic drinks machine.

Regional These generally only have second-class seating, stop at more stations, are often planned to have connections with other trains and are essential transport between small and medium size towns.

Regional lince These run only at weekends to cater for the extra traffic expected on certain routes.

Cercanías — Local trains

These are often coloured red and white, are second class only and have no facilities. They only operate from the cities already previously detailed earlier in the chapter. The identification for these is a *C* leaning at an angle.

International Services and Trains

There are not many of these and each has its own individual name. They are listed below by their station of departure in Spain, in alphabetical order.

Barcelona/Zurich and Milan/Barcelona *Pau Casals*

This is a *tren-hotel* and operates one service daily in each direction. It offers *gran clase* single and double compartments, normal class single and double compartments and *turista* class compartments for four people. The facilities include video in *gran clase*, air-conditioning, restaurant and cafeteria and newspapers and magazines.

Barcelona/Paris/Barcelona *Joan Miró*

A *tren-hotel* with all the same facilities as the *Pau Casals*.

Barcelona/Geneva/Barcelona *Catalán Talgo*

A daytime *talgo* that operates one service daily in each direction. It has first and second class seats, a restaurant and cafeteria/bar.

Lisbon/Paris/Lisbon *Surexpreso*

This is an *estrella* with one service daily in each direction and the journey time is very long. It leaves Lisbon early in the afternoon and arrives in Paris the *next* evening. It has single, double and four bed compartments, couchettes in second class, and first and second class seating. The route takes it across northwest Spain, passing through Salamanca, Valladolid, Burgos, San Sebastián and Irún.

Madrid/Paris/Madrid *Francisco de Goya*

A *tren-hotel* with all the same facilities as the *Pau Casals* that departs from Barcelona.

Madrid/Paris/Madrid *Puerta del Sol*

This is an *estrella* with one service daily in each direction, but a transfer at the border is needed by those in the first and second class seats. That does not apply, however, to those in the second class couchettes. There is also a cafeteria/bar on this train.

Madrid/Lisbon/Madrid *Luís de Camões*

This is a daytime *talgo* with one service daily in each direction and it has first and second class seats and a cafeteria. This operates via Cáceres and Valencia Alcántara, not Badajoz.

Madrid/Lisbon/Madrid *Lusitania*

This is an *estrella* with one service daily in each direction. It has single, double and four bed compartments, couchettes in second class, and first and second class seating. There is also a restaurant and cafeteria. It also operates via Cáceres and Valencia Alcántara.

Note — **Inter Rail:**
This pass is only valid for second class travel on the following trains: *Joan Miró*, *Pau Casals*, *Francisco de Goya* and *Luís de Camões*.

Glossary

Many of the terms used by RENFE will be unfamiliar to most travellers and the most frequently used ones are explained here:
Anden(es) This can be confused with *Vía*. *Anden* is the word for the whole of the platform. *Vía* is the side of the platform corresponding to the track number. Most often it is announced a train will leave from *Vía 1*, for example. Sometimes, though, it will be announced as *Anden 1, Vía 1*.
Aseo(s) Another word for toilet(s)
Asistencia al viajero/Atención al cliente An assistance office for travellers
Ayuda del joven A help office for young people
Cantina Another word for bar/cafeteria
Carritos portaequipajes Luggage trolleys. Usually operated by a 100 peseta coin that is returned when you return the trolley, but

sometimes free.

Circulación This office controls the circulation of the trains around the network. It is not a general assistance office.

Comisaría Police station

Consigna A manually operated left luggage office

Consigna automática An automatic left luggage locker. There is a variety of these. Some are cash operated but most are operated by tokens that have to be purchased from the ticket or information office. The fee is usually per 24 hours but beware, sometimes this actually only means for a period between 0000 and 2400 hours. Thus if you leave luggage overnight you incur an extra payment.

Estanco A kiosk that sells tobacco, etc

Información An office that gives timetables, information, etc

Jefe de estación/Jefe de terminal The stationmaster's office

Paseo inferior Underpass to other platforms

Sala de espera Waiting room

Servicios Another word for toilets

Vía See *Anden(es)*

Signo

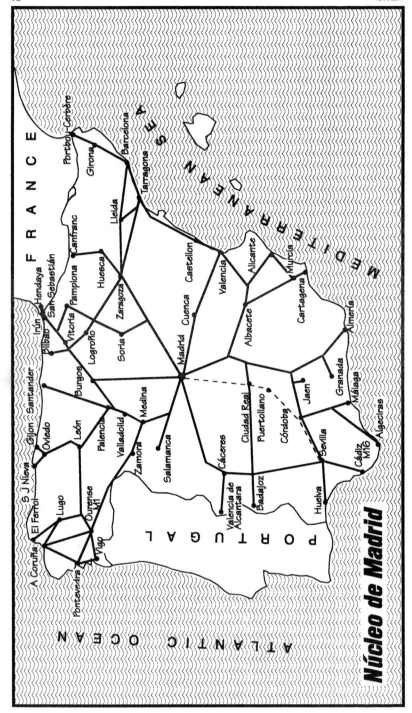

Núcleo de Madrid

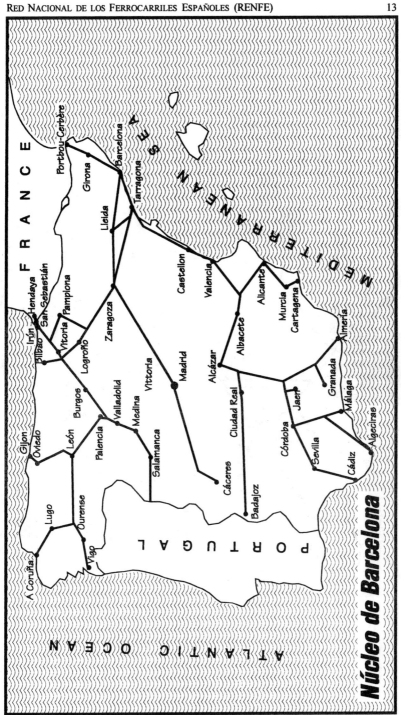

Núcleo de Barcelona

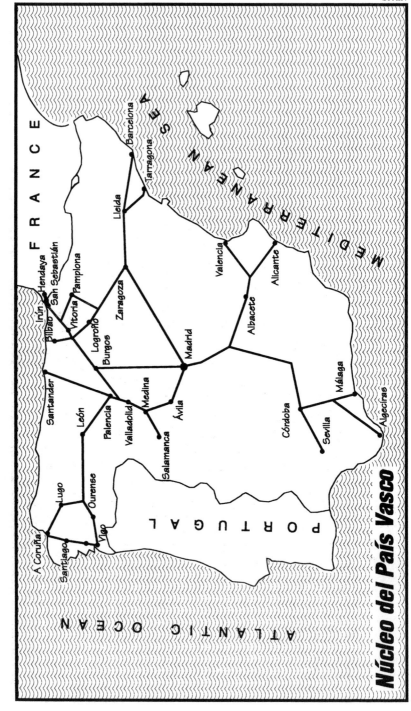

Núcleo del País Vasco

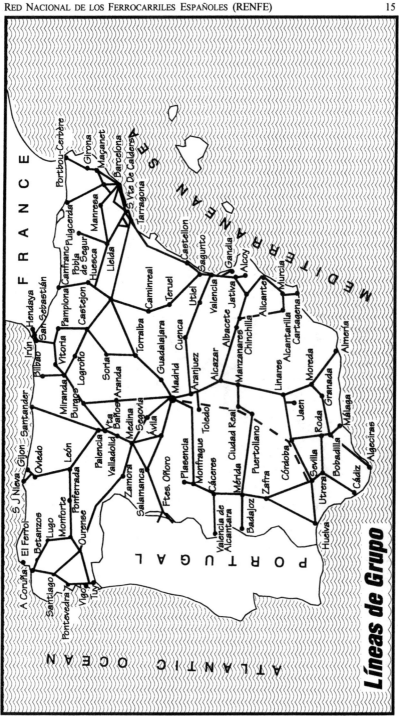

Líneas de Grupo

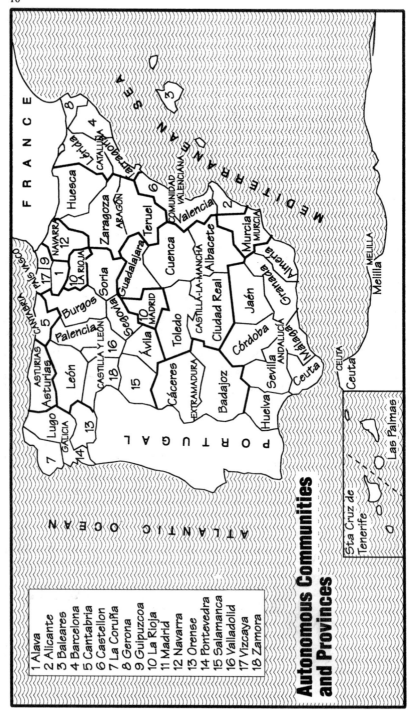

Autonomous Communities and Provinces

1 Alava
2 Alicante
3 Baleares
4 Barcelona
5 Cantabria
6 Castellon
7 La Coruña
8 Gerona
9 Guipuzcoa
10 La Rioja
11 Madrid
12 Navarra
13 Orense
14 Pontevedra
15 Salamanca
16 Valladolid
17 Vizcaya
18 Zamora

Spain: Cities and Towns

ALGECIRAS

The city

Algeciras has a strategic position on the Strait of Gibraltar — Africa is just 14km (9 miles) away — and an ancient history. Colonised by the Phoenicians and Romans, it was an important maritime centre during the years of Moorish domination which ended when it was reconquered in 1344 by Alfonso XI.

Today few signs of those times remain and, with a population of nearly 100,000, Algeciras is the principal port in Andalucía and home to a thriving fishing industry. What makes it important to most people though is that it is the gateway to Africa via the ferry services to Ceuta, a freeport and one of the two Spanish enclaves on the coast of North Africa (the other is Melilla) and Tangier. As such it is a very cosmopolitan city and the mix of peoples and cultures often surprises the first-time visitor.

Places of interest

There is really nothing in this city that cannot be missed. If there is time between ferry services, or trains, a short walk taking in the attractive Plaza Alta, the Iglesia de Nuestra Señora de la Palma — in the same square — and the unusually shaped *mercado* (market) in the Plaza Palma encompasses most of the places of interest. It is always interesting, though, to walk along the stretch of the Avenida Virgen del Carmen closest to the port entrance and watch the kaleidoscopic mix of people.

Station/location/transport to city centre

RENFE, Estación Renfe; tel: 66 36 46. Located just a short walk from the port, this is an unusually shaped and attractive whitewashed building.

Layout

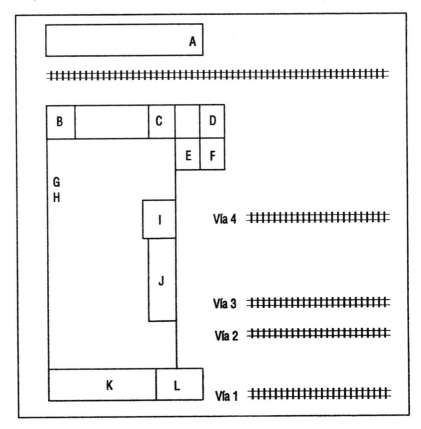

Key

A: *Consigna Automática*, open daily 0700-2300; cost 300 ptas for every 24 hours with a maximum of 15 days

B: *Kiosco* for newspapers, magazines, open 0730-2330

C: *Oficina Nacional de Imigración* An unusual office for a railway station

D: *Circulación*

E: *Información*, open 0700-2300

F: *Jefe de Estación*

G: *Servicios* — downstairs

H: *Asistencia al Viajero*

I: *Viajes Wasteels.* A travel agent which includes a *cambio* office, open Monday to Friday 0700-2200; Saturday 0700-1400

J: Ticket office

K: Cafeteria/bar, open 0645-2300

L: Restaurant, open 1400-1530, 2000-2200.

Train station to port/city centre

On foot Leave the station and take the road directly ahead. This, more or less, follows the now disused railway line straight to the port, about five minutes away. The town centre is some distance from the port but most travellers will only be interested in the area nearby where most of the accommodation is located.

Train services
To Madrid by
Estrella: via Córdoba 5¼; Madrid 12.

To Portbou/France by
Estrella: via Zaragoza 14½; Portbou 22½.

To Irún/France by
Estrella: via Madrid 10½; Pamplona 17¼; Irún 20.

To Córdoba, Granada, Málaga and Sevilla by
Regional: The first part of these trips is to Bobadilla, which takes 3 hours, where there will be a wait for a connection to Córdoba which is 2 hours more, Granada which is 2¼ more, Málaga 1½ more, and Sevilla 2¼ more. These are the fastest times; some trains are much slower, and sometimes the wait in Bobadilla can be lengthy.

Accommodation
For a town of this size there are numerous places to stay. As most are more or less of the same standard — not that good — I shall not detail them individually. They are generally located in the side streets in the area between the old railway line, the *mercado* (city market) and the port. Be aware that besides doubling as the red-light district the area directly around the *mercado* becomes noisy very early in the morning. My choice, in this area, is the Pensión Nuestra Señora del Carmen, Plaza Nuestra Señora de la Palma 12; tel: 63 24 81. For those wanting a more interesting, and upmarket, style the lovely old-fashioned Hotel Anglo Hispaño, Avenida Villanueva 7; tel: 66 01 00 — on the road between the station and the port — is the place to stay. A single is 4,500 ptas, double 6,000 ptas.

Ferry services

The largest of the companies operating services from here is Trasmediterranea, Recinto del Puerto, tel: 66 52 00, fax: 66 52 06. Tickets, which can be used on any service, can be purchased directly from the offices at the port or from any authorised travel agents, of which there are many both throughout the town and in the port itself. Many of these travel agents also double as money changers and rates can vary, so shop around. Be aware when purchasing Moroccan dirhams that you will not be able to change them back outside Morocco, so only buy what you need. This is not as big a problem as it might be because traders in Morocco will take any currency that you happen to have — at an exchange rate in their favour, of course.

Algeciras — Ceuta By ferry this takes about 1½ hours; by hydrofoil about 30 minutes, costing somewhat more.

Algeciras — Tangier By ferry this takes about 2½ hours.

General information
Car hire
Avis, Avenida Villanueva; tel: 60 24 87.

Consulate office
United Kingdom, Fzas Armadas, 11; tel: 66 16 00.

Fiestas
Annual *feria* between June 23 and July 3.

Telephone code
for Cádiz province is (956).

Tourist office
Oficina de Información de Turismo, Juan de la Cierva; tel: 57 26 36. Open Monday to Friday 0900-1400; Saturday 1000-1300. This strange glass building is on the street between the station and port, but much closer to the latter.

ÁVILA
The city

Ávila is located 122km (76 miles) northwest of Madrid on the plateau or *meseta* and, at an elevation of 1,128m (3,700ft), is the highest city in Spain. It has Celtic-iberian origins and was originally Christianised in the 1st century and reconquered from the Moors by Alfonso VI in 1085. It was then repopulated by Christian Knights who began work on what is Ávila's most dominant physical feature: Las Murallas — The Walls. These are absolutely splendid and, over the centuries, noblemen were given responsibility for defending their own particular sections. This led to the building of elegant, fortified, mansions either close to or even into the walls and many still exist today.

Another equally dominant, although in this case spiritual, aspect to Ávila is Santa Teresa. Her presence can be seen everywhere here, where she was born in 1515, in the shape of churches, convents and statues; even the main square is named after her. Helped by the advances of the Reformation, this Catholic visionary, an advocate of Carmelite thought, founded 17 convents throughout Spain, wrote prolifically and was canonised on March 12 1622.

Ávila became less important in the 16th century as the court of Carlos V in Toledo had attracted many of the noblemen, and the decline continued after the expulsion of the Muslims in the early 1600s when the population dropped dramatically.

Today with a population of about 38,000 it is the provincial capital and, unlike some places, the demands of tourism have not been allowed to spoil its natural charms.

Places of interest
Must see

Las Murallas (The Walls) The most dominant physical feature of the city and the best preserved in Spain, if not the world. In the shape of a rectangle, these heavily fortified walls have a perimeter measuring 2,557m. The average height is 12m, they are 3m thick and built into them are 90 towers and nine gateways. Construction was begun in the latter part of the 11th century, after the reconquest, and was supervised by Count Don Ramón de Borgona, the son-in-law of King Alfonso IV, although there have been later modifications — notably in the 14th century.

The most unusual feature is the prominent Cimorro, fortified

cathedral head, which is built into the narrow side of the rectangle
that is closest to the railway station. Just down from there, at the
end of the Plaza de Santa Teresa, is the important Puerta de
Alcázar. Located in the oldest part of the walls, the small gateway,
with the coat of arms of Ferdinand and Isabella above it, is guarded
by two huge towers. Just inside this gate, nestling in the corner of
the walls, is a charming little garden with a stone boar that
symbolises past cultures.

From the Puerta de Alcázar follow the outside of the walls to the
corner and then turn right on to the Paseo del Rastro, a popular
place for Ávilans to stroll. This runs along and directly under the
walls, passing on its way another gateway — the Puerta de Santa
Teresa. From this *paseo* there are views south over the town spread
out below and, in the distance, across the Ambles Valley to the
peaks — over 1,600m high and often snow covered in winter — of
the Sierra de Ávila. The walls then begin to slope downwards quite
steeply to the other end of the rectangle, and it is not possible to
follow their exact path. From the bottom of the walls take a small
diversion and walk up to a very strange monument, the Cuatro
Postes. This consists of four columns, all connected by cornices,
with a central stone cross. Besides its religious significance this spot
also offers what is undoubtedly the best view of Ávila and the walls.
It is well worth taking a taxi here at night as the walls take on a
totally different perspective when they are illuminated.

The walk back along the other long side of the rectangle is not
particularly pleasant, and is also steep, but the view of the walls
from the road is compensation for that. Turn the corner on the way
back to the cathedral, and the sights are much more varied. The
impressive Basilica San Vicente is just across the road and,
following the walls, there is the Puerta San Vicente and, at the end
of the park bearing the same name, and just before the Puerta del
Peso de la Harnia, are the Casas de Misericordia and de las
Carnicerías. At one time there were many houses incorporated into
the walls and these are the most historic of those remaining.

Inside the Walls This is a most intriguing area that is full of
surprises; churches, palaces, interesting houses and squares grace
these narrow old streets. Some of these buildings have a rather run-
down look and this, combined with few of the tourist traps that have
spoilt other places, only add to the charm. All the places that are of
any interest are located in the top half of the rectangle, that closest

to the cathedral, but unfortunately many of them are not open to the public on a regular basis. Those that are open are detailed in the regular manner and the most important of the others are described here in alphabetical order.

Catedral y Museo Catedral (Cathedral and Cathedral Museum), Plaza de la Catedral; tel: 21 16 41. Open summer daily 1000-1330, 1500-1900; winter Monday to Saturday 1000-1330, 1500-1730, Sunday and holidays 1100-1330, 1500-1730. Entrance: cathedral free, museum 100 ptas. Constructed between the 12th and 14th centuries, and considered by some to be the first Gothic cathedral in Spain, this had the dual purpose of church and fortress. The most noticeable feature of the latter is the Cimorro, the fortified cathedral head built into, and protruding from, the walls between the Puertas del Peso de la Harina and de Alcázar. On the exterior, the Puerta de los Apostoles (Door of the Apostles) at the northern end, dating from the 14th century, is most important. This was in the main façade until moved by Juan Guas in the 15th century when he redesigned the main entrance. Inside, the high altar, retrochoir and choir are particularly important and there are numerous other works of art. There are also many sepulchres of prominent people, both clerical and civil, who wanted their remains to rest within the Cathedral. The most important is that of a 15th century bishop of Ávila, Don Alonso de Madrigal, El Tostado, and this dates from the early 16th century.

Cathedral museums vary considerably in size and the importance of their exhibits. The one here, spread over several rooms with contents that are varied, interesting and important, should not be missed. Besides the normal type of paintings, sculptures, crucifixes and other religious memorabilia on display there is an El Greco portrait of Don García Ibañez, huge books of music with beautifully designed covers and, in the last room, the most precious object in the museum. This is a silver monstrance 1.7m tall (5ft 8in) made by Juan de Arfe in the 16th century, one of many made by the same craftsman. Others are on display in Córdoba, Toledo and Valladolid.

Among all these exhibits, that which attracted me most is a carved wooden sculpture of Christ on the Cross; its simplicity, when compared with the other more elaborate exhibits, made it particularly pleasing.

Convento de Santa Teresa (Convent of Santa Teresa), Plaza de la Santa; tel: 21 10 30. Open daily 0800-1300, 1530-2100. Entrance: free. Construction began on this Carmelitas Descalzas convent in 1635 and it is located on the site of the birthplace of Santa Teresa. There are many coats of arms on the façade, and inside, besides being very elaborate, there are numerous memorabilia and images of the saint as well as, reputedly, the exact place of her birth.

Capilla de Mosen Rubi (Mosen Rubi Chapel), Plaza de Mosen Rubi. This church, built in the 16th century, has an unusual design and there are many coats of arms embellishing the outside.

Casa de los Velada (Velada House), Plaza de la Catedral. Noticeable for its tower and coats of arms, this house, immediately across from the cathedral, belonged to Gomez Dávila and various monarchs have been entertained here. There is a three storey inside patio, and beamed ceilings with carvings, that provide elegant surroundings for the restaurant now located here.

Palacios de los Aguila and Verdugo (Aguila and Verdugo Palaces), Calle de Lope Nuñez. These are two excellent examples of noblemen's houses dating from the late 15th and early 16th centuries. Buildings like these, as well as being architecturally interesting, were also fortified as the owners had responsibility for defending their sections of the walls.

Palacio de los Polentinos (Polentinos Palace), Calle de Vallespin. This house was constructed in the early 16th century and is one of the most attractive in the city. The doorway is particularly ornate as it is decorated with coats of arms, shields, eagles and other motifs. Today it is a military academy and that accounts for the presence of heavily armed soldiers guarding the entrances.

Palacio de los Dávila (Davila Palace) This collection of four buildings is located between the Plazas Pedro Dávila, del Rastro and the walls by the Puerto del Rastro. These are exceptionally attractive and, dating from the 13th to 15th centuries, reflect a combination of Romanesque, Gothic, Mudejar and Renaissance styles. Today part of the buildings belong to the Episcopal Palace.

Palacio del Rey Niño (Palace of the Boy King), Plaza de la Catedral. Located just across from the cathedral, parts of this house date back to the 13th century and the name derives from the fact that King Alfonso XI grew up here. It was later used for centuries as the residence of the bishops — note the prominent bishop's coat of arms — and today it is the public library.

Palacio de Valderrabanos (Valderrabanos Palace) Today it is a very discreet and attractive four-star Best Western hotel. See *Accommodation*.

Plaza de la Victoria (Victoria Square) This is a fine example of a typical central square with the town hall (*ayuntamiento*) at one end and the Iglesia de San Juan, where Santa Teresa was baptised in April 1515, at the other. It is also known as the Plaza of the Little Market after the traditional market that is held every Friday morning.

Note: The next four places are grouped together around the Puerta and Convento de Santa Teresa.

Casas de Superunda and de los Almarza (Superunda and Almarza Houses) These two houses, standing side by side, are excellent examples of 16th century Renaissance architecture.

Palacio de los Nuñez Vela (Nuñez Vela Palace) This Renaissance palace was constructed by Blasco Nuñez de Vela, who became Viceroy of Peru, in the 16th century. It is quite large, has an elegant two storey patio, and the door and some windows are guarded by columns decorated with the family coat of arms. Today it is used as the Law Courts.

Torreón de los Guzmanes (The Guzman Tower) Built in the 16th century this tower has viewing areas on every corner and, more unusually, an overhanging battlement that protects the main doorway. There are coats of arms of each family that has owned it on the outside walls.

Outside the Walls Besides those detailed below there are other churches and convents, spread throughout the city, that are not generally open to the public. There is one place, though, that should not be missed and that is the Plaza de Italia and Plaza de Nalvillos. This double plaza is particularly charming and three interesting buildings are located here. One, the Casa de los Deanes in the Plaza de Nalvillos is described under **Museums** as it houses the Museo Provincial de Ávila. Santo Tome El Viejo, positioned between the plazas, is a church built in the 12th century but significantly altered in the 16th, while at the end of the Plaza de Italia is the 16th century Renaissance Palacio de los Serrano with the family coat of arms over the door.

Basílica de San Vicente   (St Vincent's Basilica),   Calle San Vicente. Open daily summer 1000-1300, 1600-1800; winter 1000-1330, 1600-1900. Entrance: 25 ptas. (Located just outside the walls, close to the cathedral, this was closed for restoration when I visited and therefore these details may change when it reopens.) Originally built as a Romanesque church in the early 12th century, this is dedicated to the child martyrs Saints Vicente, Sabina and Cristeta (brother and sisters), who reputedly died at the location. There have, however, been several restorations and it was not finally completed until the middle of the 14th century. One of the most important features of this church is the main doorway, considered to be one of the finest in Spain. There is also the Sepulchre de los Niños Santos (Child Saints) that itself is church shaped and covered by a very ornate decorated and tiled roof that is supported by four columns.

Monasterio de la Encarnación   (Monastery of the Incarnation), Paseo de la Encarnación; tel: 21 12 12. Open daily summer 0930-1300, 1600-1900; winter 0930-1330, 1530-1800. Entrance: 60 ptas. (This monastery is located some distance, and a rather awkward walk, outside the walls to the north. However, to compensate, it is a good place to view those walls that tower above you in the distance. By bus take the U, Green Line, fare 60 ptas, from the Plaza de Santa Teresa.) This is where Santa Teresa spent nearly 30 years of her life during which she developed her ideas of the Carmelite Reform and planned her journeys around Spain to found new monasteries. Construction began in 1513 and, coincidentally, the church was inaugurated and Teresa de Ahumada was baptised on the same day in April 1515. Santa Teresa entered the monastery in 1536 and spent 27 years as a nun and a further three as the prioress. There is little ornateness here as it was designed for those leading a monastic life. There are, though, numerous reminders of Santa Teresa, including the cell-like rooms where she lived.

Plaza de Santa Teresa (Saint Teresa Square) Located just outside the walls, and dominated by the impressive Alcázar gateway at one end and the church of San Pedro — a national monument — at the other, this is the centre of the city as far as citizen's activity is concerned. The dignified façade on the northern side, with shops, restaurants and bars in the porticos, faces a rectangular, sanded plaza with the inevitable statue of Santa Teresa at the eastern end. This plaza, which has witnessed many events over the centuries from markets to tournaments and even executions, is now the social centre of the city. Every evening and at lunchtime on weekends, especially Sundays, it seems everybody in Ávila heads for this plaza. All the bars and restaurants are full and children play in the square, creating a charming, harmonious ambience — even judged by Spanish standards.

Real Monasterio de Santo Tomás y Museo de Arte Oriental (Royal Monastery of Saint Thomas and Oriental Art Museum), Plaza de Granada; tel: 22 04 00. Open daily summer 1000-1300, 1600-1800; winter 1000-1300, 1600-1900. Entrance: Monastery and Oriental Art Museum, both 50 ptas. (By bus take the number 3, Blue line, fare 60 ptas. This has a 'circular' route so although it is not direct it offers a good chance to see the city, whichever way you go.) Although located a long way from the old town, down a steep hill, this historic complex of church, monastery and — seemingly out of place — the Oriental Art Museum should definitely not be missed. Construction of this very attractive Gothic monument was begun in 1482 and, since then, it has been managed by the Dominican Order. It was the seat of the university and was used by Isabella and Ferdinand as a summer residence. The church is particularly impressive with the sepulchre of Prince Don Juan — the oldest son of the Catholic monarchs and heir to the throne who died aged 19 — dominating the centre. As a contrast the three connected cloisters of the monastery, although rather run down, are charming and dignified. The rooms of the Royal Palace are located around the last, Kings, Cloister.

The entrance to the Oriental Art Museum, opened in 1964, is in the corner of the Kings Cloister. There are few such museums in

Spain and the exhibits have been collected, over centuries, by Dominican missionaries in the Far East.

Museums

Museo Provincial de Ávila (Provincial Museum of Ávila), Plaza Nalvillos, 3; tel: 21 10 03. Open Tuesday to Saturday 1030-1400, 1700-2000; Sunday 1030-1400. Closed Monday, holidays and alternate weekends. Entrance: 200 ptas; Spanish citizens, foreign residents and EC citizens (under 21), free on presentation of passport. This has an interesting location: a delightful double plaza, Nalvillos and de Italia, with the 12th century Santo Tome el Viejo its neighbour. The museum is housed in a typical 16th century Castilian mansion, the Casa de los Deanes, which, as the name implies, was the residence of the deans of the nearby cathedral. It houses a wide range of exhibits divided into three categories, archaeology, popular and fine arts, which are displayed in nine rooms on two floors.

Museo Teresiano (Saint Teresa's Museum), Convento de San José (Las Madres) Calle de las Madres. Open daily summer 1000-1330, 1600-1900; winter 1000-1330, 1600-1800. Entrance: 30 ptas. Located next to the Convento de San José, the first of many founded by Santa Teresa, which was inaugurated in August 1562. This is a very strangely designed museum that houses relics and memorabilia of the saint. They range from her coffin, and other personal items, to letters, books, art and even an 'authentic' replica of her cell. These are displayed in a series of rooms, around the walls, protected by both glass and bars.

Station/location/transport to city centre

RENFE, Avenida de José Antonio; tel: 22 07 81. This station is located on the outskirts of the city, some distance from the walls and old town at an elevation of 1,132.9m.

Key

A: *Consigna Automática*, open 24 hours, 200 ptas a day
B: *Jefe de estación*
C: *Jefe de circulación*
D: Underpass to other platforms
E: *Carritos portaequipajes*

F: *Librería Ferrocarriles*, news-papers, magazines, etc, open daily 0830-1400, 1600-2030
G: *Tabacalera*, cigarettes, tobacco, etc, open daily 0845-1400, 1630-2030

Layout

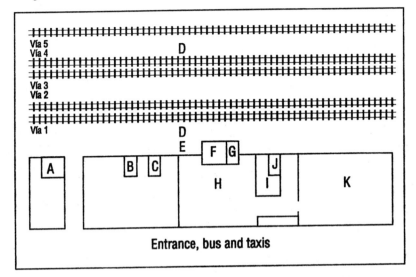

H: Booking hall
I: Ticket office and *Información*
J: *Servicios*

K: Cafeteria and restaurant, open daily 0530-0200

Train station to city centre

By bus Line 1, Red, Plaza Victoria — Hospital NS Sonsoles, direction Plaza Victoria to the last stop. Schedule: Monday to Friday 0815-1930 every 15 minutes, 1930-2230 every 30 minutes; Saturday 0745-1345 every 30 minutes, 1345-1930 every 15 minutes, 1930-2230 every 30 minutes; Sundays and holidays 0930-2230 every 30 minutes. Fare 60 ptas.

On foot Go straight out of the station and follow Avenida José Antonio to the Convento Santa Ana, then take the Calles de Isaac Peral and Duque de Alba to the Plaza de Santa Teresa de Jesús. The walls are directly ahead and the cathedral is just around the corner, to the right. Allow at least 15 minutes.

By taxi This costs about 250 ptas and takes about five minutes.

Train services
To Madrid by

	Regional/Regional Expres	*InterCity*	*Estrella*
Madrid	1¾	1½	2

To Irún/France by

	InterCity	Estrella
Valladolid	1	
Burgos	2¼	
Irún	5½	8

To Burgos by

	Regional/Regional Expres
Valladolid	1¼
Burgos	2½

To León by

	Regional Expres	Talgo Pendular
Medina del Campo	¾	¾
Valladolid	1¼	1¼
León	3¼	2¾

To Salamanca by
Regional: 1¾

To Santiago de Compostela by
Estrella: 8¼

Accommodation
There are not many places to stay in Ávila, but detailed here is a selection of the less expensive. With this in mind it may be better to call ahead and make a reservation, at any time of the year.

Close to the station
** **HR San Antonio** Avenida San Antonio, 27; tel: 22 76 89. Single 2,800 ptas, without bath 2,500; double 4,000 ptas, without bath 3,500 ptas. Located in a modern building; rather small rooms. The two-fork restaurant, El Olimpo, is modern but with a very classical style.
Fonda San Francisco Travesia de José Antonio, 2; tel: 22 02 98. Single 1,300 ptas; double 2,300 ptas. On the second floor of an old building that has, unusually, a very pleasant garden. Plain and basic but close to the station.

Just outside the walls
* **Hotel Jardín** San Segundo, 38; tel: 21 10 74. Single 2,000 ptas, without bath 1,800 ptas; double 3,600 ptas, without bath 3,100 ptas. Rather old-fashioned with a small garden in the front that presumably gives it its name.

Located just outside the walls and across from the cathedral.
Fonda Valverde Estrada, 11; tel: 21 19 70. Single 700 ptas; double 1,400 ptas. Small and very basic. No baths in rooms. In a side street off the Plaza de Santa Teresa de Jesús.

Inside the walls
**** **Hotel Palacio Valderrabanos** Plaza de la Catedral, 9; tel: 21 10 23; fax: 25 16 91. This Best Western hotel has three seasons: low January 1 to February 29 and November 1 to December 31; medium March 1 to June 30; high July 1 to October 31. Single low 9,243 ptas, medium 10,176 ptas, high 11,108 ptas; double low 12,190 ptas, medium 13,356 ptas, high 14,522 ptas. These rates include breakfast. The hotel, inside the walls and just behind the cathedral, is located in the beautiful 16th century Palacio de Valderrabanos (Valderrabanos Palace). It once belonged to the chief magistrate of Jerez, Gonzalo Dávila, who played an important role during the conquest of Gibraltar in 1462. The main doorway is particularly impressive and contains Davila's coat of arms. There are 73 rooms and each has a private bath/shower, radio, satellite colour TV, piped music, air-conditioning and mini-bar.
** **HR Continental** Plaza de la Catedral, 6; tel: 21 15 02. Single (without bath only) 1,575 ptas; double 2,900 ptas, without bath 2,250 ptas. Old-fashioned and a little run down, but interesting. Directly opposite the cathedral and next door to the tourist office.
* **Hostal Las Cancelas** Cruz Vieja, 6; tel: 22 22 49. Single 1,400 ptas; double 2,600 ptas. In a small lane close to the cathedral. Much character and an interesting restaurant. No baths in rooms; reservations particularly recommended.

General information
Car hire
Avis, Avenida de Madrid, 2. Estación de autobuses; tel: 25 06 69.

Fiestas
Easter week *(Semana Santa)*; summer *fiesta* second or third week of July and Santa Teresa October 8-15.

Hospital
Hospital Provincial; tel: 22 16 50.

Police
Comisaría, Avenida José Antonio; tel: 091.

Telephone code
for Ávila province is (918).

Public telephones
Plaza de la Catedral. Open Monday to Friday 0900-1400, 1700-2200. Closed Saturday, Sunday and holidays.

Tourist office
Oficina de Turismo, Plaza de la Catedral, 4; tel: 21 13 87. Open daily 0800-1330, 1500-1700.

BADAJOZ
The city
Located on the banks of the River Guadiana, at an elevation of
188m, Badajoz is 401km from Madrid and just 6km from the
Portuguese border. With a population of about 125,000, it is the
largest city in Extremadura and is the capital of the largest province
in Spain — 21,757 km² (8,400 sq miles).

There have been settlements here since prehistoric times and it was
a small town, under the control of Mérida, during the period of
Roman rule. After the Moorish invasion it was called Bataly under
the rule of the Córdoban Empire and when that broke up, early in
the 11th century, it became an important Taifa kingdom which was
then taken over, successively, by the Almoravides and Almohades.
The 12th century saw it being fought over between the kingdoms of
León and Portugal and it was reconquered by King Alfonso IX in
1230. Later that century there was a bitter civil war.

It has since been an important town in every Spanish War
including the Civil War. Then it was captured by Nationalist forces
in August 1936 and several thousand Republican defenders were
shot in the Plaza de Toros.

Today it is a quiet provincial city that becomes very, very hot
during the summer months.

Places of interest
As there are not many places of interest, and none really
outstanding, they are not categorised in the same manner as other
cities. Therefore all the places of any interest are listed in
alphabetical order:

Alcazaba (Fortress) This is situated on top of the steep Orinace
hill and the surrounding area, incorporating the red-light district, is
very poor and could well be unpleasant for women travelling alone.
The plaza immediately outside is, however, architecturally
interesting and extensive efforts are being made to restore it and
provide better housing for local people. The main walls were built
during the reign of Abu Yacub Yusuf, who also built the walls
around Marrakesh and the mosque in Sevilla, and enclosed the
original city which became a stronghold during the 12th century.
These were later extended during the 16th century. It is possible to
walk around the ramparts and these give a birds-eye perspective of
the city below. Otherwise, besides the Traición Tower at the main

entrance and the Duque de la Roca Palace, now housing the Museo
Arqueológico, there is not a lot to see. This is partly because an
army base takes up much of the space and the most famous sight,
the Apendiz Tower, popularly known as the Espantaperros — Dog
Frightener — is within that area. As a consequence this unusual
octagonal tower, built during the Almohade rule, is best seen from
the streets outside.

Catedral y Museo   (Cathedral and Museum),   Plaza España.
Construction began after the reconquest in 1230 when King Alfonso
IX decided that the mosque should be converted to a church
dedicated to Santa María del Castillo. The tower looks like a
fortress and the main façade was restored during the 16th century.
This is not particularly grand or ornate and, as a consequence, is
quite different from many cathedrals. The museum, entered from the
bland cloisters and open only in the mornings, was temporarily
closed when I visited.

Museo Arqueológico   (Archaeological Museum),   Plaza de Juan
Alvarez y Saez Buruaga; tel: 22 23 14. Open Tuesday to Sunday
1000-1500. Closed Monday, January 1, December 24/25/31 and
holidays. Entrance: 200 ptas, citizens of the EC (under 21) free.
This museum, founded in 1867, is located within the Alcazaba in the
16th century palace of the Duke of Roca which was built by the
powerful Súarez de Figueroa family. Actually this has been much
restored and the only original parts are the tower and façade. The
exhibits, on four floors, show the cultural and historical evolution
of the province through the prehistoric, Iberian-Tartessan, Roman,
Visigothic, Moorish and Christian medieval periods.

Museo Provincial de Bellas Artes   (Provincial Museum of Fine
Arts), Melendez Valdés, 32; tel: 22 28 45. Open Monday to Friday
0830-1430; Saturday 0900-1300. Closed Sunday and holidays.
Entrance: free. An important collection of over 600 paintings and
sculptures is located in this 19th century house/palace. They are
divided into the following categories: works from the 15th to 19th
centuries, works of 20th century regional painters and sculptures by
Perez Comendador, Cabrera and Avalos and, on the second floor,
exhibitions of more contemporary artists.

Puerta de Palmas   (Gate of Palms)   This ornately decorated gateway, protected by two large crenellated circular towers, is the symbol of the city. It was built in 1551 during the reign of King Felipe II at the end of a bridge, constructed on Roman foundations and with 32 arches, over the Guadiana river. Up until the 19th century it was used as a prison.

Station/location/transport to city centre

RENFE, Carolina Coronado; tel: 23 87 69. This rather drab and run down station is located a long way from the city centre.

Layout

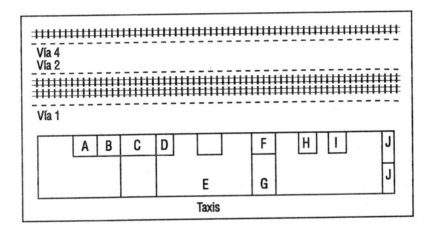

Key

A: *Comisaría*
B: *Sala de Espera*
C: *Cantina* (this seemed to be permanently closed)
D: *Estanco* for tobacco, newspapers, magazines, etc, open 0700-2200
E: *Consigna Automática*; tokens costing 300 ptas, per

24 hours, available from the ticket office. These are located in a strange position just above the entrance
F: *Información*
G: Tickets
H: *Circulación*
I: *Jefe de Estación*
J: *Servicios*

Train station to city centre

By taxi This is the most viable way and costs about 400 ptas.

Train services
To Madrid by

	Regional	Estrella	Talgo	
Mérida	¾	¾		
Ciudad Real	5	5½		
Cáceres	1¾	1¾		
Madrid	8½	6¼	9¾	5½

To Barcelona by

	Diurno	Estrella
Ciudad Real	4¾	5½
Albacete	7¼	8½
Valencia	9½	11
Barcelona	14	16

Accommodation
In the city
*** **Hotel Río** Avenida Adolfo Diaz Ambrona; tel: 27 26 00. Single 6,300 ptas; double 8,500 ptas. Located across the Guadiana river, just outside the city. All conveniences including a pool.
* **HR Villa Real** Donoso Cortes, 4; tel: 22 34 16. Single 1,270 ptas; double 2,200 ptas. Rooms without bath; clean and quiet. Close to cathedral.
* **Hostal Menacho** Abril, 12; tel: 22 18 53. Single without bath 1,100 ptas; double without bath 2,100 ptas, with bath 2,600 ptas. Close to the Puerta de Palmas. Pleasant and peaceful.
* **Pension San José** Arco Aquero, 31; tel: 22 05 68. Single 1,270 ptas; double 1,875 ptas. On the first floor. Part of private house close to cathedral.
CH Carrillo Arco Aquero, 31; tel: 22 20 14. Single 900 ptas; double 1,600 ptas. On the second floor. Same comments as for the San José.

General information
Car hire
Avis, Plaza Castelar. Hotel Zurbaran; tel: 22 43 13.

Police
Comisaría, Avenida Ramón y Cajal; tel: 23 02 53.

Telephone code
for Badajoz province is (924).

Tourist office

Oficina de Información Turística, Plaza de la Libertad, 3; tel: 22 27 63. Open Monday to Friday 0900-1400, 1700-1900; Saturday and Sunday 0900-1400. Closed holidays.

BARCELONA
The city

The modern city of Barcelona is one of intriguing contradictions, based on a 2,000 year history. It had Phoenician connections but prospered more under the Romans who built a walled town in what is now known as the Gothic Quarter. Some of the walls can still be seen and there are interesting and detailed excavations in the basement Museu d'Història de la Ciutat.

The city's importance declined during the Visigothic period and, after being captured by the Moors, it was soon recaptured by the Franks in 801, becoming part of Charlemagne's empire and the capital of the earldom of Barcelona. It was the most dominant of the Catalonian earldoms and united with the kingdom of Aragón in the 12th century. Maritime trade made it into one of the most important Mediterranean ports and when Ferdinand and Isabella married in 1469, thus joining the kingdoms of Castile and Aragón into the single nation of Spain, the central government began to suppress Catalonia's independent institutions. Throughout the Civil War, until its capture in January 1939, Barcelona was the headquarters of the Republican Government. Franco continued the suppression of all things Catalán and it was not until after his death that Catalonia was allowed the freedom to express its own identity.

However, unlike many other cities in Spain, it is not for its history that most people visit Barcelona. The city has developed a very well deserved reputation for culture and art — in many different forms. There are the unique and wonderfully weird constructions of Gaudi, the contrasting architectural styles, the paintings of Miró, Dali and Picasso, to name but a few, and the vast number of museums that cover every topic in which anyone would be interested. When you add the ever increasing influence of Catalán culture (Barcelona is bilingual), the natural vitality of the people and the Mediterranean climate, it gives the city a style and atmosphere not found anywhere else in Spain. This can be confusing to those who only visit Barcelona and nowhere else; it gives them a rather false impression of what the rest of Spain is like.

Barcelona is located 680km (425 miles) northeast of Madrid, but only 170km (106 miles) from the French border and, with a total population of around 4 million, is the second largest city in Spain. As with other large cities in Spain it is necessary to be wary of personal possessions and money, especially in the locality of La Rambla and the maze of side streets that run off it. Similarly one should be aware that prostitutes and transvestites openly ply their trade in these areas. Whilst discussing the negative aspects it is important to know that Barcelona is an expensive city. This is most notable when visiting museums, monuments, etc, where entrance fees are considerably more than elsewhere in Spain. This is compounded by so many such places to visit in Barcelona.

But do not let these things put you off Barcelona. Most people going to Spain by train will pass through the city, if only because of its geographical closeness to France, and very few will leave disappointed.

Places of interest

Barcelona is rather different from most other cities; although there are many places to visit, especially museums, not many of them can really be considered to be in *Must see* and therefore the format of this section will differ from that generally used in this guide. As it will be a matter of personal choice and, of course, time available as to what each person will want to see, this section will be tailored to the layout of the city. There are certain quarters and areas of the city where many places of interest are located in close proximity to each other and these are detailed below. All museums not located in these areas will be described, in alphabetical order, under the usual heading. This rearrangement will help visitors make the best use of their available time in this interesting city. Note also that all museums administered by the Barcelona City authority are closed on public holidays.

There is a Barcelona Tourist Bus that leaves from the Plaça Catalunya between 0900 and 1930 every day during June to September. The fare is either 1,000 ptas for all day or 700 ptas between 1400 and 2130. Included in this price are free use of the Tramvía Blau, Montjuïc Funicular and the Montjuïc Cablecar. There are also discounts for Tibidabo and Tibidabo Funicular, Poble Espanyol, Wax Museum, Golondrinas and the zoo. These buses cover 15 different stops and you can get on and off as you wish and, besides a tourist board employee to assist you, there is a free information guide.

La Rambla

On an axis between the Plaça Catalunya and the port, this is the liveliest and, arguably, the most important thoroughfare in the city. This wide, tree-lined, pedestrian walkway, separating two busy

roads, has newspaper and book *kioscos*, flower stalls, stalls selling
birds, fish and other small animals and numerous open air bars
along its entire length. It is fascinating just to sit there, at any time
of the day or night, sipping a drink, and watching the world pass
by.

On either side there are any number of places of interest — some
of which are detailed below in alphabetical order — interspersed
with shops, banks, theatres, cinemas and even a traditional food
market, Mercado la Boqueria, located about halfway down. There
are also many places of accommodation along, and to either side, of
La Rambla but beware — the area to the right hand side as you
approach the port houses the red-light district and is not very
pleasant, especially at night. The area on the other side is not that
much better but the Plaça Reial is very interesting and should not be
missed.

Gran Teatre del Liceu (Liceu Opera House), Sant Pau,. 1 bis; tel:
318 91 22. Individual visits, lasting about 30 minutes, on Monday
to Friday at 1130 and 1215 by prior arrangement with the Press and
Public Relations Department. Entrance: 200 ptas. Metro Licieu,
Line 3, Green. Located at the junction of La Rambla and Carrer de
Sant Pau this is one of the most decorative, and important, opera
houses in the world. It was opened in 1847 but was gutted by a fire
in 1861 and it reopened the following year. The ballet season is in
the spring and opera is performed between November and March.

*On Monday January 31 1994 this magnificent building was again
gutted by a fire, possibly ignited by sparks from workmen soldering
scenery for its latest production. The authorities immediately
promised it would be reconstructed on the same site, and in the
same style, but at the time of publication no timetable had been
announced.*

Museu de les Arts de l'Espectacle Institut del Teatre (Performing
Arts Museum and Theatre Institute), Nou de la Rambla, 3-5; tel:
317 39 74/317 51 98. Open Monday to Friday 1600-2000. Closed
Saturday, Sunday and holidays. Entrance: 100 ptas. Metro either
Liceu or Drassanes, Line 3, Green. Bus route 14, 18, 38 and 59.
Another example of Gaudi architecture, the Palau Güell, was built
as a residence for the Count Güell, and is worth seeing in its own
right. It is the home for the research, documentation and distribution
centre of the Theatre Institute. There are also exhibitions relating to

the world of performing arts as well as a library, open Monday to Friday 0930-1330, 1630-1930, that sells various publications. This is situated just off La Rambla, closer to its lower end, almost opposite the Plaça Reial.

The museum is currently closed for repairs, but the library remains open.

Museu de Cera (Wax Museum), Rambla Santa Monica, 4-6; tel: 317 26 49. Open July, August and September daily 1000-2000; other times Monday to Friday 1000-1400, 1600-2000, Saturday, Sunday and holidays 1000-2000. Last entrance is 30 minutes before closing time. Entrance: adults 750 ptas, youths with ID cards, senior citizens and children (5-11) 450 ptas. Metro Drassanes, Line 3, Green. Bus routes 14, 18, 38 and 59. Positioned at the bottom of La Rambla, very close to the Drassanes Metro, the Museu de Cera houses over 300 wax reproductions of famous people and the different backgrounds are enhanced by visual and audio effects. The building itself is of historical interest.

Palau de la Virreina (Virreina Palace) This interesting palace, located between the Gran Teatre and Plaça Catalunya, is now used for art exhibitions and the like.

Plaça Reial (Royal Square) Located just off La Rambla, and connected to it by the Carrer Colón, this gracious five storied, porticoed and particularly symmetrical plaza was built as a result of a competition in 1848. It has 35 palm trees but, unfortunately, the charm of the central fountain and iron lanterns, both designed by Gaudi, is not matched by many of the people who choose to gather here.

Barri Gotic (Gothic Quarter)
This, the most historic area of Barcelona, is located a short walk away from La Rambla, not far from the Liceu Metro, and has as its boundaries the Carrer Jaume I, the Vía Laietana and Avinguda Catedral.

Catedral (Cathedral and Museum), Plaça de la Seu; tel: 315 35 55. Cathedral open daily 0800-1330, 1600-1930. Entrance: free. Metro Jaume I, Line 4, Orange. Bus routes 16, 17, 19, 22 and 45. There was a cathedral in Barcelona as early as the 9th century but it was destroyed in 985. A Romanesque cathedral was consecrated in 1058 and work began on the present Gothic cathedral in 1298. However, the main façade was not completed until the late 19th century. Although not large, the inside is very imposing because of the height and elegance of the colonnades. In fact the style is very similar to that of the Santa María de la Mar, a similar but less ornate church located at the bottom of Calle Montcada near the Picasso Museum. The stained glass windows are very beautiful and the choir, also historically important as Carlos V met here with the Chapter of the Golden Fleece in 1519 — a meeting also attended by Henry VIII — can be visited for 40 ptas. An interesting feature is the chapel, directly under the altar, housing the sepulchre of Santa Eulalia, the patron saint of the city, that was carved in 1327. Personally my favourite part is the most unusual cloisters, which are open daily 0845-1300, 1600-1845. There are many small chapels around the side, and gardens in the centre that have a fish pond and, strangely, geese. In one corner there is an elaborate fountain with drinking water that has a small but charming statue of Sant Jordi (St George), the patron saint of Catalunya.

Museu Frederic Marès (Frederic Mares Museum), Plaça St Iu 5; tel: 310 58 00. Open Tuesday to Saturday 1000-1700; Sunday and holidays 1000-1400. Closed Monday. Entrance: 300 ptas; Wednesday and concessions 150 ptas. Metro Jaume I, Line 4, Orange. Bus routes 16, 17, 19, 22 and 45. Opened in 1946, this houses the collection of the sculptor Frederic Marès. The museum specialises in religious memorabilia and also has many representations of Christ on the cross. The building, including a patio with a small bar, is an absolute delight but the exhibits are rather sombre and somewhat repetitious.

Museu d'Història del Calçat (History of Footwear Museum), Plaça de Sant Felip Neri; tel: 302 26 80. Open Tuesday to Sunday 1100-1400. Closed Monday. Entrance: 200 ptas, students free. Metro Jaume I, Line 4, Orange and Liceu, Line 3, Green. Bus routes 16, 17 19, 22, 45 and 59. There are shoes from the 16th to 20th centuries and also footwear owned, and worn, by famous people in this building which once housed the Master Shoemakers Guild of Barcelona. Guided tours by prior arrangement.

Museu d'Història de la Ciutat (City History Museum), Plaça del Rei; tel: 315 11 11. Open Tuesday to Saturday 1000-1400, 1600-2000; Sunday and holidays 1000-1400. Closed Monday. Entrance: 300 ptas; Wednesday and concessions 150 ptas. Metro Jaume I, Line 4, Orange. Bus routes 16, 17, 19, 22 and 45. This is somewhat unusual as there are three separate entrances in different parts of the Plaça del Rei. From the outside these buildings are a delight, especially the tall and unusual tower, but the real surprise comes when you enter and go downstairs where subterranean excavations have exposed, and interconnected, large parts of the old Roman city. Unlike other museums there are comprehensive descriptions in English and prearranged guided tours can be arranged by calling 315 30 53.

Palau de la Generalitat (Generalitat Palace), Plaça de Sant Jaume. Open April 23, St George's Day only. Although construction of this large and impressive building began in the 15th century, during the reign of James II, it was not completed until the 17th century. It is the home of the autonomous government of Catalunya, a role it has also held throughout its history when political circumstances permitted. The staircase, in the open courtyard, is particularly impressive and the Chapel of Sant Jordi, the patron saint of Catalunya, and Orange Tree Patio should not be missed either. A modern Gothic-style bridge links it to the old canon's residence which is now the home of the Provincial Council president.

Note: The next places are located in Carrer Montcada which is about 800m from the Gothic Quarter, in the direction of Parc de la Ciutadella.

Museu Picasso (Picasso Museum), Montcada, 15-19; tel: 319 63 10/315 47 61. Open Tuesday to Saturday 1000-2000; Sunday 1000-1500. Closed Monday. Entrance: 500 ptas; concessions, students under 25 and Wednesdays 250 ptas; children under 16 free. Metro Jaume I, Line 4, Orange. Bus routes 16, 17, 22 and 45. Located in the Gothic palaces of Berenguer Aguilar, Baron de Castellet and the Palacio Meca are representative works, paintings, drawings, ceramics, etc, on the artistic evolution of Pablo Picasso (1881-1957). There is a library open 0900-1400 and guided tours are available by prior arrangement.

Museu Tèxtil i de la Indumentària   (Clothing and Textile Museum),   Montcada, 12-14; tel: 310 45 16/319 76 03. Open Tuesday to Saturday 1000-1700; Sunday and holidays 1000-1400. Closed Monday. Entrance: 300 ptas; Wednesdays and concessions 150 ptas. Metro Jaume I, Line 4, Orange. Bus routes 16, 17, 39, 40, 45, 51, 57, 59 and 64. Located in the Gothic palaces of the Marqués de Llio i Nidal are exhibits of textiles, clothing and lace. There is a specialised library, Tuesday to Thursday 0900-1400, as well as a restoration department.

Iglesia Santa María del Mar   (Church of Saint Mary of the Sea), Passeig del Born, at the bottom of Carrer Montcada. This is in an intriguing area that has maritime connections, hence the name. There was a church here in the 10th century but the present one was built during 1329-83. It is of cathedral like proportions and, in fact, of very similar design to the cathedral. The inner supporting columns are very tall and elegant and the atmosphere is one of dignified calm. It is considered to be the finest church in the city and is certainly my favourite.

El Xampanyet Montcada, 22; tel: 319 70 03. Whilst in the Carrer Montcada do not miss a visit to this bar. Founded in 1929 it specialises in *cava*, a light, sparkling, champagne-type wine that is especially refreshing and low in alcohol — only 10%. Take a bottle away with you; at around 600 ptas it is a bargain.

The port
This port, located by the Columbus Monument at the end of La Rambla, is one of the busiest in Europe and is home to the local fishing fleet as well as the medieval shipyards of which the Maritime Museum is a part.

Aerial cable cars: from Barcelona to Montjuïc   tel: 442 22 70. Open summer daily 1100-2100, October to June Monday to Friday 1200-1745, Saturday, Sunday and holidays 1130-1900. Fares: Barceloneta via Jaume I to Miramar 1000 ptas return; Jaume I to Miramar 850 ptas single, 950 ptas return.

Monument a Colón (Columbus Monument), tel: 302 52 24. Open June 24 to September 24 0900-2100; rest of the year Monday to Saturday 1000-1400, 1530-1830, Sunday and holidays 1000-1900.

Closed Monday, January 1 and 6 and December 25-26. Entrance: adults 200 ptas, children 100 ptas. This 50m iron column, with a statue of Columbus at the top, was built by Gaieta Buigas Monrava for the 1888 Universal Exhibition and to commemorate Columbus's visit to the city to be received by the Catholic monarchs, after his first voyage to the Americas. There is a lift to the viewing platform which offers a birds eye vista of the city and harbour.

Reial Drassanes i Museu Marítim (Royal Shipyards and Maritime Museum), Portal de la Pau; tel: 318 32 45/301 64 25. Open Tuesday to Saturday 0930-1300, 1600-1900; Sunday 1000-1400. Closed Monday. Entrance: 200 ptas, students free. Metro Drassanes, Line 3, Green. Bus routes 14, 18, 59 and 64. These are the most complete, and important, medieval dockyards still in existence. Originally constructed in the 14th century, there are still seven bays dating from then. It was extended in the 17th century and the bays added are closest to La Rambla. The exhibits in the museum relate to the history of navigation and include seafarers tombs, figureheads, etc, a model of *Santa María* and a life size replica of the galley used by Juan de Austria. Guided tours by prior arrangement.

Golondrinas From Moll de la Fusta to the breakwater; tel: 412 59 44. Boats run every half hour July to September 1100-2100; April to June and October 1100-1900, November to March 1100-1800. Return fare: adults 355 ptas; senior citizens 200 ptas; children 190 ptas.

Parc de la Ciutadella

Open April to September 0800-2100; October to March 0800-2000. Metro Arc de Triomf, Line 1, Red and Barceloneta, Line 4, Yellow. Bus routes 14, 16, 17, 36, 39, 40, 45, 51, 57, 59 and 64. Located some distance from the centre of the city, but close to the renovated Estacio de França railway station, this is named the 'Park of the Citadel' because it is on the site of the fort built by Felipe V in the early 18th century. The citadel was demolished in the late 19th century and, in 1888, the Universal Exhibition was held here. Today only a few of the original buildings remain and the most important of these are the Governor's Palace and the Arsenal which houses the Catalán parliament and the Museum of Modern Art. It is a pleasant place to wander around, with its lakes, including a boating lake, gardens, statues, museums and zoo, or perhaps to rent a bicycle for an hour or so.

Museu d'Art Modern (Museum of Modern Art), Parque de la Ciutadella; tel: 319 57 28. Open Monday to Sunday 1000-2100. Closed Tuesdays and January 1, Good Friday, Easter Monday, Whitsun Monday, May 1, June 24 and December 25-26. Entrance 300 ptas; senior citizens and young people aged 10-25 200 ptas; students and children under 10 free. Located in the Palau de le Ciutadella, which is also the home of the Catalunya parliament, contains paintings, engravings, drawings, furniture, sculptures and other forms of decorative arts — from the 19th and 20th centuries — by Catalán artists. By the bookstall is a very interesting computerised guide to other museums in the city.

Museu de Geologia (Geology Museum), Parque de la Ciutadella; tel: 319 68 95. Open Tuesday to Sunday 1000-1400. Closed Monday. Entrance: 300 ptas. This is the oldest of Barcelona's museums, founded in 1878 and opened in 1882. It houses collections of natural science donated to the city by Francesc Martorell. Primary exhibits include mineralogy, palaeontology, petrology and geoplanetology. The entrance is in the park.

Museu de Zoologia (Zoology Museum), Passeig Picasso; tel: 319 69 12. Open Tuesday to Sunday 1000-1400. Closed Monday. Entrance: 300 ptas. Built by Domenech i Montaner as the café/restaurant for the 1888 Universal Exhibition, this very unusual building now houses entomological, malacological, vertebrate and other zoological collections. The entrance is outside the park.

Parc Zoologic (Zoo), Passeig Picasso; tel: 309 25 00. Open daily May to September 0930-1930; October to March 1000-1700. Entrance: 900 ptas, over 65s 450 ptas, children aged 3 and under free; last tickets are sold 30 minutes before closing. This has over 400 species and more than 7,000 animals, a dolphin show and a children's section. However, it is most famous for Snowflake, the *copito de nieve*, the only albino gorilla in captivity. There is another entrance right next to the Museum of Modern Art in the park and a trip on the zoo train costs 200 ptas.

Bicitram 'Parking Rental' (bicycle rental), Avinguda Marqués de l'Argentera, 15; tel: 319 69 50/319 69 12. Open Saturday, Sunday and holidays 1000-2100. Bicycle hire is 350 ptas for the first hour and 150 for each subsequent hour; a tandem costs 950 ptas and 400 and a bicicar 1,150 ptas and 500, respectively.

Gaudi's Works

Museu del Temple Expiatori de la Sagrada Família (Museum of the Holy Family Church of the Atonement), Mallorca, 401, tel: 455 02 47. Open daily, May and September 0900-2000; June to August 0900-2100; March, April, October 0900-1900, November to February 0900-1800. Entrance: 500 ptas; students 350 ptas. Metro Sagrada Familia, Line 5, Blue. Buses 19, 34, 43, 44, 50, 51 and 54. Construction of this, Gaudi's most famous work, was begun in 1883 and was intended to be a 20th century cathedral in his inimitable style. Although this is in reality little more than a shell, the architecture is so complex and intriguing that it has become one of Barcelona's most famous sights. There is also a small museum, with exhibits that mainly detail the building process. It is possible to climb up the spiral staircases, or go up by lift, within the towers to get a different perspective of this unique building.

La Pedrera (Casa Mila) Passeig de Gràcia, 92, tel: 487 36 13. Open (patio and terrace) Monday to Friday 1000, 1100, 1200, 1600 and 1800; Saturday 1000, 1100, 1200, and **Casa Batlló** Passeig de Gràcia, 43. tel: 204 52 50. Visits by previous arrangement, Tuesday to Saturday. Both of these are served by Metro, Line 3, Green and buses 7, 16, 17, 22, 24 and 28. These are typically ornate buildings but, perhaps because they are of similar proportions to their surroundings, they do not appear to be so much out of context as many of Gaudi's works.

Parc Güell and Casa Museu Gaudi (Gaudi House/Museum), Parque Güell, Olot; tel: 284 64 46. Open Sunday to Friday 1000-1400, 1600-1900. Closed Saturday. Entrance: 150 ptas. Metro Lesseps, Line 3, Green. Bus route 24. Located in the Parc Güell, this was originally built by Francesc Berenguer but it was bought by Gaudi who lived here from 1906 to 1925. Today it houses his personal effects, furniture, drawings, etc which, as might be expected, are rather out of the ordinary. There is also a specialised library on Gaudi and Modernism which can be visited by prior

arrangement. The park itself, like everything else designed by
Gaudi, is unique and is reminiscent of a fantasy land. It is quite
large and a pleasant place to stroll through or enjoy a drink at one
of the open-air bars. Unfortunately this is some distance from the
city centre and not that easy to reach.

Montjuïc

Aerial cable cars From upper station of the Montjuïc Funicular to
Montjuïc Castle; tel: 256 64 00. Open daily June to September
1130-2130; September to June Saturday and holidays 1100-1415,
1600-1930; Christmas holidays 1100-1445, 1630-1900. Fares: 525
ptas return.

Funicular de Montjuïc From Metro, Line 3, Green, Parallel. Open
summer daily and winter (April-October) weekends and holidays
1045-2000. Trains run every 15 minutes and the return fare is 275
ptas.

Fundació Joan Miró (Joan Miro Foundation), Parc de Montjuïc,
Plaça Neptú; tel: 329 19 08. Open Tuesday to Saturday 1100-1900
(Thursday 2130), Sunday and holidays 1030-1430. Closed Monday.
Entrance: adults 500 ptas, students 250 ptas, senior citizens free.
This modern and elegant building is the work of Josep Luis Serp
and it houses the Centre for Contemporary Art Studies and a
permanent exhibition of the work of Joan Miró. The exhibits are
very avant-garde and, in 1992, included a very explicit display
featuring the human reproductive system.

Institut i Jardí Botànic (Botanical Institute and Gardens), Parc de
Montjuïc, Avinguda Montanyans; tel: 325 80 50. Visits by prior
arrangement only. Metro Espanya, Line 1, Red. Bus routes 61.
Collections of plants, flowers and other vegetation from all over the
world but with particular emphasis on those from the western
Mediterranean area. There is a library and video library and also an
advice centre for herbs.

Montjuïc Amusement Park tel: 241 70 24. Open Saturday,
Sunday and holidays 1200-2000. Entrance: 350 ptas; voucher for
entrance and rides 1,400 ptas. Access via funicular at Metro
Parallel, Line 3, Green.

Museu Arqueològic (Archaeology Museum), Parc de Montjuïc, Passeig de Santa Madrona, 39; tel: 423 21 49/423 56 01. Open Tuesday to Saturday 0930-1330, 1530-1900; Sunday and holidays 1000-1400. Closed Monday. Entrance: 200 ptas, Sundays and senior citizens free. Metro Espanya, Line 1, Red and Line 3, Green. Bus route 61. Housed in the former Palace of Graphic Arts, built for the 1929 International Exhibition, this has a wide range of exhibits from the Iberian Peninsula and the Balearics dating from prehistoric times to the medieval era.

Museu d'Art de Catalunya (Museum of Catalán Art), Parc de Montjuïc, Palau Nacional; tel: 423 71 99. Metro Espanya, Line 1, Red and Line 3, Green. Bus route 61. The most important, and largest, collection of Catalán Romanesque (11th to 13th centuries) art is on display here. There are also sections for Gothic, Renaissance, baroque and modern art. *The museum is temporarily closed for repair.*

Museu de les Arts Gràfiques (Graphic Arts Museum), Poble Espanyol, Montjuïc; tel: 426 19 99. Open Monday to Friday — Guided tours by prior arrangement only. Metro Espanya, Line 1, Red and Line 3, Green. Bus routes 9, 27, 50, 56, 57 and 61. A museum dedicated to printing and engraving with exhibits dating from the 18th to 20th centuries.

Museu Etnològic (Ethnological Museum), Parc de Montjuïc, Passeig de Santa Madrona; tel: 424 64 02. Open Wednesday and Friday to Sunday 1000-1700; Tuesday and Thursday 1000-1900. Closed Monday. Entrance: 300 ptas, Wednesdays and concessions 150 ptas. Metro Poble Sec, Line 3, Green. Bus route 55. Here there are collections from peoples and cultures from all over the world alongside special exhibitions. There is a library open on Tuesday to Saturday 0900-1400 and guided tours, by prior arrangement, are available during the same hours.

Museu Militar (Military Museum), Castell de Montjuïc; tel: 329 86 13. Open Tuesday to Sunday 0930-1400, 1530-2000. Closed Monday. Entrance: 150 ptas, senior citizens free. Funicular and aerial cable car to Montjuïc. Bus route 61. There are military uniforms, models and lead soldiers as well as antique and modern arms on display here.

Poble Espanyol (Spanish Village), Avinguda Marquès de Comillas; tel: 325 78 66. Open Monday to Thursday and Sunday 0900-2100; Tuesday 0900-0200; Friday and Saturday 0900-0400. Entrance: adults 650 ptas, children 7-14 and senior citizens 350 ptas, children under 7 free. This is very unusual. The intent, and it has more or less succeeded, has been to create a village atmosphere with streets and houses similar to those found in the different regions of Spain. Many of the houses have shops that sell regional specialities and crafts. There are also many restaurants and bars.

Tibidabo

At an elevation of over 500m this has, weather permitting, spectacular views of Barcelona. However, as the attractions are not to everyone's taste and the journey, although interesting, is rather lengthy, complicated and expensive, those with tight schedules and budgets might well decide to exclude Tibidabo from their itinerary.

The journey Ferrocarrils de la Generalitat from Plaça de Catalunya to Avinguda Tibidabo then *tramvía blau*, (Blue Tram), to the funicular — 125 ptas each way or 200 ptas return and finally the funicular — 225 ptas each way or 400 ptas return. Be warned: keep your tickets for the funicular as there is a 1,000 ptas fine if you are caught without one.

Parce d'Atraccions (Amusement Park), Plaça Tibidabo, 3-4; tel: 211 79 42. Open May to September Wednesday, Thursday, Friday 1100-2000, Saturday, Sunday and holidays 1000-2100, Closed Monday and Tuesday; October to April Saturday, Sunday and holidays only 1000-2100; Christmas and Easter holidays daily 1000-2100. Entrance: general admittance (includes cost of six predetermined attractions) 800 ptas; one-day pass (entrance, unlimited rides and entrance to Museu d'Autòmates) 1,600 ptas. A special ride, the Pasaje del Terror, is 600 ptas extra. Basically this is an amusement park but its location and spectacular views make it a little different. The Museu d'Autòmates del Tibidabo (Tibidabo Mechanical Museum), tel: 211 79 42, is located within the park and, unusually, it specialises in mechanical, moving displays of human and animal figures.

Gabinet de Físcia Experimental Mentora Alsina (Mentora Alsina Experimental Physics Museum), Ctra de Vallvidreraal Tibidabo,

56; tel: 417 57 34. This is located around the corner from the funicular and amusement park entrance, is only open for prearranged guided tours and specialises in instruments and apparatus relating to the science of physics.

Museums

Fundació Tàpies Aragó, 255; tel: 487 03 15. Open Tuesday to Sunday 1100-2000. Closed Monday. Entrance: adults 400 ptas, students 200 ptas, senior citizens and unemployed free. Metro Passeig de Gràcia, Line 3, Green. Bus routes 7, 16, 17, 22, 28 and 24. The works of Antoni Tàpies are permanently on display alongside temporary exhibitions of contemporary and modern art.

Galería de Cataláns il.lustres (Gallery of Famous Catalans), Bisbe Cassador, 3; tel: 315 00 10. Open Monday to Friday 0900-1400. Entrance: free. Metro Jaume I, Line 4, Orange. Bus routes 16, 17, 19, 22 and 45. Located in the Reial Academía de Buenas Letras (Royal Academy of Literature) this gallery, as the name implies, has portraits of famous Cataláns from the 10th to the 20th century.

Museu d'Arts Decoratives (Decorative Arts Museum), Palau de Pedralbes, Avinguda Diagonal, 686; tel: 280 50 24. Open Monday to Friday 1000-1300 by prior arrangement. Entrance: free. Metro Palau Reial, Line 3, Green. Bus routes 7, 75, BC, Bl and SJ. Exhibits include furniture, glass, porcelain, watches, gold and silver work from the 16th to 20th centuries.

Museu de Carrosses Fúnebres (Funeral Hearse Museum), Sancho de Ávila, 2; tel: 300 50 61. Open 0900-1100. Closed Sunday and holidays. Entrance: free. Metro Marina, Line 1, Red. Bus routes 6, 40 and 42. Rather macabre this; a museum dedicated — excuse the pun — to hearses and automobiles used for funeral services.

Museu i Centre d'Estudis de l'Esport 'Dr Melcior i Colet' (Sports Museum and Studies Centre), Buenos Aires, 56-58; tel: 439 89 07/430 61 18. Open Monday to Friday 1000-1400, 1600-2000. Closed Saturday, Sunday and holidays. Entrance: free. Metro Hospital Clinic, Line 5, Blue. Bus routes 6, 7, 15, 27, 34, 59 and 66. This modernist building — by Puig i Cadafalch — houses sports related memorabilia and is used for sports-related exhibitions.

Museu de Ceràmica (Ceramics Museum), Palau de Pedralbes, Avinguda Diagonal, 686; tel: 280 16 21. Open Tuesday to Sunday 1000-1400. Closed Monday. Entrance: 300 ptas, Wednesdays and concessions 150 ptas. Metro Palau Reial, Line 3, Green. Bus routes 7, 75, BC, Bl and SJ. This is located in the Palau Reial de Pedralbes, which was donated by the people of Barcelona to King Alfonso XIII. The museum has medieval ceramics from the 13th to 16th centuries and a selection of more recent examples. There is also a specialised library open 1000-1300. The palace is not open to the public.

Museu de la Ciència (Science Museum), Teodor Roviralta, 55; tel: 212 60 50. Open Tuesday to Sunday 1000-2000. Closed Monday. Entrance: 500 ptas, planetarium 300 ptas; and students and senior citizens 350 ptas, planetarium 250 ptas. Ferrocarrils de la Generalitat, Avinguda del Tibidabo and then either the *tramvía blau* or a walk up the hill. Bus routes 17, 22, 58 and 73. Here there are well laid out and inter-reactive exhibitions of optics, mechanics, computers, meteorology as well as a planetarium and, outside, a small submarine.

Museu Clarà (Clara Museum), Calatrava, 27; tel: 203 40 58. Open Tuesday to Sunday 0900-1400. Closed Monday. Entrance: free. Ferrocarrils de la Generalitat, Les Tres Torres. Bus routes 14, 22 and 26. Josep Clarà (1878-1958) was a Catalán sculptor and his works, sculpture, drawings and paintings, are displayed here in his former residence.

Museu Etnogràfic Andino-Amazònic (Andean/Amazonian Ethnological Museum), Cardenal Vives i Tutó, 2-16; tel: 204 34 58. Open first Sunday of each month 1200-1400. Closed August and September. Entrance: by donation. Metro María Cristina, Line 3, Green. Generalitat Railroad, Sarria. Bus routes 34 and 66. This evangelistically based display of geographical and indigenous technological/cultural exhibits from South America is located in the Capuchins of Sarria convent. A guide book is available for 200 ptas.

Museu del Fútbol Club Barcelona (Barcelona Football Club Museum), Aristides Maillol; tel: 330 94 11. Open April to October 1000-1300, 1500-1800, closed Sunday and holidays; November to March, Tuesday to Friday 1000-1300, 1500-1800; Saturday, Sunday and holidays 1000-1400. Closed Monday. Entrance: adults 300 ptas, students 150 ptas, children under 14 100 ptas. Metro Collblanc Line 5, Blue and María Cristina, Line 3, Green. Bus routes 7, 15, 54, 56 and 57. This stadium, with a capacity of 120,000, has only one other equal in Spain — that of its arch rival Real Madrid. It is one of the finest in Europe and puts anything in the UK to shame. There are trophies, documents and paintings detailing club history and a five-screen video show. The stadium can be viewed from the presidential box.

Museu d'Història de la Medicina de Catalunya (Museum of the History of Catalán Medicine), Ptge Mercader, 11; tel: 216 05 00. Open Thursday 1000-1300, prearranged guided tours on other days. Entrance: 250 ptas. Metro Diagonal, Line 3, Green and Line 5, Blue. Bus routes 7, 15, 16, 17 and 34. There are 2,500 exhibits demonstrating the evolution of Catalán medical science as well as personal memorabilia of eminent figures in Catalán medicine. Guided tours can be prearranged.

Museu d'Holografia (Holography Museum), Jaume I, 1; tel: 315 34 77/319 16 76. Open Monday to Saturday 1100-1330, 1730-2030. Closed Sunday and holidays. Entrance: adults 100 ptas, senior citizens and children 50 ptas. Metro Jaume I, Line 4, Orange. Bus routes 16, 17, 36, 45 and 57. Holograms, holographic techniques and applications are on display here. Prearranged guided tours are available and there are also holographic courses and souvenir sales.

Museu i Laboratori de Geologia del Seminari (Geological Museum and Laboratory of the Seminary), Diputació, 231. tel: 245 16 00. Open Monday to Friday 1100-1300, 1700-1900. Closed Saturday, Sunday, holidays and during August. Entrance: free. Metro Universitat, Line 1, Red. Bus routes 7, 14, 16, 17, 58, 59 and 64. This is a geological research centre that specialises in palaeontology (invertebrates), housing over half a million fossils.

Museu-Monestir de Pedralbes (Monastery/Museum of Pedralbes), Baixada Monestir, 9; tel: 203 92 82. Open Tuesday to Friday and Sunday 1000-1400. Saturday 1000-1700. Closed Monday. Entrance 300 ptas; Wednesday and concessions 150 ptas. Ferrocarrils de la Generalitat, Reina Elisenda. Bus routes 22, 64, 75, BC, Bl and SJ. This 14th century monastery, with an unusual three storey cloister, has been kept as much as possible in its original state allowing visitors to see how the nuns lived. One room houses the Thyssen-Bornemisza collection.

Museu de la Música (Music Museum), Avinguda Diagonal, 373; tel: 416 11 57. Closed Monday. Open Tuesday to Sunday 1000-1400, Wednesday 1700-2000. Entrance: 300 ptas; Wednesday and concessions 150 ptas. Metro Diagonal, Line 3, Green and Line 5, Blue. Bus routes 6, 15, 22, 24, 28, 34 and 39. Located in the modern Casa Quadras, a work of Puig i Cadafalch, there are musical instruments here from all over the world, dating from the 16th to 20th century. There is also a specialised library, a photographic collection and technical consultations. Prearranged guided tours are available.

Museu del Perfum (Perfume Museum), Passeig de Gràcia, 39; tel: 215 72 38. Closed Saturday, Sunday and holidays. Open Monday to Friday 1030-1330, 1630-2000. Entrance: free. Metro Passeig de Gràcia, Line 3, Green and Loine 4, Orange. Bus routes 20, 21, 22, 24, 28, 39 and 43. A very comprehensive collection of perfume and cosmetic bottles, and other containers, dating from ancient times to the 20th century.

Museu Taurí (Bullfighting Museum), Gran Vía CC, 749; tel: 245 58 03/232 71 58. Open daily during the bullfighting season (March to October) 1030-1400, 1600-1900. Closed out of the bullfighting season. Entrance: adults 300 ptas, children 100 ptas. Metro Glories, Line 1, Red, and Sagrada Familia, Line 5, Blue. Bus routes 6, 7, 18, 34, 35 and 62. This is one of the better museums of its kind in Spain. Apart from the usual collection of bulls' heads, posters, *trajes de luces* (uniforms) and photographs, it also offers limited viewing of the corrals where the bulls are kept before the *corridas*.

Museu Verdaguer (Verdaguer Museum), Ctra de les Planes (Vallvidrera); tel: 204 78 05. Open Tuesday to Sunday and holidays 1000-1400. Closed Monday. Entrance: 300 ptas; Wednesday and concessions 150 ptas. Ferrocarrils de Generalitat, Baixador de Vallvidrera. Personal belongings of the poet Jacint Verdaguer are on display here in the Villa Joana where he died. There are guided tours by prior arrangement.

The stations
Sants

This is a large, bland, modern structure where all the facilities are located on a concourse over the platforms. It is in a more modern area, some distance from the centre, and is open between 0430-2400.

Layout

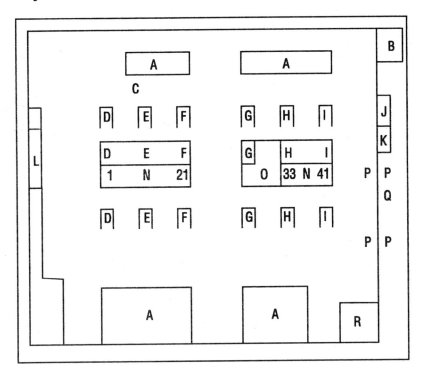

Key

A: Commercial areas. There are shops of all kinds, and plenty of telephones

B: El Minuto de Sants bar, open daily 0600-2330

C: *Barcelona Informacio Turística*, open daily 0800-2000

D: Entrance to platforms 12 and 11

E: Entrance to platforms 10 and 9

F: Entrance to platforms 8 and 7

G: Entrance to platforms 6 and 5

H: Entrance to platforms 4 and 3

I: Entrance to platforms 2 and 1

J: *Comisaría*

K: *Ayuda a la Joven*, open daily 1000-1300, 1600-2000

L: *Consigná Automática*, open daily 0630-2300, cost small 400 ptas, large 600 ptas, per 24 hour period. Fee for lost key 1,500 ptas

M: Banco Bilbao Vizcaya. Open Monday to Friday 0800-2200,

Saturday 0800-1400, 1600-2200   **P:**   Entrance to Metro
N: Ticket office   **Q:**   *Servicios*
O: *Atención al Viajero* and train   **R:**   Golden Wagon café/ restaurante,
information   open daily 0600-2300

Train station to city centre

Due to the impracticality of the bus routes and the endless traffic it is best to take the Metro from here.

By Metro Line 3, Green, Direction Montbau/Santa Coloma. Get off at Catalunya, seven stops away.

Estacio de França

This is a traditional railway station in the older part of town, that has been carefully renovated and, as such, it is in marked contrast to the style of Sants. It is open 0600-2330.

Layout

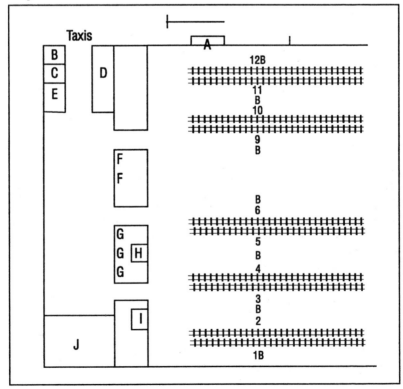

Key
A: *Consigna Automática.* There are
two sizes; large at 600 ptas and small
at 400 ptas, both for a 24 hour period
B: Bank, open regular banking
hours
C: *Barcelona Informacio Turística,*
open daily 0800-2000
D: Passenger assistance office, open
daily 0800-2400

E: Ultramar Express travel agents,
open daily 0800-2000
F: Train information offices
G: Ticket offices
H: Newspapers and magazines,
open 0700-2230
I: Men's and women's toilets
J: Cafeteria and restaurant, open
0600-2300

Train station to city centre
By Metro Line 4 (yellow) takes you to Plaça Urquinaoma, which is
as central as Plaça Catalunya.

By bus Number 14, Direction Pg Bonanova, takes you along the
harbour front and then all the way up La Rambla to the Plaça
Catalunya.

Train services
To Madrid by

	Diurno	Inter City	Talgo	Talgo Pen	Talgo Camas	Estrella
Zaragoza		4	3¾	3½	4½	6
Madrid	8½	8¼	7¼	6	8¾	10¼

To Almería by
Diurno: via Valencia 4; Linares/Baeza 9¼; Almería 13¾.

To Badajoz by
Diurno: via Valencia 4; Alcázar de San Juan 7¼; Ciudad Real 9;
Mérida 12½; Badajoz 13½.
Estrella: via Valencia 4¾; Alcázar de San Juan 9; Ciudad Real
10½; Mérida 14½; Badajoz 15½.

To Cáceres by
Diurno: via Zaragoza 4¼; Madrid 8½; Cáceres 13¼.

To Córdoba, Sevilla, Cádiz
Diurno: via Valencia 4; Linares/Baeza 9¼; Córdoba 11; Sevilla
12½; Cádiz 14½.
Estrella: via Valencia 4¾; Linares/Baeza 11¼; Córdoba 13; Sevilla
14¾; Cádiz 17½.

To Granada by
Diurno: via Valencia 4; Linares/Baeza 9¼; Granada 13¼.

Irún/France
Diurno: via Zaragoza 4½; Irún 8¾.
Estrella: via Zaragoza 5¼; Irún 12½.

To León by
Diurno: via Zaragoza 4; Burgos 7½; León 9¾.

To Málaga by
Diurno: via Valencia 4; Linares/Baeza 9¼; Córdoba 11; Málaga 13¾.
Estrella: via Valencia 4½; Linares/Baeza 10¾; Córdoba 12¾; Málaga 16.
Talgo camas: via Zaragoza 3½; Córdoba 11¼; Málaga 14.

To Valencia by
Diurno: 3¼. Inter City: 4. Talgo: 4. Estrella: 4½.

The Metro
Open Monday to Thursday 0500-2300; Friday, Saturday and the day before holidays 0500-0100; holidays, not on weekends, 0600-2300 and Sundays 0600-2400. Fare structure: single tickets 120 ptas; a ticket valid for 10 trips (controlled by a magnetic strip) costs 600 ptas and a combined train/bus 10 trip ticket 625 ptas.

The lines are identified by a number, 1, 3, 4 or 5, a colour code and the first and last stop. It is slightly confusing because the Ferrocarrils de la Generalitat de Catalunya (FGC) lines, originating at Catalunya and Espanya, are also shown in a different shade of blue on different guides. Metro tickets are also valid for FGC lines.

It is an easy system to use. First identify where you want to go and then ascertain the line number, colour code and the last stop in the direction you are going. If a change is necessary repeat the above procedure for each line until you reach your destination. To find the correct platform at the station of departure, and any subsequent changes, look for the line number, colour code and the name of the last stop in the direction you are going. These are clearly identified along with the names of all the interim stations. The lines are clearly identified in each carriage and a light comes on for each station that has been passed and another one flashes to indicate the next station. A copy of the subway guide *Metro de Barcelona* can be obtained at any ticket office.

The Metro is by far the easiest and quickest way of getting around Barcelona and the stations are generally well kept and the trains clean and neat.

As most people will usually take at least two trips, to and from the main line station, in addition to sightseeing, it is advisable to purchase a 10-trip ticket straightaway.

Accommodation

This section is different from that for other cities because firstly, there are no inexpensive places anywhere near Sants station. Secondly, if you really want to stay in the centre there are so many places of all standards, both along La Rambla and in the streets off to either side, that it is unnecessary to differentiate between them. Thirdly, many of the trains both leave and depart from the newly renovated Estacio de França and many people want to consider staying in the area nearby. This would always be my choice as the area is very interesting (although at first it might not seem so) it is only a short walk from the centre, it saves carrying heavy bags around or paying taxi fares and it can be a little cheaper. A cross-section of accommodation in this area is detailed below:

*** **Park Hotel** Avenida Marqués de Argentera, 11; tel: 319 60 00. Single 9,650 ptas; double 13,800 ptas. These rates include breakfast. Eighty-seven rooms with colour TV, radio, safe and mini-bar. Opposite the station, this is an impressive hotel.

* **Hotel Santa Marta** General Castaños, 14; tel: 319 44 27. Single 3,650 ptas; double 6,450 ptas. Left out of the station and left again. Rooms with bath/shower and colour TV. Nice, pleasant and quiet.

* **HR La Hipíca** General Castaños, 2; tel: 315 13 92. Single 2,300 ptas, 1,650 ptas without shower; double 3,850 ptas, 2,990 ptas without shower. About 100m past the Santa Marta. Clean and neat.

** **Hostal Orleans** Avda Marqués de Argentera, 13; tel: 319 73 82. Single without bath/shower 1,800 ptas; double without bath/shower 4,500 ptas, with bath/shower and TV 5,500 ptas. Directly in front of the station. The doubles are considerably better than the singles.

* **Hostal Nuevo Colón** Avenida Marqués de Argentera, 19; tel: 319 50 77. Without bath/shower: single 2,000 ptas, double 3,200 ptas; with bath/shower: single 3,200 ptas, double 4,500 ptas. Just across from the station. Plain and clean.

* **Pensión Francia** Rera Palau, 4; tel: 319 03 76. Single 2,500 ptas; double

4,000 ptas, 1,500 ptas single without bath or shower. In a small side street
about 100m across the road and to the left of the station. This is one of my
favourites. The rooms are exceptionally good for a pension. Most with
private bath/shower and toilet.

Note: By way of comparison I also list below two Grupo Husa chain hotels,
both located in a very central position, and a youth hostel.

**** **Hotel Husa Barcelona** Caspe, 1-13; tel: 302 58 58; fax: 301 86 74.
Metro Catalunya Line 1 (red) and Line 3 (green). This impressive hotel is
located in the heart of the city between the Plaça Catalunya and the Gran
Vía de les Corts Cataláns. It has 72 rooms all with bath, telephone, satellite
TV, air-conditioning, minibar and a safe box. Single, and double for single
use, 11,200 ptas; double 14,000 ptas; treble 18,700 ptas.
** **Hotel Mesón Castilla** Valldoncella, 5; tel: 318 21 82; fax: 412 40 20.
Metro Catalunya Line 1 (red) and Line 3 (green). This very dignified hotel
is located on the quiet Plaça Castilla, but only 100m from the Plaça
Catalunya. There are 60 rooms all with private bath and telephone and the
public rooms are beautifully decorated, often with wood panelling. There
is also a small outside terrace. Single 6,350 ptas; double 9,250 ptas; double,
for single use, 8,750 ptas; treble 12,450 ptas.
Youth Hostel Alberg Pere Tarres, Numància, 149-151; tel: 410 23 09.
Metro, Line 3, Green to María Cristina then walk down Avinguda Diagonal
to Carrer Numància. By bus take any of the following: 7, 15, 34, 43, 59,
66, BC or BJ.

General information
Car hire
Avis, Estacio de França, Avenida Marqués de l'Argentera; tel: 268
35 77.

Consulate telephone numbers
France: 435 55 60; United Kingdom: 308 52 01; Ireland: 576 35
00; USA: 577 44 00.

Police
Guardia Urbana, Ajuntament de Barcelona, Districte 1 — Ciutat
Vella. La Rambla, 43. Barcelona *Tourist Informatión* 301 90 60.

Public telephones
Carrer de Fontanella, 4 (on the corner of Plaça Catalunya nearest to
La Rambla and El Cortes Ingles). Open Monday to Saturday 0800-

2100. Visa, Eurocard, Mastercard, Access and American Express cards accepted for amounts over 500 ptas.

Telephone code
for Barcelona province is (93).

Tourist offices
Oficina de Turisme, Generalitat de Catalunya, Gran Vía de les Corts Catalanes, 658; tel: 301 74 43. Open Monday to Friday 0900-1900, Saturday 0900-1400. Closed Sunday and holidays.
There are other tourist offices in both of the stations.

BURGOS

The city

With a population approaching 160,000 Burgos is located 371km (232 miles) due north from Madrid, half way to the French border. It is on a plateau in the Arlanzón valley at an altitude of 900m (2,952ft) and, because of that, does not enjoy the long hot summers so common elsewhere in Spain. In fact in the winter months it is very, very cold. The city was founded in 884 as a fortification against the Moors and in 951, after the reconquest, it became the capital of Castile — until 1492 when the honour was transferred to Valladolid. Its most famous son was Rodrigo Diaz, El Cid (1026-99), who was born just 9km away in Vivar. Although married to the king's cousin, El Cid was banished from the city by Alfonso VI and became a soldier of fortune. His most famous exploit was capturing Valencia in 1094 but he was defeated by the Moors in Cuenca and died shortly after in 1099. His body was returned to San Pedro de Cardeña by his wife early in the 12th century and remained there until being moved to the cathedral early this century. In 1812 the city was a French stronghold and was put under siege by Wellington's troops. During the Civil War Franco set up a provisional government, where he was also acclaimed Head of State and Generalísimo in 1936. On April 1 1939 he proclaimed the ceasefire from La Isla palace. Today Burgos is a quiet provincial city and although there are not that many other places to see the cathedral is so spectacular that it should not be missed.

Places of interest
Must see

Catedral y Museo (Cathedral and Museum), Plaza de Santa María; tel: 20 47 12. Museum open daily 0930-1300, 1600-1900. Entrance: 300 ptas. Of all the cathedrals in Spain this is considered to be one of the most beautiful and it is also my favourite. The first stone was laid in summer 1221 by Bishop Mauricio but construction was not completed until over 400 years later. It is one of the jewels of Gothic architecture and on the World Heritage List. This cathedral is so intricate and graceful, in so many different ways, that it is impossible to do it justice in this guide. Almost everything about it is remarkable, especially the stonework — both outside and in. There are also some strange items: the *papamoscas* (flycatcher) is a clown, dating from the 15th century, that sits above a clock to the left of the main door and opens and closes its mouth at each stroke of the bell, and the Golden Staircase, built in 1519, that leads to nowhere and is only used during Easter week. This is not to forget the altars (all 38 of them), the choir, chapel of the Constable and many other aspects that must be seen.

The very best time to see the cathedral is on the holy day of the Fiesta de San Pedro and San Juan, at the end of June every year. Then all the dignitaries attend in their formal dress uniforms, while others appear in medieval costumes, and groups of women parade in traditional costume. The scene is one of solemn, dignified pageantry, at the end of which everyone files out and joins up with other, more light-hearted revellers and *gigantes* — giant figures moved around by men underneath them — in a procession around the town. Every night during this period there is a firework display and the last one comes down like a multicoloured umbrella covering the old town and cathedral — a truly memorable sight. At other times of the year the cathedral can be seen early in the morning when it is open for the first Mass. This is another of my favourite times as, more often than not, no one else is there at that time.

The museum has many treasures including a huge silver carriage, a golden monstrance and the coffin of El Cid, behind which is an interesting legend. The remains of El Cid and his wife Ximena were moved here in 1921.

Arco de Santa María (Arch of Saint Mary) This is a most impressive gateway to the city. Large, crenellated, with statues of important dignitaries set into the walls and, rather incongruously, with houses to either side. This used to be the main entrance to the city for all important visitors and also served as offices for the town hall.

By choice

Capitanía General (Military Headquarters). This is next door to the main tourist office and, although quite attractive, its main point of historical interest is that it was from here, on October 1 1936, that Franco was proclaimed Head of State and Generalísimo.

Cartuja de Miraflores (Carthusian Convent of Miraflores), 3.5km from Burgos. Open Monday to Friday 1015-1500, 1600-1800; Saturday, Sunday and holidays 1120-1230, 1300-1500, 1600-1800. By bus, Monday to Saturday, only during the summer, about every hour from 1100, fare 65 ptas (look for *Fuentes Blancas* in the

Plaza Primo de Rivera); Sunday, very limited service — check first
in the Plaza Primo de Rivera, look for *Cartuja*. This is well worth
a visit if you have the time, even though it is not that easy to get to.
This Carthusian convent was founded with sponsorship by King Juan
II of Castile, who is buried here, and the first monks arrived in
1442. Notable points of interest are the elaborate altar, a lovely
carved choir and the sepulchres of Juan II and his queen, Isabel of
Portugal.

Casa del Cordón (House of Rope) Dating from the 15th century,
this mansion/palace, considered one of the best examples in Burgos,
has been renovated over the centuries but the marvellous façade is
original. It gets its name from the cordon of rope that is carved in
stone over the entrance and time should be taken examining other
aspects of the intricate exterior. Some of the many historic events to
have taken place here are: the Catholic Monarchs received
Columbus on April 23 1497 after his second visit to the West
Indies; the annexation of Navarra was proclaimed from the palace
in 1515; and the Austrian kings stayed here when visiting the city.

Iglesia de San Nicolas (St Nicholas Church). Open Monday to
Friday 0900-1400, 1700-2100; Saturday, Sunday and holidays 0900-
1400, 1700-1800. This 15th century church, very close to the
cathedral, is notable for its very detailed and complicated altar.

Monasterio de San Pedro de Cardeña (San Pedro de Cardeña
Monastery). Located on the road past the Cartuja de Miraflores,
10km from Burgos. Open daily 1000-1300, 1600-1830; holidays
1200-1400, 1600-1830. Entrance: free. There is no bus service; you
have to take the bus to Cartuja de Miraflores and then a taxi. There
has been an abbey here since the late 9th century. El Cid was
associated with, and worked for, the abbey in the 11th century and
was buried here until his remains were moved to the cathedral many
centuries later.

Museums
Museo Arqueológico — Casa Miranda (Archaeological Museum
and Miranda House), Miranda, 13; tel: 26 58 75. Open Monday to
Friday 1000-1300, 1630-1915; Saturday 1015-1345. Closed Sunday
and holidays. Entrance: 200 ptas. Located in a quiet side street on
the opposite side of the river from the cathedral, this house, the

home of Canon Miranda, has an excellent façade and an impressive, but dirty, colonnaded patio. The rooms are very modern and the exhibits varied. There are many paintings, of all styles, but it was the unusual wooden sepulchres that fascinated me most.

Museo de Marcelino Santa María (Marcelino Santa María Museum), Monasterio de San Juan, Plaza San Juan; tel: 20 56 87. Open Tuesday to Saturday 1000-1400, 1700-2000; Sunday 1000-1400. Closed Monday and holidays. Entrance: 25 ptas. This old monastery, impressive in its own right, houses the paintings of Marcelino Santa María (1866-1952) a Burgalese painter. These paintings are generally of country scenes, with a few portraits interspersed, and are usually in a very pleasing combination of pastel colours.

Monasterio de las Huelgas y Museo de Ricas Telas (Las Huelgas Monastery and Fine Cloth Museum), Compases de Huelgas; tel: 20 16 30. Open Tuesday to Saturday 1100-1315, 1600-1715; Sunday and holidays 1100-1315. Closed Monday, and 1 and 6 January, Easter Friday, May 1, Fiestas of San Pedro and San Pablo and December 25. Entrance: 300 ptas, free on Wednesdays. As this is about 2km outside the town it may be preferable to take the bus from the Plaza de la Primo de Rivera for 65 ptas; look for those headed *Sedas — Barrio del Pilar*. This convent, founded in 1187 by Alfonso VIII and his queen Eleanor, daughter of Henry II of England, was at one time used as a summer palace for the kings of Castile. Besides the church, and rather pleasing cloisters, there are also the tombs of kings and princes. The museum has examples of fine cloth and jewellery recovered from these tombs and also the *Navas de Tolosa* Banner which was won by Alfonso VIII from the Almohads.

Station/location/transport to city centre
RENFE, Conde de Guadalhorce; tel: 20 95 20. A fairly modern bland station, at an altitude of 856.8m, located not too far from the cathedral and old town.

Key
A: *Paseo inferior*

B: *Carritos portaequipajes*

C: *Consigna Automática*, open 24 hours, cost 200 ptas per 24 hours and tokens are purchased from the ticket office

D: *Información*

E: *Kiosco* for newspapers,

Layout

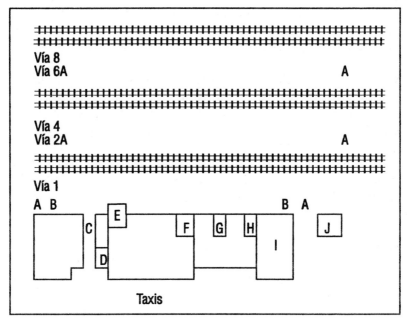

magazines, etc, open 0900-1745
F: Ticket office
G: *Circulación*
H: *Jefe de Estación*

I: Bar/cafeteria, open 24 hours daily
J: *Servicios*

Train station to city centre
On foot Go straight out of the station and straight ahead, turn right at the main road and follow the cathedral spires. It takes about 15 minutes.

By taxi This takes just five minutes and costs around 300 ptas.

Train services
To Madrid by

	Regional	Regional Express	Inter City	Estrella	Talgo
Aranda de Duero				1¼	1
Valladolid	1¾	1¼	1	1½	
Ávila	3	2½	2¼	3	
Madrid	4½	4	3¾	5	3¼

To Barcelona by

	Diurno	Estrella
Logroño	1¾	2
Zaragoza	3½	4¼
Barcelona	7¾	8½

To Irún/France by

	Diurno	InterCity	Estrella	Talgo
Miranda de Ebro	¾	¾		1
Irún	3½	3½	5	3¼

To Santiago de Compostela by
Diurno: via León 2; Santiago de Compostela 8.

Accommodation
Outside the old town
**** **Hotel Husa Puerta de Burgos** Vitoria, 69; tel: 24 10 00; fax: 24 07 07. This large hotel located in the modern part of town, about 10 minutes walk from the cathedral, is part of the Husa chain. It has 100 rooms that all have private bath, air-conditioning, telephone, satellite TV, radio, safe box and minibar. There is also a bar and coffee shop. Single 9,190 ptas; double 14,800 ptas; double, for single use, 11,840 ptas; treble 19,980 ptas.
* **HR Niza** General Mola, 12; tel: 26 19 17. Single 2,000 ptas; double 2,700 ptas. All without bath. Very pleasant. Close to station.
* **Hostal Ambos Mundos** Plaza de Vega, 25; tel: 20 61 30. Single 1,500 ptas; double 3,000 ptas; treble 4,500 ptas. All rooms without bath. Just across the river from the Arch/tower de Santa María.
* **Hostal Temino** Concepción, 14; tel: 20 80 35. Single 1,300 ptas; double 2,100 ptas. Rooms without bath. Reasonably close to station. Comfortable.
* **Pensión Ansa** Miranda, 9; tel: 20 47 67. Single 2,000 ptas; double 3,000 ptas. Rooms without bath. Doubles very nice. Singles on 4th floor, but no lift.

In the old town
*** **Hotel Mesón del Cid** Plaza Santa María, 8; tel: 20 87 15; fax: 26.94.60. A Best Western hotel. Single 8,215 ptas; double 11,289 ptas. These rates include breakfast and there is a special rate at weekends for stays of two or more nights. This elegant small hotel has a fantastic location just across from one of the most beautiful cathedrals in Spain. It also has an excellent restaurant and a bar. There are only 29 rooms and these have bath/shower, radio, satellite colour TV, balcony and a telephone. Some also have a hairdryer.

** HR Norte y Londres Plaza Alonso Martínez, 10; tel: 26 41 25. Single 4,000 ptas; double 6,700 ptas. Beautiful reception and TV lounge; nice rooms with colour TVs. Be advised the hotel stays noisy all night during the fiesta.

* Hostal Castellano Laín Calvo, 48 and San Lorenzo, 47; tel: 20 50 40. Single 1,600 ptas; double 3,000 ptas. Entrances in two streets. Interesting style. Close to Norte y Londres.

* Hostal Hidalgo Almirante Bonifaz, 14; tel: 20 34 81. Single 1,500 ptas; double 2,500 ptas. Second floor. Quiet street close to cathedral.

General information
Car hire
Avis, Avenida Generalísimo, 5; tel: 20 24 60.

Hospital
General Yague Hospital, Avenida del Cid, 96; tel: 22 18 00.

Police
Comisaría, Juan de Padilla; tel: 23 59 12.

Radio taxis
27 77 77 or 48 10 10.

RENFE city office
RENFE, Moneda, 21; tel: 20 35 60. Monday to Friday 0900-1300, 1630-1930; Saturday 0900-1300. Closed Sunday and holidays.

Telephone code
for Burgos province is (947).

Tourist office
Junta de Castilla y León, Consejería de Cultura y Turismo, Plaza Alonso Martínez, 7; tel: 20 31 25. Open Monday to Friday 0900-1400, 1630-1830; Saturday/holidays 1000-1330; Closed Sunday.
Asociación de Fomento del Turismo Información, Plaza de Santa María. Monday to Saturday 1000-1400, 1700-2000; Sunday 1000-1400. A very small office is located opposite the cathedral.

CÁCERES

The city

Cáceres is located 335km (209 miles) west of Madrid, at an altitude of 498m, and with a population approaching 70,000. The city, founded by the Romans in 34 BC, was known as Norba Caesarina and the first walls were built in that era. After the downfall of the Romans, it declined until the period of Moorish rule that lasted nearly 400 years, when it became known as Hizn Quazri; the walls were rebuilt towards the end of that period. Between the Moors and Christians the city changed hands several times before it was finally reconquered by Alfonso IX of León, in 1227. In the late 11th century the Order of Santiago, a brotherhood of knights, was founded and one of its later responsibilities was to safeguard pilgrims on their way to Santiago de Compostela. The knights built houses with defensive towers but most of these, with the exception of their favourites, were destroyed by Ferdinand and Isabella. One that was left, in the oldest part of the area, is the Casa de las Cigüeñas (storks) located in the Plaza de San Mateo. In the 14th, 15th and 16th centuries many beautiful palaces and houses were constructed and it is these that are of the most interest today. The 'Monumental Zone' is so well preserved as a medieval city that in 1986 UNESCO declared it a 'Patrimony of Humanity'. This, and the Plaza Mayor, should not be missed. Cáceres is rather isolated but, conveniently for train travellers, it is on the main rail line to Lisbon.

Places of interest
Must see

The Monumental Zone is almost totally enclosed by walls and 12 of its original 30 towers are left. The best place to begin a visit is in the Plaza Mayor. Enter the Zone through the Arco de Estrella, next to the tourist office. Once inside there are so many houses, palaces, towers and churches to see that it would be impossible to detail them in a guide like this. In any case many of them are not open to the public. To see the 'Monumental Zone' properly it is best to get a plan from the tourist office and then, if you want more information, there is a local guide in English called *Historical and Monumental Cáceres*. Armed with these you could spend hours just wandering through this almost unspoilt area. There is so much to see I have found it is best to come back a second or even third time to fully appreciate it.

Museums

Museo de Cáceres (Cáceres Museum), Plaza de las Veletas. Open Tuesday to Saturday 0930-1430; Sunday 1015-1430. Closed Monday and holidays. Entrance: 200 ptas. The museum is housed in the Palacio Veletas which has an 18th century façade and a 16th century patio. There are prehistoric exhibits and many coins but the most extraordinary thing is to be found in the basement. There you will find the old Arabic reservoir *ajibe* with its graceful horseshoe-shaped arches. The fact that it seems so out of place enhances its attractiveness. In summer 1992 a new fine arts section was opened in a nearby building. The hours of opening are the same and admission is included in the 200 ptas. The exhibits, on three floors, are of contemporary art and contrast vividly with their newly renovated, but very old, home.

Station/location/transport to city centre

RENFE, Avenida Alemania; tel: 22 08 31. A relatively modern station, at an altitude of 451.4m, that is some distance, too far to walk, from the city centre. Unusually, there is not a *consigna* office here.

Key

A: *Comisaría*	**G:** *Rail Press Librería Prodesa*,
B: *Jefe de Estación*	newspapers, magazines, etc
C: Ticket office	**H:** *Servicios*
D: Train information	**I:** Cafeteria, open 0300-2300;
E: Avis car hire	Restaurant, open 1330-1600, 2000-
F: *Tábacos*	2300

Train station to town centre

By taxi This is the most practical way and will cost about 400/450 ptas.

Train services
To Madrid by

	Regional	Diurno	Talgo	Estrella
Madrid	5	4½	3¾	4¾

To Barcelona by

Diurno: via Madrid 4¼; Zaragoza 8¾; Barcelona 13¼.

Layout

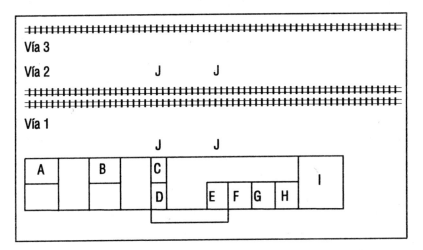

To Sevilla by
Regional: via Mérida 1¼; Zafra 2¾; Sevilla 5.

To Badajoz by

	Regional	*Talgo*
Mérida	1¼	1
Badajoz	2	1¾

Accommodation
In the city
*** Hotel Extremadura Avenida Virgen de Guadalupe, 5; tel: 22 16 00. Single 4,500 ptas; double 7,500 ptas. About five minutes from old city. All modern facilities including a pool.

All the following are close to the 'Monumental Zone':

** Hotel Álvarez Moret, 20; tel: 24 64 00. Single 3,300 ptas; double 5,700 ptas. All modern conveniences including TV and air conditioning.
* Hotel Iberia Generalísimo Franco, 2; tel: 24 82 00. Single 3,600 ptas; double 4,955 ptas. All rooms with bath. Old-fashioned hotel in a pedestrian shopping area close to the Plaza Mayor.
** HR Goya General Mola, 11; tel: 24 99 50. Single 3,000 ptas; double 3,600 ptas. On Plaza Mayor facing old city. Second floor; nice TV room.
* Hostal Castilla Ríos Verdes, 3; tel: 24 44 04. Single 1,266 ptas; double 2,266 ptas. Rooms without bath/shower. Rather plain. One street off Plaza Mayor.

* **Pensión Carretera** Plaza Mayor, 23; tel: 24 74 82. Single without bath 1,200 ptas, with bath 1,500 ptas; double 2,000 ptas. Small basic pension. Central location.

* **Pensión Márquez** Gabriel y Galán, 2; tel: 24 49 60. Double 2,000 ptas (doubles only). Second floor entrance just off Plaza Mayor.

General information
Car hire
Avis, Licencia Avis, RENFE; tel: 21 13 89.

Police
Comisaría, Avenida Virgen de la Montana, 3; tel: 21 14 51.

RENFE city office
RENFE, Plaza de la Concepción, 27; tel: 21 26 06.

Telephone code
for Cáceres province is (927).

Tele Taxi
Euro-Radio; tel: 21 21 21.

Tourist office
Oficina de Información Turística, Plaza Mayor, 37; tel: 24 63 47. Open Monday to Friday 0900-1400, 1700-1900; Saturday and Sunday 0900-1400. Closed holidays.

CÁDIZ
The city
History

1100BC	Phoenicians found Cádiz.
500-400BC	Carthaginians rule in 'Gades'.
206BC	Cádiz becomes a federal ally of the Romans.
46BC	Roman citizenship is granted to Cádiz.
400-500AD	Visigoths take control of the city.
711	Muslims take over after winning the Battle of Guadalete.
1262	Cádiz is reconquered by Alfonso X.
1493	Monopoly of trade with Africa is granted by the Catholic Monarchs. Columbus departs on his second voyage on September 25.
1502	Columbus leaves on his fourth voyage.
1587	Francis Drake attacks the Spanish fleet in Cádiz harbour.
1596	Much of the city is destroyed when an Anglo-Dutch fleet attacks the city.
1717	Chamber of Commerce is transferred from Sevilla by Felipe V beginning a period of economic expansion.
1812	Whilst the city is under siege by Napoleon's troops the national parliament meets in St Felipe Neri and, on March 19, proclaims the first Spanish constitution.

Overview

Cádiz is located 727km (454 miles) south of Madrid and has a population of about 160,000. Many cities in Spain have dramatic geographical locations but Cádiz, on a long narrow peninsula that runs parallel to the coastline, is unique. This combination of a long history and unusual geographical location has combined to give the city a very special character. The old town is at the end of the peninsula and has water on three sides. This can have a rather disorientating effect as, often, whichever way one looks down the maze of narrow streets that are prevalent in the city, the sea is visible. Adding to the charm are the many plazas, of varying sizes, spread throughout the city. Nowhere is the character more typical than in the *Populo barrio* between the cathedral and the walls separating the old from the new town. Originating in the 13th century, the lanes here are narrower, the buildings higher and the atmosphere reminds me more of what Spain was like before the advent of mass tourism changed much of the mainland. This area is guarded by three entrances and also houses several historic, or interesting, buildings. Seafood is, of course, a staple diet, in a city so close to the ocean. Along the beaches lining the Atlantic Ocean in the new town there are numerous restaurants that sell all kinds of delicious fried seafood which can often be eaten either in the restaurants or taken away. In the old town in Calle Sopranis, just off the Plaza de San Juan de Dios, there is a similar place and, although it will not work out that much cheaper than a set meal in a restaurant, the food is mouth-watering.

The city is seen at its best from the sea; if you have the time take a cruise, especially at night, or the ferry to El Puerto de Santa María.

Places of interest
Must see
Catedral y Museo (Cathedral and Cathedral Museum), Plaza Pío XII; tel: 22 22 41. Open Monday to Saturday 0930-1300, 1600-1800. Closed Sunday and holidays. Entrance: adults 200 ptas; children 100 ptas. Started in 1722 and not finished until 1838, this cathedral combines the two styles of those periods, baroque and classical. Unfortunately it is in a bad state of repair and, during 1992, only the museum was open. This is not very large but it has some interesting exhibits including a very elegant monstrance, an example of Enrique de Arfe's fine work.

Museo de Bellas Artes y Arqueológico (Fine Arts and Archaeological Museum), Plaza de Mina; tel: 21 43 00. Open Tuesday to Friday 0900-1300, 1700-2000; Saturday and Sunday 0900-1330. Closed Monday and holidays. Entrance: citizens of the EC (with ID) free; others 250 ptas. A very elegant museum that combines exhibits of local archaeological history, on the lower levels, and paintings on the upper levels.

By choice
Cruceros Turísticos (Boat cruises); tel: 22 66 27. Evenings 1900 or 2030; fare adults 500 ptas, children 300 ptas; nights 2215 or 2345 (adults only) 1,000 ptas with a drink. Cruises around the Bay of Cádiz.

Hospital de Mujeres (Women's Hospital); tel: 21 49 58. Open Monday to Friday 1000-1300. Closed Saturday and Sunday. The current building dates from 1749 and is well worth a visit. There is a classic patio and the chapel contains many works of art including a notable El Greco.

Motonave *Adriano III* (Ferry to El Puerto de Santa María) From Cádiz 1000, 1200, 1400, 1830, 2030; From El Puerto 0900, 1100, 1300, 1530, 1930. Extra service Sunday and holidays from Cádiz 1630; from El Puerto 1730. Fare: 175 ptas. The departure point is directly across from the station.

Oratorio de la Santa Cueva (Church of Santa Cueva), Rosario; tel: 21 36 09. Open Monday to Friday 1000-1300. Entrance: 50 ptas. A most unusual place. The underground chapels, built in 1783, have many works of artistic value and are rather damp. The upper chapel, built in 1796, is entirely different. Oval in shape, it is a mix of ornateness and plainness. Around the upper levels of the chapel the five semicircular paintings, three by Goya, are of particular interest.

Oratorio de San Felipe Neri (Church of San Felipe Neri), San José, 38; tel: 21 16 12. Open daily 1000-1130, 1930-2200. Entrance: free. Built in 1679 this has a most unusual elliptical shape with classical columns and a beautiful dome. One of its claims to fame is that the parliament sat there when drawing up the 1812 constitution.

Museums

Museo del Mar (Museum of the Sea); tel: 22 24 74. Open daily 1000-1400, 1700-2200. This is used for exhibitions but was closed for renovation work when I visited.

Museo Histórico Municipal (City History Museum), Santa Inés, 9; tel: 22 17 88. Open Tuesday to Friday 0900-1300, 1700-2000 (October to May 1600-1900); Saturday and Sunday 0900-1300. Closed Monday. Entrance: free. A small museum with the most interesting exhibit being a large wooden model of the city that can be viewed from above; thus giving an unusual, and helpful, perspective.

Station/location/transport to city centre
RENFE, Plaza de Sevilla; tel: 26 33 57. An unremarkable terminal that is close to both the harbour and the city.

Layout

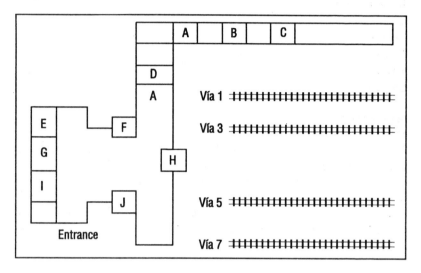

Key
A: *Consigna Automática*, open 0800-2200, 300 ptas a day, tokens from ticket office
B: *Atención al Cliente*
C: *Jefe de Estación*
D: Cafeteria, open 0900-2200
E: *Información*

F: *Servicios* — men
G: Ticket office — local services
H: *Kiosco* for newspapers, magazines, etc
I: Ticket office — long distance services
J: *Servicios* — women

Transport to city centre
On foot The closest part of the city, where all the listed hotels are, is just five minutes away.

Train services
To Madrid by

	Talgo Pen	*Talgo*	*Estrella*
Jerez de la Frontera	½	¾	¾
Sevilla	1½		1¾
Córdoba	3¼	3¾	3¾
Ciudad Real		5	

| Alcázar de San Juan | 6¼ | | 7½ |
| Madrid | 8 | 6½ | 10 |

To Barcelona by	*Diurno*	*Estrella*
Jerez de la Frontera	¾	¾
Sevilla	1½	2
Córdoba	3¼	3¾
Alcázar de San Juan	6¾	8
Valencia	10	12
Barcelona	14½	17¼

Accommodation

*** Hotel Husa Puertatierra Avenida Andalucía, 34; tel: 27 21 11; fax: 25 03 11. Only opened in 1993, this modern, elegant hotel, part of the Husa chain, is located close to both the Santa María del Mar beach and the old quarter of Cádiz. There are 98 rooms all with private bath, telephone, satellite TV, background music, air-conditioning and minibar. It also has a restaurant, bar, coffee shop and two tennis courts. Single 9,000 ptas; double 11,900 ptas; double, for single use, 9,500 ptas.

*** Hotel De Francia y Paris Plaza de San Francisco, 2; tel: 22 23 48; fax: 22 24 31. This Best Western hotel has the following two seasons: low January 1 to March 31, October 1 to December 31; high April 1 to September 30. Single low 6,042 ptas, high 6,890 ptas; double low 7,950 ptas, high 9,010 ptas. These rates include breakfast. A pleasant hotel in a very convenient location for visiting all the places of interest. It has 57 rooms with bath/shower, colour TV, direct dial telephone, and some have air-conditioning, minibar, piped music and a safe. Although there is a bar it does not have a restaurant.

** Hostal Bahía Uruguay, 5; tel: 25 90 61. Single 4,500 ptas; double 5,500 ptas. Just off Plaza de San Juan de Dios. Very nice. Single rates for double rooms.

** Hostal Carlos I Plaza de Sevilla; tel: 28 68 11. Single 3,105 ptas; double 5,800 ptas. Busy location directly above station. Rather expensive.

* Hostal España Marqués de Cádiz, 9; tel: 28 55 00. Single without bath 2,000 ptas, with bath 2,500 ptas; double with bath 3,500 ptas. Quiet street close to Plaza de San Juan de Dios. Small rooms. Interesting style.

** Pensión Centro Sol SL Padre Elejalde, 7; tel: 28 31 03. Single 4,000 ptas; double 5,000 ptas. Very pleasant. Not far from station.

CH Colón Marqués de Cádiz, 6; tel: 28 53 51. double 2,500 ptas (doubles only). Close to Plaza de San Juan de Dios.

CH La Isleña San Juan de Dios, 12. tel: 28.70.64. Single 1,100 ptas, double 2,200 ptas. Rooms without bath. Second floor overlooking plaza.

General information
Car hire
Avis, Avenida Cayetano del Toro, 16; tel: 27 11 00.

Fiestas
Easter week (*Semana Santa*) and Corpus Christi; dates are variable.

Police
Comisaría, Avenida de Andalucía, 28; tel: 28 61 11.

Telephone code
for Cádiz province is (956).

Tourist office
Junta de Andalucía, Oficina de Turismo, Calderón de la Barca, 1; tel: 21 13 13. Open Monday to Friday 0900-1400, 1700-1900; Saturday 1000-1300. Closed Sunday and holidays.

CÓRDOBA
The city
History
Córdoba is one of Spain's oldest cities:

206BC	The Romans, under Lucio Mario, invade.
152BC	The Roman municipality is given the title of 'Patrician Colony' and becomes the capital of the 'Roman Ulterior of Spain'.
45BC	Pompeii conquers the city.
572	The Visigoth king, Leovigildus, conquers the city, thus ending eight centuries of Roman rule.
711	The Moors cross from Africa, defeat the Visigoths and take control of southern Spain.
756	Abdel-Rahman I, Emir of the Ommiad dynasty, establishes Córdoba as an independent emirate.
786	Construction of the mosque begins.
929	Abdel-Rahman III renames the city a Caliphate. The city becomes one of the richest in Europe and enters its most important era. It is an admired centre of culture, science and art and has a population of between 500,000 and 1,000,000. It is considered to be one of the cultural capitals of the world.
1009	Rebellion of the Omeyan Prince Muhammad II. From now the empire breaks up into Moorish kingdoms and there is a long decline in the city's fortunes.
1236	The city is reconquered by the Castilian/Leonese King Ferdinand III, 'The Saint'. By now the city is in ruins and is repopulated by people from other areas of Spain.
1382	Alfonso XI begins construction of the Alcázar.
15th century	Late this century Isabella the Catholic lives in the Alcázar and receives Columbus before his voyage. She plans the reconquest of Granada.
1523	Carlos V begins construction of a Christian cathedral inside the mosque.

Overview
Córdoba is located in the centre/north of Andalucía, at an altitude of 123m, and close to an attractive range of small mountains, the Sierra Morena. It is a fairly flat city but with a slight incline, to the north, from the River Guadalquivir which flows on westward

towards Sevilla some 85 miles away.

With a population of over 300,000 it does not give the impression of being so large and the atmosphere is very much that of a provincial capital. Perhaps this is because most of the tourist sights are grouped together in such a small part of the city. Apart from the small shopping and tourist area, the rest of the city is residential with mainly modern apartments that are of no interest to the majority of visitors.

The area of most interest to the tourist is that around La Mezquita, the *Alcázar*, and the very attractive *barrio Judería* where there are many other places of interest. Much of the district to the east of the Mezquita has very quiet, old, residential areas interspersed with a few places of tourist interest. These streets are full of very old whitewashed houses, many of which have traditional patios, and to walk around them is a delight. After the reconquest, Fernando III founded 14 parishes and many of the churches are in this section. Although most of them are only open for services these ancient monuments, many with accompanying *plazas*, are a pleasure to see.

Places of interest
Must see
La Mezquita, La Catedral and Tesoro Catedralicio (Mosque, Cathedral and Cathedral Museum) The entrance is in the southeast corner of the courtyard; tel: 22 22 52. Open summer 1030-1330, 1600-1900; winter 1030-1330, 1530-1730. Entrance: 500 ptas. Dress: It is respectful to dress conservatively (no shorts, etc) when visiting religious places. La Mezquita stands on the site of a Visigothic cathedral on which work was started in 786 at the order of Abdel-Rahman I. Initially there were two parts, an open courtyard for ablution rituals (*Sahm*), now known as the Patio of the Orange Trees, and a covered area for over 10,000 people. It was completed in the 10th century after three expansions and, at 23,400m², it was for centuries the greatest mosque in the Islamic world. A new minaret, El Alminar, was built in the 10th century and served as a model for others such as the Giralda in Sevilla. Today parts of it are preserved within the bell tower, which is on the northwest corner of the patio.

After the reconquest in 1236, small Christian chapels were built in 1258 and 1260. Then, in the reign of Carlos V, construction of a Christian cathedral in the centre of the mosque began in 1523. The contrasting styles of mosque and cathedral make this place unique and one's attention is drawn from one to the other, in utter fascination. It is the oldest monument in day-to-day use in the Western world.

Before entering take a walk around the outside to look at the walls, doorways and the gargoyles on the roof, which serve to carry rain water to the street from aqueducts that run across the roof. You will first come to the Patio of the Orange Trees and the fountains, a very peaceful place. Entry to La Mezquita proper is in the southeast corner of the patio during the hours shown above. However there is nothing stopping you attending the religious services and, of course, there is no charge for that.

Inside you will see hundreds of columns supporting double arches. Alternate bricks in these are red, and whichever way you look the columns are accentuated by shafts of light and their shadows. The lighting effect is made even more intriguing by electric lanterns. On closer inspection it will become apparent that the columns are not only different colours but also made from different materials. It is fascinating simply to wander around; as you move in and out between the columns the colours and shades continually change, throwing up a kaleidoscope of architecture and light.

When the cathedral is reached the contrast is stunning. As ornate as the Moorish architecture and design is, the colours of La Mezquita blend well and, being Islamic, there are no human images. The cathedral, however, contains huge paintings of the saints and Christ, as well as an intricate choir by the Sevillian sculptor Pedro Duque Cornejo and a pulpit by the Frenchman, Michel de Verdiguier. There are human images everywhere in paint, stone and wood, and the colours seem less harmonious here. There are also many smaller adjoining chapels.

At the back, along the southernmost wall, there is another striking contrast in cultures. The Mihrab, a small chamber with a domed roof, was built during the second expansion of the mosque by Al-Hakam II, who was enthroned in 961. The ornamental plaster work here is simply incredible and no description can do it credit. Right next to it is the small museum of the cathedral's treasures, *Tesoro Catedralicio*, and entrance is included in the price of the ticket. There are all manner of things here dating from the 15th to 20th century, but the most important is Enrique de Arfe's monstrance. Over 2.5m high, 200kg in weight and made of solid silver, it was used for the first time in 1518 for the Corpus Christi celebrations.

This is, without doubt, a place unique in the world and once visited the memory of the contrasting styles and cultures will remain forever with you.

On a more practical note many people will want to take photographs here but flashlights are banned. Therefore it is essential to have a very fast film, even as fast as 1600 ASA. This is not readily available in Spain and when it is the price is prohibitive. If you plan to visit La Mezquita buy some fast film before you leave.

Alcázar de los Reyes Cristianos (Fortress and Palace of the Christian Kings), Campo Santo de los Mártires; tel: 29 63 92. Open summer 0930-1330, 1700-2000; winter 0930-1330, 1600-1900. Entrance: adults 200 ptas; children (under 14) 100 ptas. This fortress of the Catholic Monarchs was built in the 16th century, on the site of previous Visigoth and Muslim fortresses, by Alfonso XI. There are ancient Roman mosaics in the Hall of the Mosaics and also a Roman sarcophagus (stone coffin) dating from the 2nd or 3rd century. The rooms here have a simple elegance about them and are not at all ostentatious. There are four towers around the wall and, from those that are accessible, there are excellent views of the city and surrounding area. The gardens are also a delight, well laid out and with a series of rectangular ponds, some of which have fountains lining both sides.

Ferdinand and Isabella lived here for several years during which they received Columbus twice before his voyage, and also planned the reconquest of Granada. After the reconquest of that city, in 1492, it was used by the Court of the Inquisition, then as a civil jail and a military prison.

Palacio de los Marqueses de Viana (Palace of the Marqueses of Viana), Plaza de Don Gome, 2; tel: 48 01 34. Open summer 0900-1400; winter 1000-1300, 1600-1800. Closed Wednesdays. Entrance to museum and patios: adults 200 ptas; children 100 ptas; patios only: adults and children 100 ptas. This is one of the best preserved 16th century mansions in the city. It was acquired by the local savings bank, the Caja Provincial de Ahorros de Córdoba, in 1980 and converted to a museum. In 1981 it was declared a historic and artistic monument of national character and, in 1983, another royal decree granted it the status of Artistic Gardens. Around the building are 13 charming patios, each with a unique character. As you enter the first one through the large gates, note that the corner column has been omitted, which was to allow the entrance of horse-drawn carriages. The house itself has a marvellous collection of furniture, tapestries, porcelain and leather as well as a library.

This is one of the less well-known places to visit in Córdoba and it is very easy to miss as it blends naturally into the local environment. The only clues to its identity are the wooden entrance gates and, around the corner, large metal grille windows that allow a glimpse of one of the patios. You need to allow at least two to three hours for your visit.

Plaza de la Corredera This plaza, unique in Andalucía, was built by the Magistrate Corregidor Ronquillo Briceno and completed in the late 17th century. Rectangular in shape, the plaza has three upper floors, with galleries and balconies that are supported by semicircular arches enclosing a porticoed ground level. In its early days bullfights, and even executions, were held here. In 1896 the centre of the plaza was turned into a covered marketplace, then the roof was removed in the 1950s. Today it is still used as a general market from Monday to Saturday and as a flea market on Sundays. There are only three entrances, two through arches in the northwest and southeast corners known as the 'High and Low Arches' and the other through the southern façade where there is a fresh food *mercado*. That this historical *plaza* is today a little run-down is part of its charm. There are some interesting *rastros*, second-hand antique and junk shops, at various locations around the *plaza*.

Sinagoga (Synagogue), Judíos. Open daily summer 1000-1400, 1800-2000; winter 1000-1400, 1530-1730. Entrance free, but contributions asked for. There are only three synagogues left in Spain; the other two are in Toledo. This one is very small (7m x 6.5m) and was completed around 1315. After the reconquest of Spain in 1492, when all Jews were expelled from the country, it was converted into a hospital and later, in 1588, changed to a chapel. It was declared a national monument in 1885. The plaster work is very characteristic of Mudejar art. There is a statue of Maimonides just outside.

Medina Azahara (Medinat Al-Zahra), tel: 22 51 03. Open October to April — Tuesday to Saturday 1000-1400, 1600-1800; Sunday and holidays 1000-1330. May to September — Tuesday to Saturday 1000-1400, 1800-2000; Sunday and holidays 1000-1330. Closed Monday. Entrance: 250 ptas. On the foothills of the Sierra

Morena, just 8km west of Córdoba on the N431, you will find the remains of this intriguing old city, often referred to as 'the Versailles of the 10th century'. Work was begun in 936 during the reign of Abdel-Rahman III, and legend has it that it was constructed in honour of his favourite concubine Al-Zahra, 'the Flower'. From detailed records it can be ascertained that many of the materials were bought from distant places such as Constantinople and North Africa.

It did not have a very long life as a royal palace. Early in the 11th century the Caliphate began to break up and the city was used by different factions before being sacked. Subsequently some of the materials were used on constructions in Sevilla and other places. Excavations were begun in 1910 and still continue but enough of this city, built on three terraces, has now been uncovered to make it an essential place to visit.

By choice

Convento de la Merced (Merced Convent), Plaza del Colón. Open Monday to Friday 1000-1400, 1800-2100. These days this very ornate, and much restored, building is a local government office and only part of it is open to the public. One of its claims to fame is that Christopher Columbus stayed here while awaiting an audience with the Catholic Monarchs to discuss the voyage to the new world.

Cristo de los Faroles (Christ of the Lanterns), Plaza de los Delores. This famous statue of Christ on the cross, surrounded by eight lanterns on an iron fence, was constructed in 1794. It is a very popular monument and is in an attractive square with the old Convent Hospital of San Jacinto, dating from 1710, on one side.

Jardín Botánico (Botanical Gardens), Avenida de Zoológico. Open Tuesday to Sunday 1030-1430, 1630-1830. Closed Monday and holidays.

Parque Zoológico (Zoo), Avenida de Zoológico; tel: 47 20 00. Open 1000-1800. Entrance adults 125 ptas, children 60 ptas.

Plaza del Potro There is a 14th century inn here as well as the 15th century Hospital de la Caridad, which houses the Julio Romero de Torres and fine arts museums. In the centre of the *plaza* is a fountain, dating from 1577, with a statue of a *potro* colt in the centre. It would be a far more attractive place today if the tourist shops were removed.

Puente Romano   (Roman Bridge)   This bridge across the Guadalquivir was originally built during the times of Julius Caesar and has been restored on many occasions since then. Today none of the 16 spans is original but it still remains one of the oldest monuments in the city. There is a statue of San Rafael in the centre.

Puerta de Almodovar   Located just to the northwest of the old *barrio Judería*, this 14th century gate, which was restored in the 19th century, has two towers joined by an arch and leads from the old to the new part of Córdoba.

Puerta del Puente (Located between the Puente Romano and La Mezquita). This gate to the Roman bridge was built in 1572 during the reign of Felipe II to replace the one constructed in Roman times.

Roman Ruins   Just outside the new town hall are some Roman columns that look quite out of place.

Triunfo de San Rafael   Torrijos.   San Rafael is the guardian archangel of the city and this statue, at the top of a column, was commissioned by the cathedral authorities when the archangel saved the city from an earthquake. Completed in 1781 by Michel de Verdiguier, it was restored in 1988.

Museums

Museo Arqueológico   (Archaeological Museum),   Plaza de San Jerónimo Paez; tel: 22 40 11. Summer 1000-1400, 1800-2000; winter 1000-1400, 1700-1900. Closed Monday and holidays. Entrance free. Opened in 1965, the building is lovely, with three patios, and is in a delightful area of the city. It underwent extensive restoration in 1991-92.

Museo de Artes Cordobeses y Taurino   (Cordoban Arts and Bullfighting Museum),   Plaza de las Bulas, 5. Open summer 0930-1330, 1700-2000; winter 0930-1330, 1600-1900. Entrance adults 200 ptas; children (under 14) 100 ptas. This has two entities, the museum of bullfighting and a craft centre. The museum, not to everyone's taste, is housed in a delightful 16th century house, the Casa de las Bulas. It is one of the most interesting museums of its type in Spain. It contains a large library, many posters, *trajes de luces* (suits of lights) and bulls' heads, as well as exhibitions dedicated to famous Cordobese *toreros* Lagartijo, Machaquito, Guerrita and, arguably the most famous ever, Manolete. There are two statues dedicated to Manolete across town.

The arts section is back across the courtyard. It specialises in leather and silver; there is a small souvenir shop.

Museo de Bellas Artes (Fine Arts Museum), Plaza del Potro, 1; tel: 47 33 45. Open summer 1000-1400, 1800-2000; winter 1000-1400, 1700-1900; Sundays and holidays 1000-1330. Closed Mondays. Entrance: Spanish nationals and citizens of the EC (on presentation of passport) free; others 250 ptas. This museum of fine arts, part of the old Hospital de la Caridad (Charity Hospital), has many paintings and sculptures by Cordobese artists.

Museo Diocesano (Diocesan Museum), Torrijos, 2. Open summer 1000-1400, 1600-1800; winter 1000-1400, 1600-1800. Closed Sundays and holidays. Entrance 150 ptas. Located in a beautiful old building. The exhibits are set on floors around a classical patio. On the ground floor there are many ancient Roman artefacts and most of the paintings and other displays are in the traditional style.

Museo de Julio Romero de Torres (Julio Romero de Torres Museum), Plaza del Potro, 2; tel: 22 23 45. Open summer 0930-1330; winter 1000-1330, 1600-1800; Entrance: free. This museum, in honour of Julio Romereo de Torres who was born nearby, was opened in 1931 and contains over 50 paintings donated by the artist's family, many of them specialising in Cordobese women. Part of it is located the Hospital de la Caridad. It is a very popular museum that is not as sombre as many others. Outside there is a really beautiful patio with a fountain and busts.

Museo Vivo de Al-Andalus (Life of Andalucía Museum), Torre de la Calahorra, Puente Romano (south end); tel: 22 51 03. Open 1030-1800. The tower of Calahorra was built in 1360 by Enrique II to defend himself against attacks by his brother Pedro I. There are two parts to the tower and the one facing east displays a royal shield. These days it is a museum, and has a cinematic review of

Andalucian life over the centuries. It is best reached by walking across the Puente Romano and offers good views back to La Mezquita.

Station/location/transport to city centre

RENFE, Córdoba Central, Glorieta Conde Guadalhorce; tel: 47 76 65. Córdoba is a small city and the train station is positioned just to the north of the centre and tourist areas.

Layout

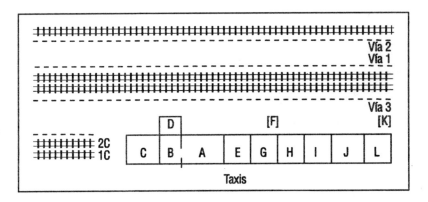

Key

A: Main entrance and booking hall
B: Various shops: grocery shop open 0900-1400, 1600-0500
C: Restaurant/bar, open 0500-0100
D: *Kiosco* for books, magazines, open 0600-2100
E: *Jefe de Estación*
F: Automatic drink dispensing machine
G: *Jefe de Circulación*
H: *Oficina de Atención al Cliente*
I: *Comisaría*
J: *Consigna Automática*; cost 200 ptas a day, open 0700-2300
K: *Carritos Portaequipajes*
L: *Servicios*

Train station to city centre

By taxi The most practical way of getting anywhere is by taxi, most places being no more than five minutes away.

Train services

To Madrid by

	Diurno	Estrella	Talgo	Talgo Pen	Talgo Camas	AVE
Linares/Baeza	1½	2½	1½			
Ciudad Real				1¼	1	
Alcázar de San Juan	3¾	4¾		3	4	
Madrid	5¾	7¾	4½	2½	6½	2

To Barcelona by

	Diurno	Estrella	Talgo Camas
Alcázar de San Juan	3½	4¼	
Valencia	6¾	7¾	
Zaragoza			8½
Barcelona	11¼	13¼	13¾

To Irún/France by

	Estrella
Alcázar de San Juan	3½
Madrid	5¾
Irún	15¼

To Algeciras/Cádiz/Sevilla/Huelva by

	Regional	Diurno	Inter City	Talgo	Talgo Pen	Estrella	AVE
Sevilla	1¾	1½	1½	1	1¼	1¼	2¾
Jerez de la Frontera	3¼	2½		2¼	3½		
Cádiz	4	3½		3	4½		
Ronda					3½		
Algeciras					5½		
Huelva				3			

To Almería by

Estrella: via Linares/Baeza 2; Almería 7½.

To Granada by

Regional: via Bobadilla 1¾; Granada 3½. These are actual travel times, in fact the overall time of the journey is dependent upon the wait for a connection in Bobadilla.

To Málaga by

	Regional	Talgo Diurno	Talgo Pen	Estrella
Bobadilla	1¼	1¾	1¼	1¾
Málaga	3¼	3	2¼	3

Accommodation
Close to the station
**** Hotel Gran Capitán Avenida de América, 5; tel: 47 02 50. Part of the Husa chain, this large, modern hotel is located a few hundred yards from the railway station (on the same street) and just 10 minutes walk from La Mezquita. It has 100 rooms all with private bath, TV, air-conditioning and safe box with some having northerly views over the Sierra Morena. There is also a restaurant, cocktail bar, coffee shop and boutique. There are two seasons: high between March 15 and October 31 and low the rest of the year. Single high 10,200 ptas, low 8,500 ptas; double high 16,200 ptas, low 13,200 ptas; double, for single use, high 12,950 ptas, low 10,500 ptas; treble high 19,700 ptas, low 16,700 ptas.

* Hotel Granada Avenida de América, 17; tel: 47 70 00. Single 1,350 ptas; double 3,000 ptas, with shower 2,600 ptas. Rather plain and old fashioned.

* HR Perales Avenida de los Mozarabes, 19; tel: 23 03 25. Single 1,000 ptas; double 1,800 ptas. A small place on the first floor of a modern block overlooking the Jardines Diego de Rivas. Can be a little noisy especially in the rooms at the front.

* Hostal Alhaken Alhaken 11, 10; tel: 47 15 93. Single 1,600 ptas, without bath 1,100 ptas; double 2,600 ptas, without bath 2,000 ptas. Located on the third floor this appears to be like the building — a little drab.

CH Córdoba Avenida de Cervantes; tel: 47 72 04. Single 1,200 ptas; double 1,700 ptas. Situated on a busy road. Rather old and unattractive.

CH Málaga Avenida de Cervantes; Single 1,200 ptas. Unattractive place on the first floor. The staff were not particularly helpful.

In the city
*** Hotel El Califa Lope de Hoces, 14; tel: 29 94 00; fax: 29 57 16. This Best Western has the following two seasons: low January 1 to February 29, July 1 to August 31 and high March 1 to June 30, September 1 to December 31. Single low 6,890 ptas, high 10,070 ptas; double low 9,010 ptas, high 13,250 ptas. These rates include breakfast. Located just 300m from the old city, has 66 rooms with bath/shower, direct dial telephone, air-conditioning and colour TV, and some have radios and balconies as well. An interesting feature is the traditional Arabic patios.

* HR Boston Málaga, 2; tel: 47 41 76. Single 1,995 ptas; double 3,320 ptas. Modern. Located on the first floor of a building adjacent to the Plaza de las Tendillas.

* HR Las Tendillas Jesús María, 1; tel: 47 30 29. Single 1,200 ptas; double 2,000 ptas. Clean, old-fashioned and located on the third floor of a building just off the Plaza de las Tendillas. There is a lift.

* Hostal Alcázar San Basilio, 2; tel: 20 25 61. Single 1,350 ptas; double 2,525 ptas; treble 3,450 ptas; four beds 5,000 ptas. Just to the west of the Plaza Campo de los Santo Martires. Clean and modern, with a wide selection of rooms and a large collection of miniature bottles in the patio. A little off the tourist beat.

* Hostal Almenzor Corregidor Luís de la Cerda, 10; tel: 48 54 00. Single 1,200 ptas; double 2,235 ptas. No patio. Very friendly people and a pleasant atmosphere.

* Hostal El León Cespedes, 6; tel: 47 30 21, Single 1,100 ptas; double 2,200 ptas. Called 'the Lion'. Very old and set around a columned patio with birds in cages and an old bull's head with broken horns on the wall. Rather basic, but acceptable, it has the advantage of being very close to La Mezquita.

* Hostal La Milagrosa Rey Herredia, 12; tel: 47 33 17. Single 1,200 ptas; double 3,500, without bath 1,800 ptas. Very attractive inside. Small bar.

* Hostal Maestre Romero Barros, 16; tel: 47 53 95. Single 1,800 ptas, without bath 1,150 ptas; double 3,300 ptas, without bath 2,300 ptas. Nice, old, with an interesting patio.

* Hostal Plaza Corredera Rodrigues Marín, 15; tel: 47 05 81. Single 1,000 ptas; double 2,000 ptas. Very pleasant and well away from the main tourist beat. Ask for a room with a view overlooking the *plaza*.

* Hostal Rey Herredia Osio, 2; tel: 47 95 59. Single 1,000 ptas; double 2,000 ptas. Quite large and very attractive indeed.

** Pensión Antonio Machado Buen Pastor, 4; tel: 29 62 59. Single 1,500 ptas; double 3,000 ptas. An exceptional place, with a lovely patio and a restaurant, for residents only, where a meal costs around 700 ptas. It is not far from the cathedral and the house next door has a series of beautiful patios.

CH Los Leones Saravia, 3; tel: 47 02 94. Single 1,000 ptas; double 1,500 ptas. 'The Lions' is very old and set around a Moorish-style, plain patio, horribly painted in blue and white.

The maze of small streets east of La Mezquita and bordered by the river has many low budget pensions and hostels that do not appear in any official guide.

General information
Car hire
Avis, Plaza de Colón, 28; tel: 47 68 62.

Fiesta
Easter week (*Semana Santa*) — variable dates; Patio Festival (*Festival de los Patios Cordobeses*) May; Flamenco Festival (*Festival de Flamenco*) every other May, and May Fair (*Feria de Mayo*) end of May.

Hospitals
Hospital Reina Sofía, Avenida de Menéndez Pidal; tel: 29 11 33.
Hospital General, Avenida de Menéndez Pidal; tel: 29 71 22.

Police
Comisaría, Avenida del Doctor Fleming, 2; tel: 47 75 00.

Telephone code
for Córdoba province is (957).

Tourist office
Oficina de Turismo, Torrijos, 10. tel: 47.12.35. Open Monday to Friday 1000-1400, 1630-1930; Saturday 1000-1400. Located in the Palacio de Congresos y Exposiciones.

CUENCA

The city

Cuenca, with a population of 43,000, is located 201km (125 miles) east of Madrid. At an altitude of 998m the city is rather isolated but the old town is in a spectacular position on a promontory between the Huecar and Jucar rivers, directly above the newer parts of the town. What there is to see is up in the old part of the town and the most famous, by far, are the Hanging Houses. However, the rest of the area, although small, is quite interesting just to wander through.

The city's isolated position is a problem for travellers by train. It is not really practical to make it a day trip from either Madrid or Valencia and therefore only those travelling between those cities, and prepared to stay overnight, can get to see it. My personal opinion is that if you are on a tight timescale Cuenca is one of the places that can be left for another year.

Places of interest
Must see

Casas Colgadas (Hanging Houses) These date from the 14th century and are perched very precariously on the steep rocks above the Hoz de Huecar. They are best seen from a distance and the Puente San Pablo across the Huecar, although a very fragile looking structure, offers the best view. If you want photographs the best time is in the morning when the sun will be behind you and not the Casas Colgadas. Unfortunately they cannot be seen from the city.

Catedral y Tesoro Catedralicio (Cathedral and Cathedral Treasure), Plaza de Pío XII (next to Plaza Mayor). Cathedral open summer 0900-1330, 1630-1930, winter, 1630-1830. Cathedral treasure (museum) open summer 1100-1330, 1630-1930, winter 1630-1830. The cathedral has a very unusual façade and with its unique Gothic/Anglo-Norman style is a national monument. However, it is very plain inside and I think that the abstract design on the stained glass windows looks rather out of place.

Old Town This is a delightful place to wander around; it is not very large and not at all spoilt by tourism. There are several interesting churches, a castle and the very unusual Torre de Mangana. This tall narrow tower used to be part of the Arab fortifications and today has been put to use, very practically, as the town's clock tower.

Museums

Museo Arqueológico (Archaeological Museum), Obispo Valero, 12; tel: 21 30 69. Open Tuesday to Saturday 1000-1400, 1600-1900; Sundays and holidays 1000-1400. Closed Monday. The museum, also known as Museo de Cuenca, currently houses collections of exhibits, mostly from the province, displayed in chronological order.

Museo de Arte Abstracto Español (Spanish Abstract Art Museum), Casa Colgadas; tel: 21 29 83. Open Tuesday to Friday 1100-1400, 1600-1800; Saturday 1100-1400, 1600-2000; Sunday 1100-1400. Closed Monday and January 1, Thursday and Friday of Easter week, Fiesta of San Mateo, December 24, 25 and 31. This is actually located in one of the Casa Colgadas (Hanging Houses). It has been restored over the ages and today is a very tasteful museum with wooden floors and ceilings that contrast with, and enhance, the exhibits.

Museo Diocesano de Arte Sacro (Diocesan Sacred Art Museum), Obispo Valero, 1. Open Tuesday to Friday 1100-1400, 1600-1800; Saturday 1100-1400, 1600-2000; Sunday 1100-1430. Closed Monday and holidays. Located in the Episcopal Palace, which is very close to the cathedral, the exhibits are very much of a religious nature and include some works of El Greco.

Station/location/transport to city centre

RENFE, Avenida General Moscardo, 10; tel: 22 07 20. This is a small and relatively modern station at an altitude of 925.4m and some distance from the old town.

Key

A: *Servicios* — men
B: *Consigna Automática*, open 0530-2300; 300 ptas per day; tokens available from the *Circulación* office
C: Waiting Area
D: *Circulación*
E: *Jefe de Estación*
F: *Comisaría*

G: *Servicios* — women
H: *Librería*: Newspapers, magazines, etc, open daily 0900-1330, 1700-2000
I: Tickets
J: Bar/cafeteria, open daily 0600-2230

Layout

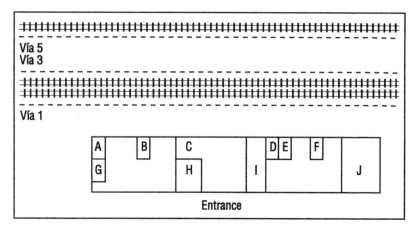

Train station to old town
By bus Line 1, Red, Estación/Plaza Mayor. Monday to Saturday 0730-2200, every 30 minutes; Sunday 0800-2200, every 30 minutes.

On foot Do not even try! It is a very long hard walk with luggage.

By taxi This can be as much as 400/450 ptas and takes up to 10 minutes.

Train services
To Madrid by
Regional: 2½.

To Valencia by
Regional: 3¼.

Accommodation
Close to the station
Fonda Marín Ramón y Cajal, 51-53; tel: 22 19 78. Single 1,100 ptas; double 2,000 ptas. Very ordinary; second floor. No baths/showers in rooms; an old and interesting façade.
Fonda Eldela Ramón y Cajal, 51-53; tel: none. Single 1,100 ptas; double 2,000 ptas. First floor. In the same building and same comments as above.

Between the station and the old town
*** **Hotel Alfonso VIII** Parque de San Julián, 3; tel: 21 43 25. Single 6,969 ptas; double 11,289 ptas; treble 13,064 ptas. Located in the city

centre this Best Western hotel has 48 rooms with bath/shower, colour
satellite TV, telephone and piped music. Some of the rooms, and the bar
and restaurant on the top floor, have panoramic views of the old town but
not, however, the Casa Colgadas which are out of sight.
* **Pensión San Julián** 18 de Julio, 1; tel: 21 17 04. Single 1,200 ptas;
double without bath 2,000 ptas, with bath 3,000 ptas. Singles without
bath/shower. Closer than others to the old town. Large bar and restaurant;
note the interesting columns in the latter.

In the old town
** **HR Posada de San José** Julian Romero, 4; tel: 21 13 00. Single
without bath 1,900 ptas, with bath 3,300 ptas; double without bath 3,300
ptas, with bath 6,250 ptas. Located just past the cathedral. An absolute
delight. A lovely old building with crooked windows and doors and uneven
floors. Restaurant has much character and an open fire. The only hotel I
have seen in Spain that reminds me of an old English country inn.

General information
Police
Comisaría, Hermanos Valdes, 4; tel: 22 35 51.

Radio taxi
Tel: 23 18 73.

Public telephones
Junction Cervantes/Castilla y La Mancha. Open Monday to Friday
0900-1300, 1700-2200; Saturday 0900-1300, 1700-2100. Closed
Sunday and holidays.

Telephone code
for Cuenca province is (966).

Tourist office
Oficina de Información y Turismo, Dalmacio García Izcara, 8; tel:
22 22 31. Open Monday to Friday 0900-1400, 1630-1830; Saturday
0900-1330. Closed Sunday and holidays.

GRANADA

The city
History
Although the Romans, Visigoths and others preceded them it was
the Muslims who had by far the greatest influence on this city. They
ruled, through one regime or another, for 781 years and for the last
250 of those Granada was the capital of the last remaining Muslim
kingdom in Spain. Amongst the many legacies from that period is
the Alhambra, a fortress/palace combination of unrivalled splendour
and magnificence, unique in the Western world. Important dates are:

711 The Moors cross from Africa, defeat the Visigoths and take
     control of southern Spain. Córdoba is established as an
     independent emirate and Granada becomes a provincial
     capital.

1009 After a rebellion by the Omeyan Prince Muhammad II the
     empire breaks up into independent Moorish kingdoms. The
     next 200 years are very unsettled. The Zirites take over
     initially and then are defeated by the Almoravids who, in their
     turn, lose out to the Almohades.

1237 Granada becomes capital of the Nasrid kingdom, destined to
     become for the next 250 years the last Muslim kingdom in
     Spain. It covers 30,000km² and has 400,000 people. This is
     the beginning of a period of great splendour, with Muslims,
     Jews and Christians living side by side. Also during this
     period, the fortress and various palaces that comprise the
     Alhambra are constructed.

1492 After many years' struggle Ferdinand and Isabella finally
     defeat Boabdil, the last Muslim king, and enter the city on
     January 2 1492. Castilians are brought in to repopulate the
     city and the Muslims are expelled to Albaicin and Las
     Alpujarras, a remote mountain region between the Sierra
     Nevada and the sea.

1502 The remaining Muslims are forced to convert to Christianity
     and become known as Moriscos. They are, however, very
     badly treated.

1504 Isabella dies and her remains are kept in the San Francisco
     convent in the Alhambra, until the Capilla Real in the city is
     completed.

1516 Ferdinand dies and his remains are put, with those of his
     wife, in the Alhambra. Carlos I, his grandson, becomes king.

1519 After the death of Maximiliano I, his paternal grandfather,

Carlos I takes the title Carlos V (Holy Roman Emperor).

1521 The remains of Ferdinand and Isabella are transferred ceremoniously to the Capilla Real.

1526 The University of Granada is founded by Carlos V.

1527 Carlos V begins construction of the new royal palace, Casa Real Nueva, in the Alhambra. Parts of the old palace are destroyed in the process.

1568 The Moriscos rebel, are repressed harshly and deported to other parts of Spain. Christians from the north are brought in to replace them.

Overview

Granada, with a population of about 275,000, is located towards the southeast of Andalucía at an elevation of between 660m and 780m, and is only a few miles north of the Sierra Nevada mountains. These are the largest in Spain, Mulhacen at 3,482m (11,400ft) being the highest. The peaks are usually snow covered all year, and provide Granada with a background unrivalled by any city outside of the Alpine areas. The ski resort of Sol y Nieve — Sun and Snow — is not far away and, even as late as Easter, it is common to see people walking around with skis. Meanwhile some of the most attractive sections of the Costa del Sol are only 70km (44 miles) away.

Granada also has the third most important university in Spain and possibly as much as a sixth of the population are students. However, tourist-wise, it is a different matter and this is demonstrated by the number of hotels — more than in either Sevilla or Córdoba. Unfortunately so many tourists bring other problems and there are more beggars and street traders here than in other cities. Petty crime is not at all uncommon so take special care of cameras and valuables, etc.

The city is geographically diverse and far and away the most dramatic parts are the large steep hills separated by the River Darro and its narrow valley. If you walk from the Plaza Nueva along the river, away from the more modern districts, the city suddenly changes and becomes much more pleasant and the surrounding houses and churches are a reminder of centuries past.

The hill to the left of the river rises very steeply and is known as Albaicin. Here there are many narrow lanes and streets full of charming old houses; the area also housed the fortresses and palaces of the first kings. If you have the energy to walk up to the Mirador San Nicolas, you will not be disappointed. Across the valley the world famous Alhambra sits on top of the other tree-covered hill (La Sabica) with the Generalife palace even higher to the left, in isolated splendour. Moreover, if the day is clear, the snow-covered peaks of the Sierra Nevada in the background complete a truly unique and world-famous vista. The scene is especially breathtaking in the autumn, late in this part of the world, when the colours are more varied.

Most of the rest of the city, the area directly under the Alhambra being a notable exception, is surprisingly bland and few visitors will venture far from the centre where the majority of the tourist sights and the commercial and shopping districts are located.

Besides those sights listed under **Places of interest** there are other churches and convents not usually open to the public except for services, but many of which are of historical and architectural interest.

Places of interest
Must see
Alhambra y Generalife Calle de la Alhambra; tel: 22 75 27. Open for day visits — summer (April to September), Monday to Saturday 0900-2000; winter (October to March), Monday to Saturday 0900-1800; all year Sunday 0900-1800. Night visits — summer Tuesday, Thursday and Saturday 2200-2400; winter Saturday 2200-2400. Entrance 600 ptas. The most visited monument in Spain, after the Prado museum in Madrid, and very few people leave disappointed. There are very many books on the subject, by eminent authors, but none can adequately describe the Alhambra. Video tapes are sold in the tourist shops in every combination of language and system available but even this mixture of visual effects and dramatic music fails to do the place justice.

It is simply a place that one has to see for oneself. Wander through and savour the contrasting styles of architecture; marvel at the intricacy of the Moorish designs; be cooled by the running water and ponds; be amazed by the spectacular gardens. Most people will want a souvenir of their visit and the local tourist guides will offer, by their nature, a more comprehensive explanation of what there is to see, along with many beautiful illustrations, than is possible here. The following is a very general description.

The Alhambra, which is derived from an Arabic root meaning 'red castle', and the Generalife occupy most of one of the two large hills that overlook the city of Granada. A fortress has existed on the site since the 9th century but the first kings of Granada had their palaces and fortifications on the other hill of Albaicin. It was not until the early 13th century that work was begun on the Alhambra, and further palaces were added by Yusef I and Muhammad V during the 14th century. Effectively this made it a fortified city, palace *alcázar* (fortress) and small town all in one.

The Generalife, a palace and residence of the Nasrid kings, and the extensive gardens were also constructed earlier in this period. After the reconquest in 1492 it was used as a Christian court. Later Carlos V built a palace, the design of which is entirely at odds with its surroundings. Then in the 18th and early 19th centuries it was allowed to fall into decline and was even used a barracks by Napoleon's troops. It was not until 1870 that this unique place was designated a national monument. Today there are four principal component parts.

Alcazaba (Fortress within a walled town) This is the fortress part and the oldest towers date from the mid 13th century. In basic terms it is the remains of a castle and it is interesting to note the large cracks in the towers. From the top of the Torre de la Vela (watchtower) there are very good views down over the city, though the perpetual smog usually spoils the scene.

The Casa Real Vieja This is the Moorish Old Royal House, or Palace, and what most people come to see. Actually it is a combination of palaces with their own courtyards and other attendant buildings. These are simply incredible. Once seen, the intricacy and beauty of the designs are never forgotten and the various patios and pools enhance them even more. The *Patio de los Leones* (Court of the Lions) is particularly stunning and world famous in its own right. There is also a bath area and a series of terraced gardens, just outside the palaces, that have their own pools. Here the *Torre de las Damas* (Tower of the Ladies) has five elegant arches and a pool with two large lions acting as fountains at the other end. The gardens are a cat-lover's paradise, as there are dozens of them living wild here.

The Casa Real Nueva This is the New Royal Palace. Construction began on it in 1527 under Carlos V and its design looks totally out of place. From the outside it is square with many motifs, figures and coats of arms sculpted into the brickwork. The inside holds another surprise. Here there is a large, two storey, terraced circular patio supported on both levels by impressive columns; this is altogether more elegant. Today there are two museums located in the building and it is also sometimes used for concerts.

The Generalife This is higher up on the hill behind the Alhambra, and reached through interconnecting gardens protected by towers along the walls. Strangely these towers are only open on certain days and, even then, the numbers of visitors at any one time are limited. The Generalife is a combination of a palace, the summer residence of the kings, extensive gardens and a small amphitheatre. Walking through these gardens and looking back down to the Alhambra and across to Albaicin, with the ever-present Sierra Nevada as a backdrop, one gets a feeling of serenity and peace. This is enhanced considerably by the constant sound of water from the fountains or water running down the channels on both sides of the steps through the gardens.

Capilla Real (Royal Chapel), Oficios; tel: 22 92 39. Open daily 1030-1300, 1600-1900. Entrance: 150 ptas. Ferdinand and Isabella were so taken by Granada that they decided to found, in 1504, a royal chapel to house their tombs. Isabella died in that year and her husband, Ferdinand, followed her in 1516, but since the chapel had not been completed their remains were kept at the San Francisco Convent in the Alhambra. Their grandson, Carlos V, completed the building and the remains were ceremoniously transferred in 1521. Other members of the royal family were buried here at later dates, but Felipe II had some removed to El Escorial, and only their daughter Juana, her husband Felipe and grandson Prince Miguel were left with them.

Today the Capilla Real is a fascinating mixture of mausoleum, church and museum, with many personal items of the monarchs on display.

Museo Catedralicio (Cathedral and Cathedral Museum), Gran Vía de Colón; tel: 22 29 59. Open daily 1030-1300, 1600-1900; Sunday afternoons only. Entrance 150 ptas. This is considered to be one of the leading Renaissance churches in Spain. Construction began in 1518 and finished early in the 17th century. At 115m long, 67m wide and with a ceiling height of 45m, it is very large and, unlike some cathedrals, gives a feeling of light and space. There are many small chapels around the sides and the combined effect is aesthetically pleasing. The Treasury museum houses tapestries, paintings and other religious artefacts.

By choice

Basílica de San Juan de Dios   (St John of God Basilica), Convalecencia, 1; tel: 22 21 44. Open Monday to Saturday 0900-1300. Closed Sunday. Entrance is free, but donations are accepted. This has a collection of paintings, sculptures, sacred art and crafts dating from the 15th to 20th centuries. There is also contemporary art, including 27 oil paintings by the Granadino artist Manuel Lopez Vasquez.

Casa de los Tiros   Plaza del Padre Suárez. Open Monday to Friday 1000-1400. Constructed for the Grana Venegas family in the early 16th century the Casa de los Tiros houses their coat of arms as well as five statues of warriors. Today the home of the Museum of History and Handicrafts of Granada, it includes a newspaper and magazine library, and the tourist office can be found here.

Corral del Carbón   (House of Coal),   Plta. Tovar; tel: 22 45 50. Open Monday to Saturday 1000-1330, 1600-2000. Dating from the 12th century this is the oldest Arabic monument in the city. It was originally a warehouse and lodging place for merchants and, after the reconquest, was used as a theatre. Today there is a market selling typically Granadino arts and crafts. Unfortunately this is located in such a position that it is difficult to take photographs.

El Bañuelo   Carrera del Darro, 31; tel: 22 23 39. Open Tuesday to Saturday 1000-1400. Entrance is free. Dating from the 11th century, although restored in 1928, these are considered to be the best preserved Arabic baths in Spain.

Hospital Real   (Royal Hospital),   Ancha de Capuchinos. Open Monday to Friday 1100-1300. Overlooking the Triunfo gardens and fountain (Fuente del Triunfo), this impressive building was founded in 1504 as a royal hospital by the Catholic Monarchs. It has been restored and now houses the administrative offices of the university.

Monasterio de la Cartuja   (Carthusian Monastery), Carretera de Alfacar; tel: 20 19 32. Open Monday to Saturday 1000-1300, 1600-

1900; Sunday 1000-1200, 1600-1900. Entrance: 150 ptas. This is about one mile out of town and if you do not have a car, and don't fancy a long walk, take the No 8 bus from Reyes Católicos or Gran Vía de Colón, which is supposed to run every 10 minutes between 0630 and 2315. Positioned on the site of a Roman cemetery, this monastery was founded in 1506. However, construction did not begin until 1516 and continued for nearly 300 years. The monastery is very ornate and the sanctuary and sacristy are important examples of Spanish baroque architecture. There are also many paintings, sculptures and ornaments from the 17th and 18th centuries.

Palacio de la Madraza (Madraza Palace), Oficios. Open during business hours. Originally an Arabic university founded in 1349, the Catholic Monarchs converted it to a town hall (*ayuntamiento*) and it remained as such until the mid 16th century. Today it belongs to the university and is used for meetings.

Chancillería Real (Royal Chancery), Plaza Nueva. Open Monday to Friday 1000-1300. Construction of this very attractive building began in 1530 and the patio is particularly noteworthy. It used to be the Royal High Court of Justice and today is the Provincial High Court.

Sacromonte Famous for both the gypsies and the caves that some of them live in. By night this becomes a tourist area, with all the negative aspects that that brings, as there are several *tablaos* (flamenco bars), here and such events as 'typical gypsy marriage ceremonies' are well advertised in the city. I tend to think that it is more interesting during the day, when the caves can be seen more clearly. However, in any event, unless you enjoy a long, hard walk it is advisable to travel by taxi or bus.

Torre Bermejas Located in the Alhambra park but separate from the main complex. Called the 'Red Tower', it is one of the oldest military fortresses in Granada.

Mirador San Nicolas (St Nicholas Viewpoint) The best views of the Alhambra and the Sierra Nevada are from here. If you want to take pictures do not go in the morning as the sun will be in your face; the best time is in the afternoons when the sun will be at your back and might turn the snow a pink colour.

Museums

Museo Arqueológico (Archaeological Museum), Carrera del Darro, 41; tel: 22 56 40. Open Tuesday to Sunday 1000-1400. Closed Sunday and Monday. Entrance: Spanish nationals and citizens of the EC (on presentation of passport) free; others 250 ptas. The museum is located in a beautiful Renaissance palace, the Casa de Castril, the façade of which dates from 1539. Actually, the best view of this is from the Alhambra, from where it can be seen in context with the other buildings in the area. There are exhibits from prehistoric, Roman, Visigoth and Moorish times.

Museo Nacional de Arte Hispanomusulman (National Museum of Spanish/Muslim Art), Palacio de Carlos V; tel: 22 62 79. Open Tuesday to Saturday 1000-1400. Closed Sunday and Monday. Entrance: Spanish nationals and citizens of the EC (on presentation of passport) free; others 250 ptas. Located in the Palacio de Carlos V in the Alhambra complex this houses Spanish/Arabic exhibits from the Granada area. There are many small rooms and some overlook the old royal palaces.

Museo Provincial de Bellas Artes (Provincial Fine Arts Museum), Palacio de Carlos V; tel: 22 48 43. Open Tuesday to Saturday 1000-1400. Closed Sunday and Monday. Entrance free. Contains many paintings and sculptures from the 15th to 20th centuries. Particular emphasis is paid to the 17th century Granadino school of artists, among them Alonso Cano and Sanchez Cotan.

Casa Museo Federico García Lorca Fuentevaqueros; tel: 44 64 53. West of the map close, to the airport. Open Tuesday to Sunday 1000-1300, 1600-1800. Closed Monday. Located in Fuentevaqueros, a small town to the west of Granada. By car, take the N342 Granada/Málaga road, turning off at Chauchina, which is just across from the airport. This is the family home of the most celebrated of Spanish poets. He was killed in 1936, early in the Spanish Civil War, by political enemies. One of his best known works is *The Lament for Ignacio Sanchez Mejias*, a matador friend who was killed in the Plaza de Toros of Manzanares on August 11 1934. It is a stark, haunting, poetic description of the type of death that is never far away for any matador.

Station/location/transport to city centre
RENFE, Avenida de los Andaluces, 12; tel: 20 41 00. This terminal is located in a rather nondescript area a long way to the west from the city centre.

Layout

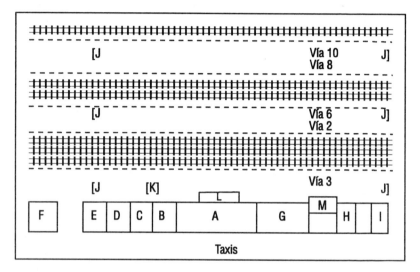

Key
A: Main entrance and booking hall
B: *Sala de Espera*
C: *Jefe de Terminal*
D: *Comisaría*
E: *Servicio de Atención al Viajero*
F: *Servicios*
G: Cafe/bar, open 0700-2330
H: *Consigna Automática.* There are three sizes. There is an attendant on hand and the price is either 400 or 200 ptas a day; open 0730-2300
I: *Jefe de Circulación*
J: Foot subways between platforms
K: *Carritos Portaequipajes*
L: Kiosco for newspapers, magazines
M: *Tabacos Kiosco*; This sells tobacco, cigarettes and postage stamps

Train station to city centre
By bus Several buses go to and from the centre via the Avenida de la Constitución. However, given the usual traffic jams, this can be a slow journey.

By taxi This is by far the most convenient way of getting to and from the centre, 5-10 minutes away and about 300 ptas.

Train services
To Madrid by

	Talgo	Talgo Pen	Estrella
Alcázar de San Juan	4½	4½	5¾
Madrid	6¼	6¼	8½

To Barcelona by
Diurno: Via Alcázar de San Juan 2¼; Valencia 8¾; Barcelona 13¼.

To Algeciras/Córdoba/Málaga/Sevilla by
Regional/Regional Expres: Via Bobadilla 1¾ Algeciras 3¾. Córdoba 3¼. Málaga 3. Sevilla 3¾. These are actual travel times, and the overall time of the journey is dependent upon the wait for a connection in Bobadilla.

To Almería by
Regional: Almería 3.

To Cádiz by
Regional/Regional Expres: This is rather complicated as it involves a double change at Bobadilla and Utrera. It is more straightforward, and sometimes faster, to go via Sevilla.

Accommodation
Close to the station
* Hostal Terminus Avenida Andaluces, 10; tel: 20 14 23. Single 1,000 ptas; double 1,500 ptas. Basic. Located in an old block close to the station.
CH Camas Avenida Andaluces; tel: 29 19 76. Single 800 ptas; double 1,400 ptas. Just to the right as you come out of the station. Old and unpleasant.
CH Las Dos RR Cisne, 6. Apart from the beautiful front door, this appears to be a run of the mill guesthouse.

In the city
**** Hotel Rallye Paseo de Ronda, 107; tel: 27 28 00; fax: 27 28 62. Single 10,070 ptas; double 14,628 ptas. These rates do not include breakfast but there is a 20% discount at weekends. A new Best Western hotel, with restaurant and bar, located about 10 to 15 minutes walk away from the cathedral. There are 80 rooms and they all have bath/shower, hair dryer, satellite TV, direct dial telephone, safe, minibar and air-conditioning.
* Hotel Casablanca Frailes, 3; tel: 25 76 00. Single 1,800 ptas; double

3,500 ptas. On a small back street close to the centre. There is a fountain in the lobby.

** **HR León** Alvaro de Bazán, 2; tel: 27 65 00. Single 1,350 ptas; double 2,700 ptas. Modern, clean and pleasant place; on first floor.

** **HR Sacromonte** Plaza del Lino, 1. tel: 26.64.11. Single 2,000 ptas; double 3,500 ptas; parking 1,000 ptas. Very modern. Close to the shopping centre. Colour TVs in all rooms.

* **HR Britz** Cuesta de Gomerez, 1; tel: 22 36 52. Single 1,300 ptas; double 3,100 ptas, without bath 2,500 ptas. Very pleasant, but being next to the Plaza Nueva the front rooms can be noisy.

* **HR Don Lupe** Avenida de los Alijares; tel: 22 14 73; fax: 22 14 74; telex: 78498. Single 1,450 ptas; double 2,900 ptas. A little smaller than other hotels in the area next to the Alhambra, but the owner is delightful and that counts for a lot in itself. The parking is free and there is also a pool.

* **HR Florida** Principe, 13; tel: 26 37 47. Single 1,484 ptas; double 2,332 ptas. A strange place with toy models hanging from the ceiling in the reception area. Very central.

* **HR San Joaquín** Mano de Hierro, 14; tel: 28 28 79. Single 1,300 ptas; double 1,600 ptas. An amazing place, over 500 years old and set around a series of lovely patios. There is a restaurant (with a set meal for 700 ptas) and the tables are set in an open patio during the summer. There is a TV room and the bedrooms are certainly more than adequate. The owner is a charming, friendly man. If you want something different this is it.

* **HR Sevilla** Fábrica Vieja, 18; tel: 27 85 13. Single 1,200 ptas; double 3,180 ptas, without bath 2,200 ptas. Neat and clean inside. Situated on a quiet street near a plaza.

* **HR Valencia** Alhóndiga, 9; tel: 26 44 12. Single 1,800 ptas; double 2,850 ptas, without bath 2,000 ptas. Medium sized. On the edge of the shopping district.

** **Hostal El Rocio** Capuchinas, 6; tel: 26 58 23. Single 2,500 ptas; double 4,950 ptas; parking 800 ptas. Of medium size, just north of the Plaza Trinidad.

** **Hostal Landazuri** Cuesta de Gomerez, 24; tel: 22 14 06. Single 1,100; double 2,700, without bath 1,900. Located in a modern building halfway up the street.

* **Hostal Granadina** Párraga, 7; tel: 25 87 14. Single 1,600 ptas, without bath 1,200 ptas; double 3,000 ptas, without bath 2,600 ptas. Nice and clean. On the first floor. Near the centre.

* **Hostal Las Nievas** Sierpe Baja, 5; tel: 26 53 11. Single 2,000 ptas; double 3,500 ptas. Modern; in the heart of the shopping centre. The restaurant is closed in winter and there are no lifts. Good value.

* **Hostal Veracruz** San Antón, 39; tel: 26 27 70. Single 1,500 ptas; double 2,200 ptas. Located on a fairly quiet street in a nice old house. There is a

small restaurant where the Menu del día is 700 ptas.

* **Pensión Gran Capitán** Plaza Gran Capitán, 4; tel: 27 21 24. Single 1,500 ptas; double 2,000 ptas. Located on the third floor of an apartment building. There is a lift; old-fashioned decor and atmosphere.

CH Muñoz Mesones, 53; tel: 26 38 19. Single 900 ptas; double 1,800 ptas. Located on the second floor. Old-fashioned but nice.

CH Portugos Lucena, 8; tel: 27 89 75. Single 800 ptas; double 1,600 ptas. An old building, but pleasant enough inside.

CH Reina Laurel de Tablas, 13; tel: 28 03 95. Single 800 ptas; double 1,600 ptas. Clean and modern.

There are many more low budget places of accommodation in the maze of streets within the boundaries of the Gran Vía de Colón, San Juan de Dios, Alhóndiga and Reyes Católicos.

General information
Car hire
Avis, Recogidas, 31; tel: 25 23 58.

Dry cleaners
La Estrella de Oro, Puentezuelas, 2; tel: 26 46 10. Translated as 'The Golden Star', this is one of a chain of dry cleaners/laundry shops that offer a 24-hour service.

Fiestas
Easter week (*Semana Santa*) variable dates, Corpus Christi variable dates.

Hospitals
Hospital Clinico, Avenida del Doctor Olóriz; tel: 27 02 00.
Hospital General, Avenida del Coronel Muñoz; tel: 27 64 00.

Police
Comisaría, Plaza de los Campos;. tel: 091.

Telephone code
for Granada province is (958).

Tourist office
Patronato Provincial de Turismo, Plaza Maríana Pineda, 10; tel: 22 35 27; fax: 22 39 15; telex: 78753 PIGR. Open Monday to Friday 1000-1330, 1630-1900; Saturday 1000-1330.

JEREZ DE LA FRONTERA
The city

Located 678km (424 miles) south of Madrid, and at an altitude of only 56m, Jerez de la Frontera has a population of over 200,000. It has a very long and rich history and the centuries of Moorish influence are typified by the large and impressive Alcázar. However, its fame derives principally from wine and horses, in that order.

The city's most famous product is sherry — in all its variations — but brandy is important as well. Jerez's proximity to the sea has enabled it more easily to export these products throughout the world, a process that developed rapidly in the 17th to 19th centuries. The names of many of the *bodegas*, literally a place where the barrels of sherry are stored but also commonly used to identify a particular company, will be familiar to everyone. This, in turn, has given Jerez an affluence that can readily be seen throughout the city giving it a style and character that is entirely different from other places.

Horses are also traditionally important and the two ways most visitors are likely to see this is at the Royal School of Equestrian Art — an absolute must — and in May during the annual *Feria del Caballo* (Horse Fair).

Another unusual custom here is the way beer is served. The glasses generally used in the city's bars are totally different from those I have seen anywhere else in Spain. Rather wide and tall, with straight sides, they have a line, often blue, around the middle and the beer is never poured above it.

Of all the cities I have visited, Jerez de la Frontera was one that I had no strong feelings about before I went, but it turned out to be the one that gave me the most pleasant surprise. There are no absolutely wonderful monuments or museums but the city has a distinctly different, and rather charming, atmosphere. Besides the places listed below there are several interesting churches and my favourite is the San Miguel, close to the Alcázar. This dates from the 15th-16th centuries and has a rather lovely altar. Remember, in the summer months it is very, very hot.

Places of interest
Must see

Catedral (Cathedral), Plaza Encarnación. Open Monday to Friday 1800-2030; Saturday and Sunday 1100-1200, 1800-2030. Entrance:

free. Built over the old Mosque, this dates from the 17th century and, as cathedrals go, is not very interesting. The altar is fairly plain, the dome is quite high and the side chapels are fairly unusual in that they are not closed in. The most dominant feature is the tower that is located away from the main structure. Note that the opening hours are rather strange.

Gonzalez Byass (Sherry *bodega*), Manuel María González; tel: 34 00 00. Visits 0930-1100. Entrance: 200 ptas. Of all the *bodegas* in Jerez, Gonzalez Byass is one of the oldest and most famous. One of its products, *Tio Pepe*, is sold worldwide. The process of cultivating the grapes and producing these wines is complicated and best left to the tour guide to explain. A visit to Jerez de la Frontera would be incomplete without a visit to Gonzalez Byass.

Real Escuela Andaluza del Arte Ecuestre (Royal Andalusian School of Equestrian Art), Recreo de las Cadenas, Avenida Duque de Abrantes; tel: 33 11 11. Open Monday to Friday (except Thursday) 1100-1300. Entrance: adults 425 ptas; children 170 ptas. Thursday (shows only) 1200. Entrance: adults 2,200, 1,750 or 1,400 ptas, children 800 ptas. *Galas de Verano* (summer gala evenings) 2230. Entrance: 2,550, 1,950 or 1,525 ptas. Located just outside the centre, this is an absolute must. The grounds are very extensive and there are two large buildings: the old mansion and an indoor stadium that leads on to the stables. On all days except Thursday everything is open for inspection and it is possible to watch the horses in training. Thursday is show day and it is not possible to visit the stables and tack rooms. This is more than compensated for by the splendour of the show which lasts about one and a half hours. There are also a limited number of night-time shows during July and August (four in 1992), but the dates are not announced very far in advance.

By choice

Convento de Santo Domingo (St Domingo Convent). Located just across from the tourist office this structure, dating from the reconquest, is notable for its fine cloisters, used nowadays for various exhibitions.

Fundación Andaluza de Flamenco (Foundation of Andalusian Flamenco), Palacio Pemartín, Plaza San Juan, 1; tel: 34 92 65.

Open Monday to Friday 0930-1330, 1800-2100; Saturday 1000-1330. Closed Sunday and holidays. Entrance: free. Located in an 18th century palace in the old Barrio de Santiago, this is one of my favourite places. The building, with a lovely small patio, is quite small and attractive and the rooms and exhibits are both tasteful and interesting. If you visit when the dancers are practising in the dance classroom you will be fascinated. You can sit at the back of the long room looking straight into a wall length mirror watching yourself watching the dancers watch themselves practise their steps, accompanied by, and usually instructing in timing, an accomplished guitarist.

Mezquita (Mosque) Manuel María González. Open Monday to Friday 1100-1400, 1600-1900 (August-September 1700-2100); holidays 1100-1400. Closed Saturday and Sunday. Entrance: free. To date, winter 1992, this is the only part of the Alcázar open to the public. The entrance is on the side closest to the cathedral and it dates from the 11th century. Of Almohade design, this is small but very dignified.

Parque Zoológico y Jardín Botánico 'Alberto Duran' (Zoo and Botanical Gardens), Taxdirt; tel: 18 23 97/18 42 07. Open Tuesday to Sunday 1000-1800. Closed Monday. Entrance: adults 400 ptas, children (under 14) 200 ptas.

Museums
Museo de Relojes (Clock Museum), Fundación Andres de Ribera, Cervantes, 3; tel: 18 21 00. Open Monday to Saturday 1000-1400. Closed Sunday and holidays. Visits outside these hours by prior arrangement. Entrance: 200 ptas. Do not be put off that this is a little difficult to find, it is worth the effort. The museum itself, considered to be one of the best of its kind in the world, takes up one wing — the rest cannot be visited — of a remarkable mansion. There are 302 pieces all in working order and the best time to visit is, of course, just before the hour. For about five minutes you are treated to a continuous chiming with many different tones. Take some time in the garden where there are peacocks, black swans and many other species of birds. The small gift shop, by the gate house, has a wide ranging stock including the Cadiz ballpoint pens which have a novel design and make good gifts.

Station/location/transport to city centre

RENFE, Plaza de la Estación; tel: 34 23 19. This station. located a
short distance from the city centre and at an altitude of 489.4m, is
really very beautiful. The only other station that compares with it is
in Toledo.

Layout

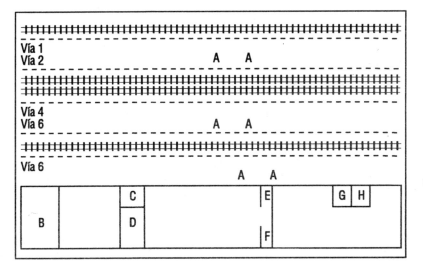

Key

A: *Paseo Inferior*
B: Cafeteria, open 0630-2300
C: *Información*
D: Ticket office

E: *Servicios*, women
F: *Servicios*, men
G: *Jefe de Estación*
H: *Circulación*

Train station to city centre

By bus Number L8, CIRCUNVALACIÓN - I. The stop is in the
street just to the left of the station and buses run between 0600 and
2300 every day of the week. On weekdays they run every 11
minutes; on Saturday every 15 minutes in the morning and every 30
minutes in the afternoon, and every 30 minutes all day on Sunday.
The fare is 60 ptas and don't worry, you will not be able to miss the
buses, they are painted a light purple! Get off at the Plaza de las
Angustias and most of the listed accommodation is nearby.

By taxi Just a few minutes away and about 350 ptas.

Train services

Jerez is about halfway between Sevilla and Cádiz and there are regular services to those cities. For longer distance journeys see either the Cádiz or Sevilla chapters.

Accommodation

*** **Hotel Doña Blanca** Bodegas, 11; tel: 34 04 03. This hotel has three seasons, low: January and December, medium: February, March and November and high: the rest of the year and such times as Easter, fiestas and when there is motor, bike or car racing; prices are shown in this order. Single 6,000 ptas, 7,000 ptas, 8,500 ptas; double (for single use) 6,500 ptas, 8,000 ptas, 10,000 ptas; double 8,500 ptas, 10,000 ptas, 12,500 ptas. Very nice in city centre. All rooms with air-conditioning, colour TV and radio, minibar and an individual safe.

** **Hotel Joma** Medina, 28; tel: 34 96 89. Single 4,000 ptas; double 7,000 ptas. Clean and comfortable. Small rooms with bath/shower and colour TV.

** **Hotel Serit** Higueras, 7; tel: 34 07 00. Single 6,000 ptas; double 8,000 ptas. All rooms with air-conditioning, music and colour TV and telephone.

* **Hotel Trujillo** Medina, 36; tel: 34 24 38. Single 2,500 ptas; double 3,500 ptas. Very pleasant. Rooms with music, bath, air-conditioning and telephone.

* **HR El Coloso** Pedro Alonso, 13; tel: 34 90 08. Single 4,335 ptas; double 7,000 ptas. Good size rooms. Bath/shower and colour TV. In a quiet location.

* **Hostal Gover** Honsario, 6; tel: 33 26 00. Single 2,500 ptas; double 4,000 ptas. In a quiet street. Rooms with a shower. English-speaking manager.

* **Hostal San Miguel** Plaza León XIII, 4; tel: 34 85 62. Single 1,900 ptas; double 3,300 ptas. Very old-fashioned. Small rooms with no bath/shower. Away from the other places to stay.

* **Pensión Las Palomas** Higueras, 17; tel: 34 37 73. Single 1,800 ptas; double without bath 3,000 ptas, with bath 4,000 ptas. Quite large, with an interesting patio.

* **Pensión Los Amarillos** Medina, 39; tel: 34 22 96. Single 1,300 ptas; double 2,000 ptas. Small and plain. No bath/shower in rooms.

General information
Car hire

Avis, Sevilla, 25; tel: 34 43 11.

Fiestas

The two main fiestas are Easter week (*Semana Santa*) and the May Horse Fair, early in the month. In the first two weeks of September there is the Wine Harvest Festival and it can be difficult to get accommodation in that period.

Radio taxi
Tele-Taxi, 34 48 60.

Telephone code
for Cádiz province is (956).

Tourist office
Oficina Municipal de Turismo, Alameda Cristina, 7; tel: 33 11 50. Open Monday to Friday 0800-1500, 1700-1900; Saturday 1000-1400. Closed Sunday and holidays.

LEÓN

The city

Located 421km (263 miles) northwest of Madrid, at an altitude of
823m, León has a population approaching 130,000. It was founded
in 68 AD by the Roman 7th Legion — Gemina Pia Felix — who
built on the hill where the cathedral is now located. The Romans
succumbed to the Visigoths in the middle of the 6th century and in
the early 8th century the Moors conquered the area. It was often
fought over and by the 10th century it had become the most
important Christian town in Spain, the court of the Kingdom of
León, and was repopulated with Mozarabs — Christian refugees
from Córdoba and Toledo. In 996 it was sacked by Almanzor and
it was not until the 11th century that it was finally reconquered.
During that century its strategic position, on the road to Santiago de
Compostela, opened the city to new influences and styles,
particularly Romanesque. During the 12th century its influence
began to decline and in 1235 it joined forces with Castile.

Today it is a city that although modern and affluent has a
somewhat old-fashioned atmosphere. Besides the places listed below
there are quite a few old palaces and houses, as well as churches,
that can be seen from the outside. The Plaza Mayor is also of some
interest and so are the remains of the walls.

I was rather disappointed with León when I first visited. I had
expected far more. My views were not changed after a second visit
either and I suspect that like myself, many people on a short visit
will only really be interested in the cathedral.

Places of interest
Must see

Catedral y Museo (Cathedral and Museum), Plaza de Regla, 4.
Museum open Monday to Saturday 0930-1330, 1600-1945. Closed
Sunday and holidays. Entrance: 250 ptas museum and cloisters; 100
ptas cloisters only. The main sections of the cathedral were built
between the 13th and 14th centuries. It is Gothic in style, and can
be seen from most parts of the city. It is one of the most famous
cathedrals in Spain and its many stained glass windows are
magnificent and unique. To see them at their best the cathedral
should be visited at different times of the day. The Door of Our
White Lady, on the western portico, should be studied and the inside
is very impressive without being too elaborate. There are also many
ancient sepulchres, with that of Ordono II being particularly ornate.

The cloister is worth a visit on its own and the museum exhibits, which are many and varied, are housed in several rooms — themselves different in style — around the cloister.

Museo de San Isidro (San Isidro Museum), Real Colegiata, Plaza de San Isidro, 4. Open Tuesday to Saturday 1000-1330, 1600-1830; Sunday and holidays 1000-1330. Closed Monday. Entrance: 200 ptas. A main feature of this small museum is the Pantheon of Kings. This is one of the earliest Romanesque buildings in Spain and there is a series of beautiful frescoes on the ceilings, with gospel and other scenes. There are also many sepulchres and a large, but rather plain, cloister. The entrance is to the left of the church which was originally built in the 11th century but has been much restored. In the Chapter Treasury Room, reached up a spiral staircase, there are many very special exhibits with the most important being the Chalice of Doña Urraca.

By choice
Casa de Botines (Botine House), Plaza de San Marcelo. Located just opposite the Palacio de los Guzmanes, this house could not be more different in style. Built by Gaudi at the end of the 19th century, it is full of his typical idiosyncrasies and looks rather out of place. Today it is used by the Caja España, a bank.

Palacio de los Guzmanes (Guzman Palace), Generalísimo Franco. Built in 1571, today it is the home of the Provincial Council and the only part that can be visited is the patio, impressive both in size and architecture.

Museums
San Marcos Museo Arqueológico y Provincial (San Marcos Provincial Archaeological Museum), Convento de San Marcos, Plaza de San Marcos. Open Tuesday to Saturday 1000-1400, 1700-1900; Sunday and holidays 1000-1330 (May to September only). Closed Monday. Entrance: free. Originally this was the Primate House of the Knights of St James who guarded the pilgrim route to Santiago, but the present elaborate façade was not added until the mid 16th century. It has also been used as a political prison and barracks. Today it has a very unusual double use: as a hotel (a Parador Nacional), and a museum. There is also a church with a beautiful cloister that is shared by all of them. The museum is very

small — just one room separated by a glass partition from the hotel lounge — and the church is plain but elegant. One different aspect is that all of the side chapels, on both sides, are connected by a passageway.

It is the cloister though that is most attractive; this is double levelled with sarcophagi and busts around the outside lower level, a rather overgrown but beautiful central garden and four very large statues in the arches facing the hotel.

Station/location/transport to city centre
RENFE, Astorga; tel: 23 37 00. A rather modern station, at an elevation of 824.2m, this is located about 10 minutes walk from the cathedral.

Layout

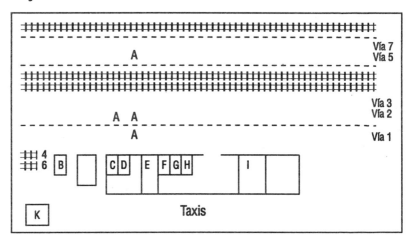

Key
A: *Paseo Inferior*
B: *Servicios*
C: *Comisaría*
D: *Jefe de Estación*
E: Ticket office
F: *Librería*, newspapers, magazines, etc, open 0700-2030
G: *Estanco*, tobacco, etc, open

0830-2100
H: *Información*
I: Bar/cafeteria, open 24 hours daily
J: *Carritos Portaequipe*, free
K: *Consigna Automática*; tokens are purchased at *Información* 200 ptas per 24 hours

Station to town centre
On foot Bear right out of the station, follow the road around to the

left and continue straight on; cross the river, pass the large fountain and the cathedral is about 10-15 minutes away.

By taxi five minutes and about 300 ptas away.

Train services
To Madrid by

	Regional Expres	Talgo Pen	Estrella
Valladolid	1¾	1½	2¼
Ávila	3	2¾	3¾
Madrid	4¾	4¼	5¾

To Barcelona by
Diurno: via Burgos 1¾; Zaragoza 4½; Barcelona 9¼.
Estrella: via Burgos 2; Zaragoza 7¼; Barcelona 12¼.

To Santiago de Compostela by
Diurno: via Monforte de Lemos 3; Ourense 4¼; Santiago de Compostela 6.

Accommodation
Close to the station
* **HR La Barra** Avenida de Palencia, 2; tel: 22 10 84. Single 1,200 ptas; double 2,200 ptas. Plain and basic. Rooms without baths.
* **Hostal Covadonga** Avenida de Palencia, 2; tel: 22 26 01. Single 1,500 ptas; double 2,500 ptas. Very similar to La Barra, but smaller.

In the city
** **HR Don Suero** Suero de Quiñones, 15; tel: 23 06 00. Single 2,800 ptas; double 4,000 ptas. Large modern building. Close to Plaza San Marcos. Good value.
* **HR Londres** Avenida Roma, 1; tel: 22 22 74. Single 1,700 ptas; double 2,600 ptas. Clean small rooms; all without bath.
* **HR Paris** Generalísimo, 20; tel: 23 86 00. Single 3,550 ptas; double 5,500 ptas. Central, close to cathedral. Historic building. Rooms with TV.
* **HR Quindos** Avenida José Antonio, 24; tel: 23 62 00. Single 4,490 ptas; double 7,400 ptas. Very nice but a little expensive; quiet. Close to Plaza de San Marcos.
* **Hostal Padre Isla** Joaquín Costa, 2; tel: 24 03 77. Single 3,000 ptas; double 5,500 ptas. All rooms with bath. Surprisingly modern inside. A little expensive.

118

SPAIN: CITIES AND TOWNS

General information
Car hire
Avis, Paseo Condesa Sagasta, 34, Bajo; tel: 27 00 75.

Police
Comisaría, Villa Benavente, 6; tel: 20 73 12.

RENFE city office
RENFE, del Carmen, 4; tel: 22 05 25. Open Monday to Friday 0930-1400, 1700-2000; Saturday 1000-1330. Closed Sunday and holidays.

Public telephones
Calle del Burgo Nuevo, 15. Open Monday to Friday 0900-1430, 1600-2230; Saturday 0900-1400, 1600-2100. Closed Sunday and holidays.

Telephone code
for León province is (987).

Tourist office
Oficina de Información de Turismo, Plaza de Regla, 3; tel: 23 70 82. Open Monday to Friday 0900-1400, 1600-1730; Saturday 1000-1300. Closed Sunday and holidays. Located just across from the cathedral.

MADRID
The city

Madrid, the capital of Spain and the largest city, with a population of over 3,200,000, is located in the geographical centre of the country on the Castilian plateau and, at an elevation of 655m (over 2,100ft), is also the highest capital city in Europe. As such it has a Continental type climate which gives it very hot summers and cold, sometimes long, winters.

Although built close to where prehistoric remains have been found, Madrid had no particular importance for many centuries. In the mid 9th century the Visigoths were defeated by Mohammed I and it was not until 1083 that the city was finally reconquered from the Moors by Alfonso VI. Although Alfonso X gave it royal rights in 1262, a parliament was convened by Fernando IV at the end of the 14th century and Ferdinand and Isabella visited the city in 1477, it was not until 1561 that Felipe II moved the capital from Toledo to Madrid. The city then began growing to meet the new demands and the most important addition during this, Hapsburg, era was the Plaza Mayor. However, it was not until the House of Bourbon succeeded the Hapsburg dynasty that many of the grand buildings and monuments that still adorn the city were constructed. The most prominent of these are the Royal Palace, the Palacio de Oriente, the Prado Museum and the nearby Puerta de Alcalá. The latter was built in 1778 to honour Carlos III's entry into the city as king. Later still wide avenues lined with impressive buildings, such as the Gran Vía, delightful statues and cooling fountains were added. Another architectural element — office towers and exclusive hotels interspersed with modern fountains — has been added in the last quarter century. The most interesting examples line the Paseo de la Castellana, a wide avenue running northwards from its junction with the Gran Vía, Alcalá, and the Plaza de Cibeles. The latter takes its name from one of the most important, and beautiful, fountains in the city. Incidentally the large building on the east side of the Plaza de Cibeles must be one of the world's most attractive post offices.

Historically the city has not been immune from the ravages of war. In the early 19th century the French occupied the city and the uprising of May 2-3 1808, which failed in itself but was a forerunner to the Wars of Independence, has been immortalised by Goya, whose paintings *El Dos de Mayo* and *El Tres de Mayo* can be seen in the Prado. More recently, after being initially taken by the Republican forces in the Civil War, the Nationalists arrived and began a siege that was to last from November 1936 to the end of the war in March 1939, causing immense suffering for the citizens.

Surprisingly, for such a large and important city, there are not that many specific places for tourists to visit. There are, however, numerous museums covering a very wide range of subjects. But Madrid has plenty to offer: besides the interesting mix of architectural styles, perhaps the most important attraction is the way of life.

Every evening the Madrileños take to the streets, whether it is in their own neighbourhoods or in the centre of the city — often these are the same — to walk, meet their family and friends and take a drink and *tapas* in a favourite bar. It will then be late enough to eat, usually not before 2130, and often in one of the many restaurants that have mouthwatering displays of fish, shellfish and, a local favourite, octopus (*pulpo*). Many of these places are found in the Plaza Mayor and the surrounding areas, which are the older parts of Madrid.

Sunday, especially before lunch, is a special day and, besides the *Rastro* (flea market), the Parque Retiro is especially popular and perhaps the best place to see the local citizens enjoying themselves most. On those afternoons when there are *corridas* (bullfights) at the Plaza de Toros Monumental Las Ventas, the most important in the world and with a capacity of over 23,000, the atmosphere in the surrounding area is quite electric. Another popular event on Sundays in the winter is soccer; Real Madrid is one of the most famous soccer clubs in the world and their stadium, Estadio Santiago Bernabeu, is located in the heart of the business section on the Paseo de la Castellana. It holds over 110,000 people and is in the process of even more expansion.

At one time or another, all visitors to Madrid will pass through the Puerta del Sol. Located close to the Plaza Mayor, this is the social centre of Madrid and, indeed, it is considered the centre of the country. In fact, all main roads in Spain radiate from here and distances are measured from the 0km point in the plaza. It is also on the edge of the shopping area, with the large El Corte Ingles department store on the northwest side. Seven streets radiate from here, and these are used in a most dramatic fashion at Easter. Sombre and immensely impressive processions from local churches, carrying their saints very slowly on huge platforms, and accompanied by their own bands as well as by penitents who are often hooded, barefoot and carrying huge wooden crosses, enter the

Puerta del Sol from one street and depart back to their own church via another.

During the daytime this plaza, with its small fountains, is a meeting place for both locals and tourists and it is also used for demonstrations and protests. Beware of the latter occasions as they can sometimes turn violent; you will know that they are about to happen by the presence of numerous paramilitary police. At night the character changes, and not for the better. Rather more unsavoury characters gather around the fountains, and also in the local backstreets, and one must become somewhat cautious. Drugs are a fact of life here, as elsewhere in the world, and it is not uncommon to come across both their use and the subsequent problems that they cause.

Places of interest
Note: After the Prado these are listed in alphabetical order.

Must see
Museo Nacional del Prado (Prado National Museum), Paseo del Prado; tel: 420 28 36. Metro between Banco de España Line 2 (red) and Atocha Line 1 (blue). Open Tuesday to Saturday 0900-1900; Sunday and holidays 0900-1400. Closed Monday. Entrance: 400 ptas; Wednesday EC citizens (under 21) and students free. Tickets bought here are also valid for El Casón del Buen Retiro.

The imposing building was built in 1785 and was originally intended to be the home of the Natural Science Museum. However, in 1819 the Prado Museum was inaugurated here to house the royal collection. Today you will find one of the world's greatest museums with a huge collection of over 6,000 paintings, not all of which are on permanent display. There are sections for Spanish, Flamenco, Dutch, Italian, French and German schools of art as well as areas for sculpture and temporary exhibitions. Perhaps the most famous paintings are those by Goya (1746-1828); the collection started with only three which were part of the royal collection donated by Ferdinand VII, the founder. The rest have been acquired, through various means, over the years and a comprehensive guide to them can be purchased for 100 ptas. The Prado is the most visited national monument in Spain.

El Casón del Buen Retiro Alfonso XII, 28; tel: 420 26 28. Metro Banco de España or Retiro Line 2 (red). Open the same hours as the

Prado and tickets, also the same price, are valid in the Prado. This is another part of the Prado and is located in a separate building a little behind the main museum and just across from the Parque Retiro. It houses paintings from the 19th century and is much smaller than the Prado.

Catedral de Nuestra Señora de la Almudena (Our Lady of Almudena Cathedral) Open daily 1000-1400, 1800-2030. Located directly opposite the entrance to the Royal Palace, this is a very unusual church. The structure is 19th century Gothic but inside is totally different as all the decorations and chapels are thoroughly modern. This makes for an intriguing contrast that is fascinating to see.

Descalzas Reales Monasterio (Royal Descalzas Monastery), Plaza de las Descalzas, 3; tel: 248 74 04. Metro between Callao Lines 3 (yellow) and 5 (green) and Sol Lines 1 (blue), 2 (red) and 3 (yellow). Open Tuesday, Wednesday, Thursday and Saturday 1030-1230, 1600-1730; Friday 1030-1230; Sunday and holidays 1100-1330. Closed Monday. Entrance 500 ptas, foreign students 400 ptas; Wednesday free for EC citizens with passport or ID card. No solo visits, only organised tours that last for about 45 minutes. Juana de Austria, daughter of Carlos V, was born here in 1536 and founded the monastery in 1559. It then became a retreat for the kings of Castile. Today, although unattractively located immediately behind the large El Corte Ingles department store, it is a very dignified museum with important works of art accumulated since its foundation in the 16th century. In 1987 it was named 'European Museum of the Year'.

Museo Thyssen-Bornemisza   (Thyssen-Bornemisza Museum) Palacio de Villahermosa, Paseo del Prado, 8; tel: 420 39 44. Metro Banco de España Line 2 (red). Open Tuesday to Sunday 1000-1900. Closed Monday. Entrance: 600 ptas; students 350 ptas. Advance bookings can be made on Tuesday to Sunday 1600-1800. Opened in October 1992 and located in the specially renovated Villahermosa Palace, this museum houses nearly 800 paintings of the great masters from the 13th century to date, representing the best pictures from the collection of Baron Hans Heinrich Thyssen-Bornemisza.

Palacio Real, Museo de la Real Armería y Real Farmacia (Royal Palace, Royal Armoury Museum and Royal Pharmacy), Bailén; tel: 248 74 04. Metro Opera, Line 2 (red) and Line 5 (green). Open Monday to Saturday 0900-1900, last ticket 1800; Sunday and holidays 0900-1600, last ticket 1500. Closed when palace used for royal receptions. Entrance 750 ptas, foreign students 600 ptas; Wednesday free for EC citizens with passport or ID card.

Palacio Real (Royal Palace) Free tours are available, in different languages, and the last leaves 45 minutes before closing time. Built on the site of the Alcázar of the House of Austria, the Palacio Real was begun in 1738 by Felipe V and was completed by Carlos III in 1764. With 2,800 rooms this huge building, on seven levels, is the second largest palace in Europe after the Hermitage in St Petersburg. Although it is still used for state occasions and receptions, the present king prefers to reside in the more modest Zarzuela palace and his grandfather, Alfonso XIII, was the last monarch to live here, up to 1931. It is reputed that no one has ever been in to all the rooms and only a limited number can be visited. These are splendid indeed, sumptuously decorated with many fine works of art, tapestries, beautifully painted ceilings and numerous chandeliers. The Throne Room, anachronistic as it is, holds a special fascination.

Museo de la Real Armería (The Royal Armoury Museum) Founded by Felipe II, the Royal Armoury has been on its present site since 1893. The collection of armour, some of which belonged to such famous historical figures as Ferdinand and Isabella, Boabdil, the last Moorish leader of Granada and Spain, Maximilian of Austria and many other kings of Spain, is considered to be one of the finest in the world. Apart from the armour for horses, men, children and even dogs, there are many mementoes of famous battles.

Real Farmacia (Royal Pharmacy) Apart from a reproduction of a 17th century laboratory there is cupboard after cupboard filled with original porcelain jars, strange-shaped glass vessels and chemical apparatus. All very interesting for the chemically minded but possibly rather monotonous for others.

Plaza Mayor This classical square, one of the best of its kind, was constructed at the wishes of Felipe III during 1617-19. It is 200m long, 100m wide and has three levels above the porticoed ground floor. The most important buildings are the Casa de la Panadería (the Bakers' Guild) where some of the city archives are kept and the Casa de la Carnicería (the Butchers' Guild). The large equestrian statue in the centre is of Felipe III. At one time there were 136 houses around the square and their balconies offered the residents a grandstand view of public events — from bullfights to executions — held there. Today it has less dramatic uses but still remains a fascinating place to visit, especially on weekend nights. There are numerous bars and restaurants under the porticos and many spread into the plaza itself. Sometimes there are stalls in the plaza — at Christmastide they sell a strange combination of religious decorations and practical jokes — and always small crowds of people and artists, portrait and other. In the southwest corner steps lead down to the Arcos de Cuchilleros and the *cuevas* (caves). These are actually restaurants and bars built back under the plaza and they have a character all of their own. Amongst the varied cuisine found here — and in the rest of the city — fish is predominant, rather strange in a city so far from the sea. The windows of the restaurants are full of huge octopus (*pulpo*) and other exotic creatures and even the downmarket bars are not left out. In these squid (*calamara*) sandwiches (*bocadillos*) are available to take away for about 200 ptas and they can be washed down with litre cups of beer or any other drink of your choice.

By choice
El Rastro (Flea Market) Located in the streets below the San Isidro Cathedral (a little south of the Plaza Mayor) and as far as Ronda de Toledo. Metro Tirso de Molina Line 1 (blue) or La Latina Line 5 (green). Open Sundays from about 0800 until mid afternoon. Although the location is not as distinguished as for the *rastros* in Sevilla and Córdoba, this is far larger. It covers a whole network of steeply sloping streets and, as usual, the range of goods for sale is vast. If at first the stalls you see are selling only new items, just persevere and you will not be disappointed.

Museo de la Real Academia de Bellas Artes de San Fernando (The San Fernando Museum and Royal Academy of Fine Arts), Alcalá, 13; tel: 522 14 91. Metro Sevilla Line 2 (red). Open daily summer 0900-1500; winter Tuesday to Friday 0900-1900, Saturday, Sunday, Monday and holidays 0900-1500. Entrance: 200 ptas. A traditional museum that has a large and varied collection of art from many eras.

Museo Nacional 'Centro de Arte Reina Sofía' (National Museum and Queen Sofía Art Centre), Santa Isabel, 52; tel: 467 50 62. Metro Atocha Line 1 (blue). Open Monday and Wednesday to Saturday 1000-2100, Sunday 1000-1430. Closed Tuesday. Entrance: 400 ptas, students free. Located in a large, traditional building that has had modern glass lifts added to the exterior; it is a matter of taste whether you think these improve, or detract from, the original architecture. Inside, the large central patio has fountains and a modern art windmobile. Named after the present queen, the museum specialises in 20th century art by both Spanish and foreign artists and all Picasso's works once housed in El Casón del Buen Retiro are now exhibited here.

Parque Retiro (The Retreat Park) In the centre of Madrid, just behind the Prado, this park was created by King Felipe IV and its 143 hectares are surrounded by decorative railings and 12 gateways. Amongst the many monuments are the equestrian statue of Alfonso XII standing high over the ornamental lake (*estanque*) and boating pool, a small Crystal Palace used as an exhibition hall. There are numerous other statues, fountains and gardens and the best time to visit is on a Sunday, when the Madrileños bring this charming park to life with art exhibitions, musicians and, more importantly, their natural exuberance.

Real Jardín Botanico (Royal Botanical Gardens), Plaza de Murillo, 2; tel: 420 35 68. Metro Atocha Line 1 (blue). Open daily; the hours change according to the season and vary from 1000-1800 and 1000-2100. Entrance: 100 ptas, students 50 ptas. Located just south of the Prado this was founded by Carlos III in 1781 and today has over 30,000 different species of plants from all over the world. A tranquil place to spend an hour or so away from the hustle and bustle of the city.

Museums
Note: Most of the details have been collated from Tourist Office and other official documentation.

Museo Arqueológico Nacional (National Archaeological Museum), Serrano, 13; tel: 577 79 12. Metro Colón or Serrano Line 4 (brown). Open Tuesday to Sunday 0915-1345. Closed Monday and holidays. Located close to the impressive Puerta de Alcalá, this museum was founded by Royal Decree from Isabella II in 1867. Exhibits cover the prehistoric, classic and medieval times, with extensive collections of coins from all over the world and of ceramics.

Museo de Arte Contemporaneo Española (Museum of Spanish Contemporary Art), Avenida Juan de Herrera, 2; tel: 549 71 50. Metro Ciudad de Universitaria Line 6 (grey) or Moncloa Line 3 (yellow). Open Tuesday to Saturday 1000-1800; Sunday 1000-1500. Closed Monday and holidays. Founded in the late 19th century this has had a variety of different names and homes. Today it is located on the university campus and has works of art, mainly by Spaniards, from the 19th and 20th centuries.

Museo Cerralbo (Cerralbo Museum), Ventura Rodriguez, 17; tel: 247 36 46. Metro Plaza de España Lines 3 (yellow) and 10 (dark blue) or Ventura Rodriguez Line 3 (yellow). Open Tuesday to Sunday 1000-1500. Closed Monday, holidays and August. The exhibits in this building, which used to belong to the Marqués de Cerralbo, range from small armaments to porcelain and paintings, including an El Greco.

Museo de Ciencias Naturales (Natural Science Museum), Paseo de la Castellana; tel: 411 13 28. Metro República Argentina Line 6 (grey). Open Tuesday to Saturday 1000-1800; Sunday and holidays 1000-1430.

Museo Ejercito (Army Museum), Mendez Nuñez, 1; tel: 531 46 24. Metro Banco de España Line 2 (red). Open Tuesday to Sunday 1000-1400. Closed Monday and holidays. Located in the Buen Retiro palace, built 1631, this has an extensive array of exhibits. Among the most interesting is El Cid's 'Tizona' sword and a part of the cross Christopher Columbus had when landing in the New World.

Museo Etnológia (Ethnological Museum), Alfonso XII, 68; tel: 230 64 18. Metro Atocha Line 1 (blue). Open Tuesday to Saturday

1000-1800; Sunday 1000-1400. Closed Monday and holidays. A few mummies and many other exhibits from the Philippines.

Museo Lazaro Galdiano (Lazaro Galdiano Museum), Serrano, 122; tel: 261 60 84. Metro Nuñez de Balbao Lines 5 (green) and 9 (purple). Open Tuesday to Sunday 1000-1400. Closed Monday, holidays and August. This houses the important private collection of Sr José Lazaro, who gave the works to the Spanish government in 1948, and includes furniture, silverware and sculptures as well as paintings. The building, a neoclassical mansion with lovely gardens, was the private residence of this affluent merchant.

Museo Municipal (Municipal Museum), Fuencarral, 78; tel: 522 57 32. Metro Tribunal Lines 1 (blue) and 10 (dark blue). Open Tuesday to Saturday 1000-1400, 1700-1900; Sunday 1000-1430. Closed Monday and holidays. Dedicated to the history of Madrid.

Museo Nacional de Artes Decorativas (National Museum of Decorative Arts), Montalban, 12; tel: 521 34 40. Metro Banco de España Line 2 (red). Open Tuesday to Friday 0930-1430; Saturday and Sunday 1000-1400. Closed Monday and holidays. The exhibits here are mainly of Spanish origin from the 15th to 19th centuries.

Museo Naval (Naval Museum), Paseo del Prado, 5; tel: 421 04 19. Metro Banco de España Line 2 (red). Open Tuesday to Sunday 1030-1330. Closed Monday, holidays and August. The name speaks for itself.

Museo Romántico (Romantic Museum), San Mateo, 13; tel: 448 10 45. Metro Alonso Martínez Lines 4 (brown), 5 (green) and 10 (dark blue) or Tribunal Lines 1 (blue) and 10 (dark blue). Open Tuesday to Sunday 1000-1500. Closed Monday, holidays and August. The Marqués de la Vega-Inclan left as legacy to the nation this collection of 19th century furniture and paintings.

Museo Sorolla (Sorolla Museum), Paseo General Martínez Campos, 37; tel: 410 15 84. Metro Iglesia Line 1 (blue). Open Tuesday to Saturday 1000-1400. Closed Monday, holidays and August. This museum, built as a combined house/studio for the painter Joaquín Sorolla y Bastida, now houses his works.

Museo Taurino (Bullfighting Museum), Alcalá, 237; tel: 255 18 57. Metro Ventas Line 2 (red) or Line 5 (green). Open Tuesday to Friday and Sunday 0900-1400. Closed Monday, Saturday and on days that bullfights are held. For those interested in the subject this is a must. It is part of the Plaza de Toros Monumental de Las Ventas, the largest bullfighting arena in Spain, seating over 22,000, and the most important in the world.

Planetario de Madrid (Madrid Planetarium) Parque de Tierno Galvan. tel: 467 34 61. Metro Mendez Alvaro Line 6 (grey). Open Tuesday to Sunday 1130-1345 1700-2045. Closed Monday.

Real Fábrica de Tapices (Royal Tapestry Factory), Fuenterrabia, 2; tel: 551 34 00. Metro Atocha Renfe and Menéndez Pelayo Line 1 (blue). Monday to Friday 0930-1230. Closed Saturday, Sunday, holidays and August. Exhibits from the 18th and 19th centuries and visits to see carpets and tapestries being made.

The stations
Madrid has three principal mainline railway stations. Chamartín, a modern station in the north of the city, is the most important and long distance trains leave for all destinations in Spain. It is also the administrative headquarters for RENFE.

Atocha, much closer to the centre of the city, is complex — in more than one meaning of the word. The original building, a classic old-fashioned railway station, used to be a terminal. That was closed and an ultramodern tri-level station was built nearby. This is on the same line as Chamartín (to the north) and many through trains stop at both stations. The old station has been restored to become the station for Spain's new high speed line, AVE (*Alta Velocidad Española*), between Madrid and Sevilla and certain other types of trains to various destinations.

The third one has two names, Principe Pío or Norte, and is rather a strange, if traditional, station. It serves destinations in northwest Spain and the overnight trains leave from here instead of Chamartín.

These stations are connected both by the Metro and the *cercanías* (local train system) and the most convenient ways between them are detailed under each station.

Chamartín
Located in the north of the city in a residential area, a long way

from the city centre. It is modern and the concourse, where all
the facilities are located, is positioned over the platforms. There is
also a commercial area with cafeterias and shops, one open 24
hours, on the same level. The exit to the Metro is on the Platform
1 side of the station close to Facility A, or by underpass from the
platforms.

Layout

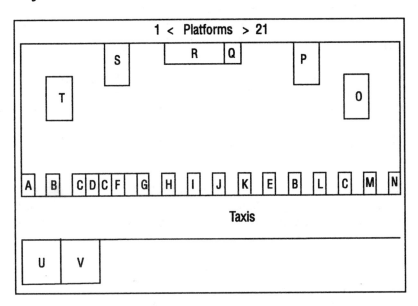

Key

A: *Telefónica*, open daily 0730-
2300
B: *Librería Prodesa* Rail Press,
newspapers, magazines, books, open
daily 0700-2300
C: *Regalos*, a gift shop, open daily
0800-2300
D: Deli-Express, a fast food outlet,
open daily 0700-2300
E: *Tábacos*, cigarettes, tobacco,
stamps, etc, open daily 0700-2330
F: Hertz car rental, open Monday
to Saturday 0730-2230
G: *Información y Reserva Hotelera*,
hotel information and reservations,
open Monday 0715-2130; Tuesday to

Sunday 0730-2300
H: Bank, cash dispenser and
currency machine, Caja de Madrid.
The bank is open Monday to Friday
0830-1400, the Cash dispenser takes
Visa, Access, Mastercard and
Eurocard and the currency machine
automatically changes foreign bank
notes
I: *Correos* and *Telegrafo*, post
office, telegram office, open Monday
to Friday 0830-2100
J: Bank, cash dispenser and
currency machine, Banco Bilbao
Vizcaya. The bank is open on
weekends as well as regular hours;

the cash dispenser is on the Servired system and takes all major credit cards and the currency machine automatically changes foreign banknotes

K: Burger Express, a fast food outlet, open daily 0800-2300

L: Cash dispenser, Banco de Fomento. This is on the Telebanco system and takes all major credit cards

M: *Communidad de Madrid Oficina Turismo*, tourist office, open Monday to Friday 0800-2000; Saturday 0800-1300. Closed Sunday

N: *'Romi 88' Bombonería and Heladería*, an ice-cream and sweet shop, open daily 0730-2300

O: *Restaurante Costa Brava*, open

daily 1330-1545, 2000-2230

P: Cafeteria/Bar Mataro, open daily 0700-2330

Q: Train information, open daily 0730-2330

R: Ticket office, same day tickets only

S: Cafeteria/bar, open daily 0700-2400

T: Restaurante El Jardín, open daily 1300-1600, 2000-2300

U: Ticket office, *Oficina de Ventas* open 0900-2000, for future days tickets

V: *Consigna*, both automatic and manual, open daily 0730-2330, price 300 ptas small, 600 ptas large. All luggage has to go through an automatic security machine

Note: If you have to wait around for a train, either at lunchtime or in the evening, and you want a meal there is an excellent Chinese restaurant just five minutes away. Go down the escalators to the street, cross over and walk through what looks like a small pedestrian shopping centre and, at the far end, you will find the China Imperial restaurant at Mauricio Legendre, 16; tel: 315 44 08. The food is delicious and the lunchtime special is amazingly good value. Beware, though, of the bars in the shopping arcade; these are actually brothels.

Chamartín to Atocha RENFE
- **by RENFE** Any main-line or *cercanía* service between the stations. This is by far the fastest and easiest way.

Chamartín to Principe Pío/Norte
- **by RENFE** The easiest, but slightly longer and more expensive way, is a *cercanía*, of which there are four trains an hour. The fare is 165 ptas and the journey takes about 45 minutes.
- **by Metro** The Metro is cheaper and a little quicker, but more complicated. Line 8, Pink, Fuencarral to Avenida de América. Direction Avenida de América and change at Plaza Castilla, the first stop. Then Line 1, Blue, Plaza Castilla to Portazago. Direction Portazago change at Cuatro Caminos. Then Line 2, Red, Cuatro

Caminos to Ventas. Direction Ventas change at Opera, the fifth stop; then Line R, a shuttle service between Opera and Norte.

Chamartín to Puerta del Sol

- **by bus** The slowest, especially during the rush-hours, but probably the most interesting way. Number 5, a red bus, from the station concourse all the way to Puerta del sol.

- **by Metro** Line 8, Pink, Fuencarral to Avenida de América; direction Avenida de América change at Plaza Castilla, the first stop. Then Line 1 (Blue) Plaza Castilla to Portazgo. Direction Portazgo and Sol is the tenth stop.

- **by taxi** This is a long journey anyway but traffic conditions can vary considerably and therefore it is difficult to estimate the fare. Expect a minimum of 1,100 ptas and possibly as much as 1,500 ptas.

Atocha

The new station is a complicated, tri-level, modern structure that is not possible to depict in diagram form. The platforms, for all trains except the AVE, are on the lowest level and the following facilities are on the middle level. *Croissentería*, open daily 0700-2300; BRIEF, a combination of cafeteria, restaurant and shop, open daily 0630-2300; *Cajero*, a cash dispensing machine that takes Visa, Mastercard, Eurocard and Access cards; the ticket office, *Consigna automática* machines at 300 ptas and a variety of automatic drink machines, etc, are on the upper level. Exits from the platforms are controlled by electronic gates which open when the ticket is put in. Those without such tickets exit by a special gate next to the ticket office.

The original station is now used for the high speed AVE trains that run on new tracks between Madrid, Ciudad Real, Puertollano, Córdoba and Sevilla and other services that use these new tracks. The building has been most beautifully restored in a unique and imaginative style; the trains have been left outside and the old-fashioned high ceiling concourse has been left for the passengers. The startlingly attractive result is enhanced by groups of tall palm trees and unusual fountains emitting a very fine spray that gives both a soothing and cooling effect.

Layout

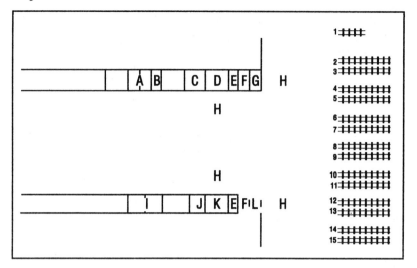

Key (lower level)

A: *Atención al Cliente* office
B: Train information office, open daily 0600-2400
C: Ticket office
D: Ticket services, *Venta Personalizada*
E: Stairs to upper levels
F: Lifts to upper levels
G: *Servicios*, men

H: Escalators to upper levels
I: *Consigna Automática*, open daily 0600-2400, price, per 24 hours: small, 300 ptas; medium, 400 ptas; large 500 ptas
J: Cafeteria, open daily 0600-2400
K: *Gabinete de Circulación*
L: *Servicios*, women

The second level is basically a waiting area, including the special Club AVE room, and overlooks the trains and the elegant new interior; taxis are found on the third level.

Atocha RENFE to Chamartín
- by RENFE Any main-line or *cercanía* service between the stations. This is by far the fastest and easiest way.

Atocha Renfe to Principe Pío/Norte
- by Metro Line 1, Blue, Portazgo to Plaza Castilla. Direction Plaza Castilla to Sol. Then Line 2, Red, Ventas to Cuatro Caminos. Direction Cuatro Caminos to Opera, just one stop; then Line R, a shuttle service between Opera and Norte.

Atocha RENFE to Puerta del Sol
- **by Metro** Line 1, Blue, Portazco to Plaza Castilla. Direction Plaza Castilla and Sol is the fourth stop.

- **by taxi** This depends upon the time of day and traffic conditions. Allow for 300 ptas minimum to perhaps 500 ptas maximum.

Principe Pío/Norte
A small, only nine platforms, and rather old-fashioned terminal that is almost underneath the walls of the Royal Palace in a pleasant part of Madrid. It is more commonly known as Norte and a plaque on the wall indicates it is at a height of 592.2m above sea level.

Layout

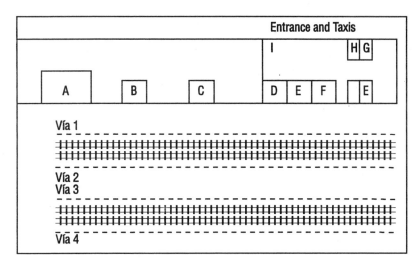

Key
A: Cafeteria, open daily 0700-2330
B: *Servicios*
C: *Comisaría*
D: *Tábacos*, cigarettes, tobacco, stamps, etc, open daily 0800-1400, 1700-2030
E: *Librería Prodesa Rail Press*, newspapers, magazines, etc, open daily 0700-2300

F: *Bombonería Regalos*, sweets and gifts, open daily 0700-1330, 1500-2300
G: Ticket office
H: *Información y Atención al Viajero*
I: *Consigna Automática*, price 300 ptas per machine

Norte to Chamartín
- **by RENFE** The easiest, but slightly longer and more expensive way, is a *cercanía* of which there are four trains an hour. the fare is 165 ptas and the journey takes about 45 minutes.
- **by Metro** Line R a shuttle service between Norte and Opera. then Line 2, Red, Ventas to Cuatro Caminos. Direction Cuatro Caminos to the last stop. Then Line 1, Blue, Portazgo to Plaza Castilla. Direction Plaza Castilla and again change at the last stop. Then Line 8, Pink, Avenida de América to Fuencarral. Direction Fuencarral and Chamartín is the next stop.

Norte to Atocha RENFE
- **by Metro** Line R a shuttle service between Norte and Opera. Then Line 2, Red, Cuatro Caminos to Ventas. Direction Ventas one stop to Sol. Then Line 1, Blue, Plaza Castilla to Portazgo. Direction Portazgo and Atocha RENFE is four stops on.

Norte to Puerta del Sol
- **by Metro** Line R Norte to Opera, a shuttle service between Opera and Norte. Then Line 2, Red, Cuatro Caminos to Ventas. Direction Ventas and Sol is the second stop.
- **by taxi** As usual this depends upon the time of day and traffic conditions but the fare should be between 250 to 400 ptas.

Train services
Note: These are listed in clockwise order, starting at the route closest to the 12 o'clock point.

To Irún/France by

	InterCity	Talgo	Estrella
Ávila		1½	1¾
Valladolid	2½		3¼
Burgos	3¾	3	4¾
Irún	7	6¼	9¾

Barcelona by

	Diurno	Inter City	Talgo	Talgo Camas	Estrella
Zaragoza	3½		3¼	3½	4
Tarragona	7	7½			
Barcelona	8¼	8½	7½	8¾	10¼

To Valencia by

	Regional	Inter City	Estrella
Cuenca	2¾		
Albacete		2¼	4¼
Valencia	5½	4¼	8¼

To Almería/Granada by

	Talgo	Talgo Pen *	Estrella
Alcázar de San Juan	1½	2	2
Moreda	5½	6½	7½
Almería	7½	9	
Granada	6¼		8¾

* These trains split at Moreda

To Algeciras/Málaga by

	Diurno	Talgo	Talgo Pen	Talgo Camas	Estrella
Alcázar de San Juan	1¾	1½	2	2¼	2¼
Ciudad Real		1¼			
Córdoba	5	2½	4½	6¼	6 6
Algeciras				11½	
Málaga	8¼	5	7	9½	10¼

To Sevilla by

	Regional	Talgo	Talgo Camas	Estrella	AVE
Alcázar de San Juan	2				
Ciudad Real		1¼			
Cáceres	4½				
Mérida	5½				
Zafra	6½				
Córdoba			2½	6	2
Sevilla		9½	3½	8	2¾

To Badajoz by

	Regional	Talgo	Estrella
Ciudad Real	3		3½
Cáceres	5¼	3¾	
Mérida	7½ 6¼	4½	8¾
Badajoz	8½ 7½	5½	10¼

To Salamanca by
Regional: via Ávila 1¾; Salamanca 3¼.

To Santiago de Compostela by
	Talgo	Estrella
Ávila	1¼	1½
Zamora	3	3½
Santiago de Compostela	7½	10

To León by
	Regional	Talgo Pen
Ávila	1¾	1½
Valladolid	3	2½
León	5	4¼

The Metro
Open 0600-0130. Fare structure: single tickets cost 125 ptas; a ticket valid for 10 trips (controlled by a magnetic strip) costs 450 ptas.

The lines are identified by a number, 1 to 10, and R for the Norte/Opera shuttle, a colour code and the first and last stop. This system is easy to use. First identify where you want to go and then ascertain the line number, colour code and the last stop in the direction you are going. If a change, or changes, is necessary repeat the above procedure for each line until you reach your destination. To find the correct platform at the station of departure, and any subsequent changes, look for the line number, colour code and the name of the last stop in the direction you are going. These are clearly identified along with the names of all the interim stations. The lines are clearly identified in each carriage, too, and a recording (male voice) tells you the name of the next stop whilst a female voice identifies any connecting lines at the forthcoming station.

There is a clock on each platform indicating how long it has been since the last train departed and, in the centre of the platform, a notice board that gives the average times between trains at different times of the day.

A copy of the subway guide *Plano de Madrid Metro a Metro* can be obtained at any ticket office.

The Metro is by far the easiest and quickest way of getting around Madrid. The stations are generally well kept and the trains clean and neat.

As most people will usually take at least two trips, to and from the mainline station, without considering sightseeing it is advisable to purchase a 10-trip ticket straightaway.

Accommodation
Close to Chamartín
**** Hotel Chamartín Agustín de Foxa; tel: 323 30 87; fax: 733 02 14. This large hotel, part of the Husa chain, is ideally located for train travellers as it is located directly above Madrid's main station of the same name. There are 360 rooms and 18 suites which all have a private bathroom, telephone, satellite TV, air-conditioning, minibar and private safe. Singles 13,500 ptas; double 17,900 ptas; double, for single use, 14,300 ptas; treble 24,675 ptas.

Close to Atocha
Posada de San Blas Atocha, 117; tel: 429 10 99. Metro, this is between Atocha and Antón Martín, both on Line 1 (blue). Single 1,200 ptas; double 2,000 ptas. The entrance is in a large, plain patio. Many rooms but rather basic.

Close to Principe Pío/Norte
Note: Metro — both of these are close to Norte, Line R, the shuttle service from Opera.
** HR O'Ribeiro Paseo de la Florida, 15; tel: 542 12 76. Single 1,600 ptas; double 2,800 ptas. Directly across from the station. Second floor; rather old-fashioned.
* Hostal Mieres Paseo de la Florida, 15; tel: 248 50 11. Single without bath 1,400 ptas; double 2,300 ptas. Same building as the O'Ribeiro but first floor; also old-fashioned and clean.

In the city
**** Hotel Arosa Salud, 21. (Edificio Gran Vía, 29); tel: 532 16 00; fax: 531 31 27. Metro Callao, Line 3 (yellow) and Line 5 (green). A Best Western hotel. Single 13,833 ptas; double 19,928 ptas. These rates include breakfast. Located in a very central position just off the Gran Vía and north of the Puerta del Sol this has 140 rooms, some with balcony, all fully equipped with bath/shower, satellite colour TV, direct dial telephone, radio, piped music, safe and minibar, and some also have a hairdryer. There is also a restaurant and bar.
Note: There are literally dozens of places to stay in the centre of Madrid but the cheaper district is south and east of the Plaza Mayor and all of the following are located in that area. Almost all lower budget places share the following characteristics. There will be a bell, with an intercom system,

outside the front door. When a voice answers and you ask for a *habitación*
the proprietor will automatically open the front doors. Then pass into the
lobby and walk (there is rarely a lift) up the wooden stairway to the
required floor. There, another door, usually with a small round metal grille,
will have the name of the place on it. If it is not open ring the bell and
either someone will open the door or the metal grille will be revolved, from
the inside, allowing the proprietor to check you out first.

** **HR Gonzalo** Cervantes, 34; tel: 429 27 14. Metro Antón Martín, Line
1 (blue). Single without bath 2,000 ptas, with bath 3,200 ptas; double with
bath 4,000 ptas. On a quiet street across from the Prado. Clean and rather
nice. Third floor with lift.

* **HR Arbol del Japón** Conde de Romanones, 10; tel: 369 31 94. Metro
Tirso de Molina, Line 1 (blue). Single without bath 2,200 ptas; double
without bath 3,600 ptas. The entrance is at the back of a large patio.
Apparently run by Japanese people. Expensive.

* **HR Blas** Mesón de Paredes, 5; tel: 369 01 15. Metro Tirso de Molina,
Line 1 (blue). Single 1,200 ptas; double 2,000 ptas. Plain and ordinary. In
a pedestrian-only street, close to the Metro.

* **HR Dos Naciones** Conde de Romanones, 8; tel: 369 35 42. Metro Tirso
de Molina, Line 1 (blue). Single without bath 1,700 ptas; double without
bath 2,700 ptas, with bath 3,200 ptas. On the third floor with a lift. Same
building as the Hostal Muñoz but somewhat nicer.

* **HR Ferñandez** León, 10; tel: 429 56 37. Metro Antón Martín, Line 1
(blue). Single without bath 1,600 ptas, with bath 2,500 ptas; double with
bath 3,500 ptas. Located in a quiet street on the first floor. Run of the mill
place.

* **Hostal Amaika** Esparteros, 11; tel: 531 52 78. Metro Sol, Lines 1
(blue), 2 (red) and 3 (yellow). Single without bath 1,500 ptas, with bath
2,500 ptas; double without bath 2,500 ptas, with bath 3,500 ptas. On third
and fourth floors of a very large building. Lift up but not down. Between
the Puerta del Sol and Plaza Mayor.

* **Hostal Commercial** Esparteros, 12; tel: 522 66 30. Metro Sol, Lines 1
(blue), 2 (red) and 3 (yellow). Single without bath 1,500 ptas, with bath
2,000 ptas; double without bath 2,800 ptas, with bath 3,000 ptas. On second
floor. Plain building with no lift. Between the Puerta del Sol and Plaza
Mayor.

* **Hostal Muñoz** Conde de Romanones, 8; tel: 369 05 16. Metro Tirso de
Molina, Line 1 (blue). Single without bath 1,800 ptas; double without bath
2,600 ptas, with bath 3,300 ptas. On fourth floor with lift. In the same
building as the Dos Naciones but not as nice.

* **Hostal Tirso** Tirso de Molina, 13; tel: 369 34 08. Metro Tirso de
Molina, Line 1 (blue). Single without bath 1,800 ptas; double without bath
2,300 ptas. Located right on the plaza. Second floor and no lift; very dark

and dingy inside.

* Pensións Abulense y Viguesa Mesón de Paredes, 13; tel: 539 89 73 and 530 74 22. Metro Tirsa de Molina, Line 1 (blue). Single 800 ptas; double 1,600 ptas. Two small pensions on first and second floors. Run by the same people. Plain and basic. In a pedestrian only street and next door to the oldest bar in Madrid.

CH Cordero Bolsa, 10; tel: 522 88 07. Metro Sol, Line 1 (blue), Line 2 (red) and 3 (yellow). Single without bath 1,800 ptas; double without bath 2,000 ptas. Second floor without lift. Off the southeast corner of Plaza Mayor. Plain and ordinary.

CH Rosado Bolsa, 10; tel: 532 51 75. Single without bath 1,500 ptas; double without bath 2,000 ptas. Apart from being one floor higher the comments here are the same as for the Cordero.

General information
Car hire
Avis, Estación Atocha, Terminal AVE, Glorieta de Atocha; tel: 530 01 68.

Fiestas
Easter week (*Semana Santa*), variable dates, and San Isidro in early May.

Police
The most central police station is inside the Sol Metro station; the most convenient entrance is on the south side of the Puerta del Sol.

RENFE city office
Alcalá, 44. Open Monday to Friday 0930-2000. Closed Saturday, Sunday and holidays.

Public telephones
Gran Vía, 30. Open Monday to Saturday 0900-2400; Sunday and holidays 1200-2400.

Telephones and Fax
Espoz y Miña (just off the south side of the Puerta del Sol). Open Monday to Friday 0930-2200; Saturday 1000-2200. Closed Sunday and holidays.

Telephone code

for Madrid is (91).

Tourist office

Oficina Municipal, Plaza Mayor, 3; tel: 266 54 77. Open Monday
to Friday 1000-2000; Saturday 1000-1400. Closed Sunday and
holidays.

MADRID — DAY TRIPS

There are three places that are worth seeing within a short distance of Madrid and it is ideal to see these on day trips from the capital.

El Escorial and the Valle de los Caídos (Valley of the Fallen)

El Escorial is 52km (32.5 miles) west of Madrid and is reached by either *Regional* or *Cercanía* services which depart from Chamartín or Atocha. From the station you can either take a L1 San Lorenzo/Estación (green) bus that costs 60 ptas to the monastery, or walk. The latter is uphill all the way but as it is through a pleasant park it is enjoyable.

Monastery of San Lorenzo el Real del Escorial Open Tuesday to Sunday 1000-1900. Closed Monday. Entrance: 500 ptas; student 350 ptas. There are two parts: Zone A has the Museo de Pintura, Palacio de Asturias, Pantheons and *Sales Capituleres*, and the last admission is one hour before closing; Zone B has the library and Basilica and last entry is 20 minutes before closing. The recommended time to allow for visiting is two hours for Zone A and 30 minutes for Zone B.

This huge building was commissioned as a monastery by Felipe II to commemorate his victory over the French on St Lawrence's Day, August 10 1557. It was built between 1563 and 1584 and also includes a royal palace and pantheon. Its location, 1,065m (3,494ft) up on the foothills of the Sierra de Guadarrama, enhances its beauty.

The inside is no less impressive. The Museum of Art consists of many rooms of important paintings and many people will find the Gallery of Battles intriguing. The kings quarters are actually quite austere even though there are many fine examples of furniture. It is the pantheons that will attract most people's attention. The Pantheon of the Kings is nothing short of spectacular, while the Pantheon of the Infants is very different in style, but perhaps more moving.

In Zone B the Basilica is very large indeed and rather splendid. In the midst of all this splendour my personal favourites are the particularly beautiful murals on the ceiling of the library. Really, El Escorial should not be missed. For those wanting more information the tourist office is at Floridablanca 11 (tel: 890 15 54) and is open Monday to Friday 1000-1400, 1500-1800 and Saturday 1000-1330.

Valle de los Caídos (Valley of the Fallen) This is nearby and it is convenient to include a visit after seeing the monastery. Buses run by Autocares Herranz leave daily from San Lorenzo, except Monday, at 1515 and return from Valle de los Caídos at 1730 and tickets can be purchased at Reino Victoria, 3, in San Lorenzo. The journey is pretty and does not take very long. The Valle de los Caídos was built as a memorial to the dead of the Civil War and is in a very beautiful location. The huge cross is 150m (492ft) high and 46m (150ft) across at the fingertips and a funicular takes you up on to the plinth. (This is open on Saturday, Sunday and holidays and costs 250 ptas.) The view back down the valley is simply spectacular and it is easy to be overawed by the size of the cross.

No less spectacular, but in an entirely different way, is the Basilica. This occupies a space that has been hollowed out of the granite hill, is of immense proportions, and is very ornate. The tombstones of José Antonio Primo de Rivera, the founder of the Falangist Party, and of Franco are prominent, whilst in the crypt, which is closed to the public, there are ossuaries containing the remains of tens of thousands of dead, of both sides, from the Civil War.

Aranjuez

Aranjuez is 49km (30 miles) south of Madrid and is reached by either *Regional* or *Cercanía* services from Atocha. Turn right out of the station then left at the first junction and the palace is directly ahead.

Palacio Real (Royal Palace) Open Tuesday to Sunday 1000-1900 (summer) 1000-1730 (winter). Entrance: 400 ptas; free to EC citizens on Wednesdays. Only guided tours allowed; these are in Spanish and last about 45 minutes.

Aranjuez has been a royal favourite for centuries; the Catholic Monarchs often visited the town and there were previous palaces before the present one was constructed in the early 18th century. Each of the rooms is lavishly furnished in different styles and there are two that are very strange indeed. One of these is decorated with Chinese ceramics and the other is similar to a room in the Alhambra in Granada. They certainly add character but do look out of place. The sound of water running over a weir outside just adds to the charm. There are extensive gardens that are a delight to walk through and in the *Jardín del Príncipe* (Prince's Garden) one can find the following:

Casa de Marinos (Sailor's House) Open the same hours as the palace but the entrance (combined with the Casa del Labrador) is an extra 300 ptas. Again, guided tours only. The Sailor's House is rather incongruous with its surroundings as the exhibits are the sovereign's royal vessels.

Casa del Labrador (Labourer's House) Same details as for the Casa de Marinos. This is located at the far end of the gardens and is not at all like a labourer's house — it is actually named after the workhouse that used to be on the site. In fact it is rather grand and today houses an art museum.

As these places are rather far apart there is a little 'train', *Chiquitren de Aranjuez*, that runs between them and costs 300 ptas.

Aranjuez is not the most important of places to visit but it is interesting and the surroundings, very pretty and peaceful, make a lovely change from the bustling, crowded city.

MÁLAGA
The city
This area has a long history. There are prehistoric caves nearby and
Málaga itself was an important trading centre for the Phoenicians,
Greeks, Carthaginians and Romans before the invading Moors
captured the city from the Visigoths in 714. Initially it was
controlled by the Caliphate of Córdoba but, after that collapsed in
the 11th century, power passed to the Kingdom of Granada and it
was not until 1487 that the city was finally reconquered by
Ferdinand and Isabella.

Today Málaga is a large city, with a population of about 600,000,
and it is most important as an international gateway to the world
famous resort area of the Costa del Sol. This coastline, from
Gibraltar in the west to Almería in the east, with its numerous
beaches and pleasing climate — hot in the summer, cool and
pleasant in the winter — attracts millions of people annually. Many
of these pass through Málaga, either its large international airport,
the railway station or even the busy port but, surprisingly, this has
not changed the character of the city all that much. It has though, as
in other large cities, brought its own problems and unsuspecting
tourists are likely to become easy victims. Always pay particular
attention to bags, shoulder bags and cameras, etc as youths on
mopeds are very adept at snatching these as they go by. This type
of crime is so prevalent that there are full time interpreters at the
main police station.

Do not let such problems put you off visiting Málaga as the city
has an interesting character. The wide, tree-lined Paseo del Parque
that stretches from the Plaza de la Marina — with its large new
fountain — to the Fuente (fountain) Genovesa and the nearby Plaza
de Toros is particularly delightful. This is a long narrow park with
numerous trees, statues, small fountains, duck ponds, an open-air
theatre and, on the north side, two very attractive buildings: the
Ayuntamiento (Town Hall) and *Aduana* (Customs House). Running
north from the Plaza de la Marina is the most important shopping
street, Calle Marqués de Larios; this celebrated its centenary in
1991 and a huge cake was baked for the residents. For the more
adventurous, those seeking the more traditional Málaga, a walk
through the back streets up to the Plaza de la Merced is rather
interesting. There, at number 14 in the northeast corner, is the
birthplace of Pablo Picasso.

Málaga is rightly famous for its seafood and, besides restaurants, the small bars along and off the north side of the Alameda Principal, close to Larios, should not be missed. These sell octopus (*pulpo*) squid (*calamara*) and all kinds of shellfish, particularly shrimps (*gambas*) — the latter are particularly delicious when grilled in garlic. Do not forget to follow the local custom and simply throw the shells on to the floor. For those wanting to try the local wine the most famous variety is called Málaga Wine, but beware, this is not to everyone's taste as it is very sweet (*dulce*).

The city changes its character three times a year. Firstly at Easter (*Semana Santa*) when the traditional processions are somewhat less sombre than those in northern cities. The second is during the August Fair, when the Malagueños really let their hair down. The women wear their traditional, and very colourful, dresses and the men their *Trajes de Campo*, traditional ranch wear. They then converge on the centre on horseback (the horses are rented and stabled by the beach), gypsy caravans that are brightly decorated and even on foot. Once there they drink mainly *fino* (dry sherry) — note the small metal containers on a chain around the men's necks — and dance *Sevillianos*. Each night the large funfair on the edge of the city is equally crowded. These celebrations go on for about ten days and last well into the early hours of the morning.

The third celebration, Christmas, is the one least seen by tourists and, perhaps, most incongruous to the traditions of those from colder climates. The palm trees of the Paseo del Parque are covered with decorations and lights and it is possible, some years, to sit out in shirt sleeves at 2230 in temperatures close to 70F. Also the Alameda Principal is lined with stalls that either sell religious decorations or practical jokes; a strange combination but one that says a lot about the Spanish personality.

Places of interest
Must see
Alcazaba, Teatro Romano and **Museo Arqueológico** (Fortress, Roman Theatre and Archaeological Museum), Calle Alcazaba; tel: 221 60 05. Open Monday to Saturday 1000-1300, 1700-2000. Closed Sunday and holidays. Entrance: 20 ptas. Three for the price of one here and all for a bargain 20 ptas. The Teatro Romano (Roman Theatre) is not very impressive and, in any event, can be seen from the road without paying. The Alcazaba, an Arab fortress and palace dating from the 11th century, was undergoing major renovation and many parts of it were out of bounds when I visited.

The museum has Neolithic, Eneolithic and Roman exhibits, amongst others.

Museo de Artes y Tradiciones Populares (Museum of Popular Arts and Traditions), Pasillo Santa Isabel, 10. tel: 221 71 37. Open Tuesday to Friday 1000-1330, 1700-2000, Saturday 1000-1330. Closed Monday, Sunday and holidays. Entrance: free. This beautiful old house is in marked contrast to its rather undistinguished surroundings. It is an absolutely charming place with a patio full of large plants. The exhibits are a cross section of all things pertinent to life in Málaga in days gone by: crafts, carriages, paintings, wine-making utensils, clothes and even a boat — to name just a few. For me this is the most interesting museum in Málaga and it should not be missed.

Museo de Bellas Artes (Fine Arts Museum), San Agustín, 6; tel: 221 83 82. Open Tuesday to Friday 1000-1330, 1700-2000, Saturday, Sunday and holidays 1000-1330. Closed Monday. Entrance: foreign residents in Spain and citizens of the EC under 21 free, others 250 ptas. Photography not allowed. Located in an interesting but rather plain building dating from the 16th century. There are two patios and the exhibits are generally very formal and sombre. However they are enlivened by a small room of colourful modern paintings, including some by Picasso who was born in Málaga. In case the need arises the toilets are impeccable here.

Museo Catedralicio (Cathedral Museum), Molina Lario; tel: 221 59 17. Open Monday to Saturday 1000-1245, 1600-1900. Closed Sunday and holidays. Entrance: 100 ptas. A large, formal cathedral built between the 16th and 18th centuries with one unfinished tower and some beautiful stained-glass windows. There are small, but attractive gardens in the quadrangle and around the outside.

By choice
Gibralfaro Of Phoenician origin, today there are only the remains of a Moorish castle and nearby the modern Parador Nacional hotel. There are magnificent views of the city and surrounding countryside from here and it also offers a free view of the bullfights held in the *plaza de toros* directly below. It is possible to walk up and down but the pathway is steep and difficult. Much better to get a taxi up and walk down.

Museums

Fundación Pablo Ruiz Picasso (Picasso Foundation), Plaza de la Merced, 14; tel: 228 39 00. Open Monday to Friday 1100-1400. Entrance: free. Located in the house where Picasso was born this is more of a research centre than a museum, although there are some exhibits.

Museo Diocesano de Arte Sacro (Sacred Arts Museum), Plaza del Obispo; tel: 222 25 52. This museum is located in the elegant Episcopal Palace very close to the cathedral. However it was closed for extensive restoration at the time of research.

Museo de Semana Santa (Holy Week Museum), Plaza de San Pedro/Iglesia de San Julián; tel: 231 23 94. Open Monday to Friday 1030-1230. Closed Saturday, Sunday and holidays. Entrance: free. A museum strictly for those interested in religious festivals. Located directly across from the El Cortes Inglés department store.

Station/location/transport to city centre

RENFE, Cuarteles; tel: 231 25 00. The station is located a mile or so to the west of the city centre and is adjacent to the bus station. Beware, the pedestrian area directly outside the station provides a home for the city's down and outs and is none too pleasant.

Layout

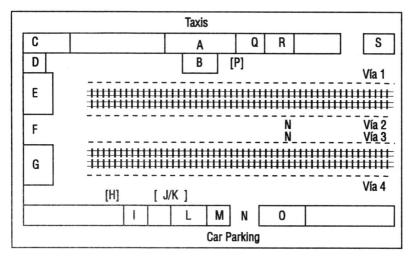

Key

A: Main entrance, booking hall and entrance to Málaga/Fuengirola line
B: *Kiosco* for books, magazines, open 0730-1900
C: Restaurant/bar; a large place, recently renovated, with toilets, open 0700-2300
D: Automatic cash dispenser for Visa/Servired/Electron/ Eurocard Access/Caixa Oberja/ Mastercard/ Tarjeta 4B/ Eurocheque
E: *Tienda Picasso*; a general shop that sells souvenirs, cigarettes etc. It also has a *Cambio* (bureau de change), open 0800-2245
F: There is a strange piece of modern art here based on one of Picasso's works (this has now been moved into the booking hall)
G: Tabernas los Gitanillos; advertised as typical of Andalucía this is a small café/bar with outside tables. It accepts Visa cards, open 0700-2245

H: Business card *tarjeta* machine
I: *Consigna Automática*; there are two sizes, large and small and the price is 400 and 200 ptas respectively, per day, open 0700-2300
J: Automatic drink dispensing machine
K: Train composition board; most stations have these, showing the format, in engines and carriages, of all trains
L: *Comisaría*
M: A very small bar that, strangely, has an automatic\drink dispensing machine
N: *Carritos Portaequipajes*
O: *Aduana*
P: Automatic cigarette machine
Q: *Jefe de Terminal*
R: *Oficina de Atención al Cliente*
S: *Servicios*

Train station to city centre

By bus The number 19 *Aeropuerto* bus passes the railway station on its route to and from the airport. As with taxis, the journey on most days is very slow.

By taxi Without any traffic problems the journey to the centre takes only 3-4 minutes and costs about 225 ptas. It is wise though, on weekdays up until about 2100 and on Saturdays until 1500, to assume that it will take a lot longer and cost up to 400-450 ptas.

By train The C1 line, Málaga to Fuengirola, goes one stop further past the railway station towards the centre. However, apart from the fact that it only runs every half hour, the terminal is some distance from the actual centre. It is next to the Post and Telecommunications building, the most prominent in Málaga, and across from El Cortes Inglés, on the opposite side of the River Guadalmedina from the older part of the city where the hotels and monuments are located.

Train services
To Madrid by

	Diurno	Talgo	Talgo Pen	Talgo Camas	Estrella
Córdoba	2¾	2½	2	2½	2¾
Ciudad Real		3½			
Alcázar de San Juan	6½		5¼	6½	7
Madrid	8½	5	7	9¼	9¾

To Barcelona by

	Diurno	Talgo Camas	Estrella
Córdoba	2¼	2¼	2¾
Alcázar de San Juan	6		7
Zaragoza	10¾		
Valencia	9½		10½
Barcelona	14	16	16

To Algeciras/Córdoba/Granada/Sevilla by

	Regional	Regional Expres	InterCity
Bobadilla	1¼	1	1
Ronda	2¼		
Algeciras	4		
Córdoba	2¾		
Granada		2¾	
Sevilla	3	3½	2½

Note: The times shown for Algeciras and Granada are those for the train journey. The actual time varies according to how long the wait for a connection is in Bobadilla.

To Cádiz by
Regional: This is rather complicated as it involves a double change at Bobadilla and Utrera. It is more straightforward, and sometimes faster, to go via Sevilla.

Accommodation

For those who want to relax on the Costa del Sol for a few days but still avoid all the crowds, the **** **Hotel Husa Mijas** Costa del Sol, Málaga (tel: 952 48 58 00; fax: 952 48 58 25) is an ideal place. This hotel, part of the Husa chain, is located on the foothills of the Sierra de Mijas between Málaga and Marbella. Set in lovely gardens overlooking the Mediterranean, there is a swimming pool and tennis court, facilities for golf and horse riding and a beauty centre with gymnasium, sauna, jacuzzi and massage available. The restaurant is either indoors or out on the terrace where there is a barbecue. There are 100 rooms and five suites, all with modern facilities. There are two seasons: low, November 1 to March 31, and high the rest of the year. Double, low 10,000 ptas, high 12,000 ptas; double, for single use, low 8,000 ptas, high 10,000 ptas; treble, low 12,000 ptas, high 15,000 ptas.

Close to the station

*** **HR Terminal** Pasaje de Noblejas, 2/4; tel: 231 82 00. Single 3,200 ptas; double 4,000 ptas. About 100 yards from the station off the right hand side of Cuarteles. On second floor of a building in a small passage. Clean and neat but a shade expensive.

** **Hostal Las Américas** Cuarteles, 62 (Edificio Cantabria); tel: 231 93 74. Single 3,000 ptas; double 4,500 ptas. A little expensive. The entrance is in a small arcade diagonally across from the station.

** **Pensión La Hispanidad** Explanada de la Estación. tel: 231 11 35. Single without bath 1,700 ptas, with bath 2,100 ptas; double without bath 2,900 ptas, with bath 3,750 ptas. Opposite the end of the station. Attractive reception area with many photographs, etc. Many rooms named after South and Latin American countries.

* **Pensión Los Gitanillos** Estación de RENFE (Andenes), Málaga; tel: 233 28 89. Single 2,000 ptas; double 3,800 ptas. Located above the station restaurant. It also has a ladies' hairdressers (*peluquería*). Very neat and clean; small TV room.

In the town

* **HR Andalucía** Alarcón Lújan, 12; tel: 221 19 60. Single 2,000 ptas; double 3,000 ptas. Located in a passageway just off Larios — to the left near the Alameda Principal. On fourth floor with a lift; old-fashioned but pleasant.

* **HR El Ruedo** Trinidad Grund, 3; tel: 221 58 20. Single 1,500 ptas; double 3,000 ptas. Located close to the port entrance. Eighteen rather basic rooms.

* **Hostal Europa** Martinez, 3; tel: 221 74 62. Single 1.300 ptas; double 2,600 ptas. Centrally located and old-fashioned. On the second floor. All rooms with shower.
* **Hostal La Palma** Martinez, 3; tel: 222 67 72. Single 1,800 ptas; double 3,000 ptas. On first floor, pleasant and clean. Also centrally located.
* **Pensión Juanita** Alarcón Lújan, 8; tel: 221 35 86. Doubles only 2,000 ptas. In the same passage as the HR Andalucía. On fourth floor with a lift; plain and clean.
* **Pensión la Mundial** Hoyo de Esparteros, 1; tel: 221 06 18. Single 1,200 ptas; double 2,000 ptas. In an open plaza close to the *mercado*. Plain, old-fashioned and cheap.
* **Pensión Rosa** Martinez, 10; tel: 221 27 16. Single 2,000 ptas; double 3,500 ptas. Very central — just off Larios. Old-fashioned and simple.
CH Córdoba Bolsa, 9; tel: 221 44 69. Single 1,000 ptas; double 2,000 ptas. Plain and basic — second floor but no lift. No baths or showers in rooms. Located between Larios and the cathedral.
CH Pepe Mar Pasaje de Chinitas. No phone. Single 1,000 ptas; double 2,000 ptas. Located off the Plaze de la Constitución just past the tourist office; very small.

Ferry services
Trasmediterranea, Estación Maritima; tel: 222 43 91. These offices are located in the port and the entrance is close to the Plaza de la Marina, an important junction which is also very close to the centre of town.

The only ferry service is to Melilla, one of the two Spanish enclaves (the other is Ceuta) on the coast of North Africa. In summer 1993 there were departures Monday, Wednesday, Friday and Sunday. The one-way fare was adult 5,000 ptas, children 2,500 ptas; Visa, Mastercard and Eurocard are accepted.

Layout

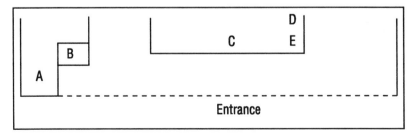

Key

A: Bar/cafeteria, open 0730-2300
B: *Consigna*, open (summer)
Sunday and Wednesday 0800-1700;
Monday, Tuesday, Thursday and
Saturday 0800-1300 1700-2300;

Friday 0800-1300 1700-1900. Cost:
150 ptas a piece
C: Ticket office
D/E: *Servicios*

General information
Car hire
Avis, Cortina del Muelle, 13; tel: 222 49 49.

Fiestas
Easter week (*Semana Santa*) variable dates, *Feria de Agosto* (August Fair) begins second weekend in August and lasts about 10 days.

RENFE city office
RENFE, Strachan, 2/4; tel: 221 25 00. Open Monday to Friday 0900-1330, 1630-1930. Closed Saturday, Sunday and holidays.

Telephone code
for Málaga province is (95).

Tourist office
Junta de Andalucía, Oficina de Turismo, Pasaje de Chinitas, 4; tel: 222 89 48 and 221 34 45. Open Monday to Friday 0900-1400, Saturday 0900-1300. Closed Sunday and holidays. Located in a small passageway just off the Plaza de la Constitución — on the Calle Larios side.

MÉRIDA

The city

Located 408kms (255 miles) from Madrid (by train) at an altitude of 221m (725ft) and with a population of about 60,000, Mérida, in the province of Badajoz, is the capital of the autonomous region of Extremadura.

Roman Spain was divided into three provinces, Lusitania, Tarraconensis and Baetica, and at the end of the Cantabrian Wars Caesar Augustus decided to settle veteran legionnaires in the former. A strategic site was chosen and in 25 BC Augusta Emerita was founded for the veterans of the 5th and 10th Legions. Before very long it became the capital of the province, the most important city in the Iberian Peninsula and one of the most important in the Roman world.

Christianity was very important here; it is possible that St James the Apostle preached in the province. In 304 AD Saint Eulalia and others were martyred, Mérida was appointed as one of three ecclesiastical centres in Hispania by the Edict of Milan and in 1119 a papal bull removed the See to Santiago de Compostela.

After the period of Roman rule Mérida retained some of its importance under the Visigoths but declined greatly when Moorish domination began in 713. After the Caliphate of Córdoba broke up early in the 11th century, Mérida even lost its position of provincial capital to Badajoz. Alfonso IX reconquered the city in 1230 but this did not stop the decline and, during the middle ages, many traces of previous greatness were lost when the city was practically demolished.

The city became important again in the 19th century when the advent of the railway made it a communications centre, and its fame today centres upon the marvellous Roman monuments that have been meticulously excavated, renovated and preserved. It has the distinction of being the only Spanish town to be named a *Conjunto Historico Arqueológico* (Historical Archaeological Complex).

Places of interest
Must see

Note: There is a combined entrance fee of 200 ptas for the Teatro y Anfiteatro Romano, the Alcazaba Arabe and the Casas Romanas del Mithreo y Anfiteatro.

Alcazaba Arabe, Casas Romanas del Mithreo y Anfiteatro (Arab Fortress and the Roman Houses of the Mithreo and Amphitheatre), tel: 31 73 09. Open summer (April 1 to September 30) 0900-1400, 1700-1900; winter (October 1 to March 31) 0900-1400, 1600-1800. Closed Sunday, holiday afternoons, December 25 and January 1.

Arab Fortress This is on the site of Roman fortifications built to defend the bridge and traces of the original walls can still be seen. Abdel-Rahman II constructed the fortress in 835 AD and little, besides the walls, still remains. However, the ramparts offer excellent views of the bridge and the Guadiana river. The two other points of interest are the *ajibe* (water cistern) in the walls by the river and the recently restored cloister of the 16th century monastery that was built by the Knights of Santiago. Imaginatively, the Regional Government of Extremadura uses part of the exterior as office accommodation.

Roman House of the Mithreo This house, found only in the 1960s, is located next to the Plaza de Toros, some distance from the other monuments. It is important because of the mosaics that have been found there, particularly the Cosmic Mosaic.

Roman Houses of the Amphitheatre Located just across the road from the Roman Theatre and Amphitheatre these are still in the process of excavation. It is thought that there were two houses here dating from sometime during the 3rd and 4th centuries AD. Besides the layout of the houses, which are extensive, and some mosaics, there is not a lot to see.

Museo Nacional de Arte Romano (National Museum of Roman Art), José Ramón Mélida; tel: 31 16 90. Open summer (June 1 to September 30) 1000-1400, 1700-1900; winter (October 1 to May 31) 1000-1400, 1600-1800. Closed Sunday afternoons, Monday, May 1, December 24/25/31. Entrance: 200 ptas; EC students (under 21) free. Visits to the crypt, for no more than 40 people, take place at 1030, 1200, 1230, 1300, 1730 and 1800. This museum, one of the most important of its kind in the world, was inaugurated by the King and Queen of Spain and the President of Italy on September 9 1986. In 1989 it received a special commendation as European Museum of the Year. The building has been brilliantly designed, both in style and practicality, so that its illustrious exhibits — many from the Roman Theatre and Amphitheatre, to which it is connected via the crypt — can be viewed to their best advantage.

Teatro y Anfiteatro Romanos (Roman Theatre and Amphitheatre), tel: 31 25 30. Open daily summer (June 1 to September 30) 0800-2200; winter (October 1 to May 31) 0800-1800. Closed December 25 and January 1.

Roman Theatre This, the most impressive monument in Mérida, was originally built in 16-15 BC by Agrippa, the son-in-law of Augustus, but was reconstructed several times up to the 4th century when the elegant façade, with colonnades and statues, was added. It seated 6,000 in the semicircular shaped auditorium. Excavation began early this century but it was not until the 1960s that the important work of renovation began. It is used every July during the International Festival of Classic Drama.

Amphitheatre Completed in 8 BC this is elliptical in shape and had a capacity for up to 14,000 spectators. Although, naturally, in some state of disrepair there is more than enough remaining for one to imagine gladiatorial shows taking place here. The gates, entrances and passageways are particularly interesting.

Temple of Diana Located in a side street, not far from the Plaza España, this imposing structure is entirely at odds with its environment. Reputedly built between the 1st and 2nd centuries, the temple is very large and, because much of it was used by a nobleman as part of his private house, it is fairly well preserved.

By choice
Acueducto de los Milagros (The Miraculous Aqueduct) This incomplete, but still very impressive, aqueduct carried water to Mérida from the Proserpina reservoir 5km away. It was probably built just after the founding of the city and is 830m long and 25m high. Unless one wants to study it in detail there is an excellent view from the train.

Arco de Trajano (Trajan's Arch) Located just off the Plaza de España this decorative arch, 15m high and 13m wide, is larger than its immediate environment. Previously called the Santiago Arch this was a monumental gate on the most important street and used to be the symbol of the city.

Puente Romano (Roman Bridge) This is 792m (866 yards) long, has 60 granite arches, and is now used only by pedestrians.

Roman Circus Also known as the Hippodrome, this is where the chariot races were held. It is very large (440m x 155m), and could hold 30,000 people. There is not that much to see and, if one did not know better, at first glance it seems little more than waste ground. It is located about ten minutes' walk from the Roman Theatre/ Amphitheatre in a very bland area.

Museums
Museo de Arte Visigodo (Museum of Visigothic Art), Santa Julia, 1; tel: 30 01 06. Open summer 1000-1400, 1700-1900, winter 1000-1400, 1600-1800. Entrance: free. An important collection of Visigoth art.

Station/location/transport to city centre
RENFE, Cordero; tel: 31 20 05. A modern station, fairly close to the town centre, that is effectively a terminal.

Layout

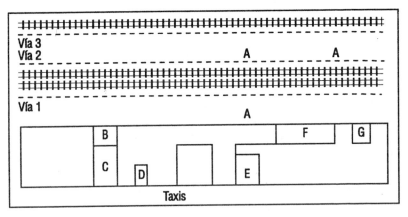

Key
A: *Paseo Inferior*
B: *Información*
C: Ticket office, open 0800-2100

D: *Consigna Automática*, 300 ptas per 24 hours, the tokens are sold at the ticket office

E: *Kiosco* for newspapers, magazines, etc, open 0700-1200, 1500-2100

F: Bar/cafeteria, open 0630-2300
G: *Comisaría*

Train station to city centre
On foot Not too far, but a little complicated. Follow the street up the hill to the left of the station forecourt. Cross the main road and continue up the hill to the top and then follow the road down to the Plaza España. About 10-15 minutes.

By taxi A lot easier and only about 5 minutes and 300 ptas away.

Train services
To Madrid by

	Regional	Estrella	Talgo
Cáceres	1	1	
Ciudad Real	4¼	4¼	
Madrid	7½ 5½	8¾	4¾

To Barcelona by

	Diurno	Estrella
Ciudad Real	3¾	4½
Albacete	6¼	7½
Valencia	8½	10
Barcelona	13	15

To Sevilla by
Regional: via Zafra 1¼; Sevilla 3¾.

Accommodation
There are not that many places to stay here and, to complicate matters, they are not easy to find either. As most people will only stay one night I highly recommend the *** Hotel Emperatriz. It is not often that one can afford to stay in a palace and, if you want to treat yourself, this is the place to do it.

Close to the station
* **HR Salud** Vespaciano, 41; tel: 31 22 59. Single 1,900 ptas; double 3,500 ptas. Quite close to the station and the aqueduct. No baths in rooms; clean, in a side street.

In the city
*** **Hotel Emperatriz** Plaza de España, 19; tel: 31 31 11. Single 4,500

ptas; double 6,500 ptas. A genuine 16th century palace that has seen kings, emperors and many other noblemen as visitors. In a delightful location — the terrace is a charming place to have a drink and watch the local people in the attractive plaza — and with an excellent restaurant. Superb value; TVs in rooms.

** **Hotel Lusitania** Oviedo, 12; tel: 31 61 12. Single 4,000 ptas; double 6,000 ptas. Rooms with baths; modern and clean. Close to Alcazaba.

* **Pensión el Arco** Santa Beatriz de Silva, 4; tel: 31 01 07. Single 1,350 ptas; double 2,300 ptas. In a quiet plaza and with interesting decor. Small rooms, no baths or even washbasins.

General information
Car hire
Avis, Estación RENFE, Bajo; tel: 30 16 13.

Police
Comisaría, Almendralejo, 48; tel: 091.

Telephone code
for Badajoz province is (924).

Tourist office
Oficina de Información Turística, Pedro María Plano; tel: 31 53 53. Open summer Monday to Friday 0900-1400, 1700-1900, Saturday and Sunday 0900-1400; winter Monday to Friday 0900-1400, 1600-1800, Saturday and Sunday 0900-1400. This is located just outside the National Museum of Roman Art and the Roman Theatre and Amphitheatre.

SALAMANCA
The city
Located 233km (145 miles) west of Madrid at an altitude of 800m
(2,624ft), Salamanca has a population of 170,000. In the 3rd century
BC it was conquered by Hannibal and became his most westerly
outpost. Known as Helmántica by the Romans, it was of strategic
importance because of its position at the centre of the *Ruta de la
Plata* (Route of Silver) that connected the northern ports and mines
with the south of the peninsula. The bridge over the River Tormes
is a reminder of this era.

Following rule by the Visigoths and Moors, the city was
repopulated in 1102 after Alfonso VI had reconquered Toledo. In
1218 a university was founded by Alfonso IX and this, the first in
Spain, achieved an international reputation. Since then the fortunes
of the city and the university have been closely matched.

The golden age, for both, was between the late 15th and early
18th centuries. In this period Salamanca was the main cultural centre
in the Spanish Empire and one of the most important in Europe. At
one time when the city only had a population of 20,000 there were
nearly 7,000 students enrolled at the university. As the city was
strategically situated between France and Portugal it suffered badly
during the War of Independence and it was entered by Wellington
just before he fought the important Battle of Salamanca, just south
of the city, in the summer of 1812. As a consequence the city and
university suffered a decline that has only been reversed this
century; there are now over 25,000 students at the two universities.

In recognition of its cultural importance, UNESCO has declared
Salamanca to be Patrimony of Humanity.

Besides all of the places listed below, many others are not open to
the public and this also applies to the churches, most of which are
only open during services. The church of San Marcos, about five
minutes walk in the opposite direction to the cathedrals, away from
the Plaza Mayor along Calle de Zamora, is my particular favourite.
This small church dates from the 12th century, is circular in shape
with a small tower, and its lack of pretentiousness makes it all the
more charming. There is also another Romanesque church, the
Iglesia de Santo Tomás de Canterbury, which is reputed to be the
first in the world to be dedicated to that Saint.

Salamanca is an absolutely delightful city and every effort should
be made to see it.

Places of interest
Must see

Catedral Nueva, Catedral Vieja, Patio Chico, Museo y Claustro — Capillas (New Cathedral, Old Cathedral, Patio Chico, Museum and Cloisters and Chapels), Plaza de Anaya; tel: 21 74 76. Open summer (May to September) daily 1000-1400, 1600-2000; winter (October to April) daily 0930-1330, 1530-1800 — last admission 30 minutes before closing time. Entrance: 200 ptas, free on Tuesday. The entrance fee does not apply to the New Cathedral. Built because the old one had become too small, the New Cathedral was started in 1513 and has Renaissance and Baroque additions. It is large, imposing, and considered to be one of the last Gothic structures in Spain. The entrance to the Old Cathedral and museum is in the New Cathedral and one passes through into a different era. Construction was begun in 1114, although not completed until a century later, and it is considered to be one of the most important Romanesque buildings in Spain. Of particular interest is the marvellous altar. Dating from the middle of the 15th century it consists of two contrasting parts which were created by two Italian brothers. There are many other fine examples of artwork, sepulchres, etc, in the various chapels around the cloisters which, together, make up the museum. The Patio Chico is a small tranquil square where the Old and New cathedrals meet and the contrast of styles is fascinating.

Convento de San Esteban (Convent of St Stephen), Plaza de Santo Domingo; tel: 21 50 50. Open summer (May to September) daily 0900-1330, 1600-2000; winter (October to April) daily 0900-1300, 1600-1830. Entrance: 100 ptas. Work on this Dominican church was begun in 1524. It is very ornate indeed and the main, plateresque-style façade — the last part of the church to be completed, in 1610 — should not be missed. The King's Cloister, completed in 1544, is also a delight and the central area has many plants and trees. The Pantheon of the Theologians is the final resting place for many of the university's most famous theologians, and there is also a sacristy and chapter room which are quite similar, as well as a staircase of some merit. Christopher Columbus stayed here when presenting his plans to the Dominicans who assisted in influencing the Catholic Monarchs.

Museo de Bellas Artes, Arqueológico y Etnológico (Fine Arts, Archaeological and Ethnological Museum), Patio Escuelas

Menores; tel: 21 22 35. Open Monday to Friday 0830-1430. Closed Saturday, Sunday and holidays. Entrance: 200 ptas; EC citizens (under 21) and foreigners resident in Spain free. This museum is located in the 15th century mansion of Dr Alvárez Albarca who was a physician to Queen Isabella. There is a small garden with stone pigs and an old cart before one enters a most beautiful and unusual patio. There are exhibits around the sides and in the rooms around the patio and *Sala 1* has a most ornate ceiling. There are fewer paintings on the upper level and they are much more modern in style.

Plaza Mayor This is considered the most beautiful plaza of its kind in Spain. Construction was begun in 1729 during the reign of Felipe V and it was completed in 1755. It has three storeys with a porticoed lower level and the Town Hall and Royal Pavilion are particularly elegant. Like others of its kind this has been used over the centuries for a variety of activities and, today, is very much the social centre of the city. In 1992, this was actually used for a bullfight, one of the traditional activities once held regularly.

Universidad y Museo de Escuelas Menores (University and Young Scholars Museum), Libreros; tel: 29 44 00 ext. 1150. Open Monday to Friday 0930-1330, 1630-1830; Saturday 0930-1330, 1630-1800; Sunday and holidays 1000-1300. Entrance: 125 ptas.

University This was founded in 1218 by Alfonso IX and is the oldest in Spain. The building, though, dates from the middle of the 15th century and the main façade is elaborate and beautiful, with three parts based upon the Pope at the time, the Catholic Monarchs and Carlos V. Inside, the rooms around the patio are quite different as they are used for a variety of functions, some of the ceilings are magnificent and there is a fossil/mineral display. Upstairs there is a library with around 40,000 books dating from before the 19th century.

Museo de Escuelas Menores (Museum of Minor Schools) This is a separate entity that is found in the elegant Patio de Escuelas Menores about 100m away. It is very small with robes, chests, chairs and busts, etc, but its main feature is the unusual ceiling — half wooden and half domed and painted.

By choice

Casa de las Conchas (House of the Shells), Rúa Mayor. This house, dating from the late 15th century, belonged to Dr Talavera Maldonado, a Knight of Santiago. The shells on the exterior were copied from Santiago and it also has noteworthy window grilles. It is directly across from the Clerecía. There is also a fine patio, but at the end of 1992 the house was closed for restoration and it was not possible to view it.

Clerecía Compañia, 5; tel: 21 59 66. Open Monday to Friday 0800-1300, 1600-2000. Closed Saturday, Sunday and holidays. Entrance: free. This is considered to be the grandest building in the city. Work was begun in 1617 and completed in 1755. It has a huge façade, a grand church and a very large baroque cloister. Today it is the headquarters of the Pontifical University.

Convento de las Dueñas (Las Dueñas Convent) Plaza Concilio de Trento; tel: 21 54 42. Open summer (April to September) daily 1030-1300, 1615-1900; winter (October to March) daily 1000-1300, 1600-1730. Entrance: 80 ptas. This convent was founded in 1419 by Doña Juana Rodríguez Maldonado whose husband was an accountant to Juan II of Castile. Although not large, it is particularly charming. There is a small garden before one enters the beautiful and irregular shaped patio of which one side is built into a wall. The upper level is covered and very ornate.

The nuns have a small shop in the garden that sells homemade sweets and cakes; open 1000-1300, 1600-1700.

Convento de Santa Clara (Santa Clara Convent) Santa Clara; tel: 26 96 23. Open Monday to Friday 0930-1400, 1600-1900; Saturday and Sunday 0930-1400. Closed holidays. Entrance: 100 ptas. There is a most unusual combination of things to see here. It was originally founded in the 13th century but the building has been changed since then. The paintings in the lower choir (*coro*) date from the 14th to 16th centuries and are important. The cloisters are rather different, with semicircular arches, and the wooden painted ceilings are worth attention. From the upper *coro* one can look down into the ornate 18th century church and also, strangely, walk over the preserved wooden beams of the church. A viewing platform gives an excellent view of the cathedral, but unfortunately it is not very good for photography as it is glassed in with protective bars on the outside.

Note: Just outside in the Plaza de San Roman, the Colegio Mixto has a most interesting façade.

Convento y Museo de las Ursulas (Ursuline Convent and Museum) Ursulas; tel: 21 98 77. Open daily 1000-1300, 1630-1900. Entrance: 70 ptas. This Gothic church, located close to the Plaza Mayor, was commissioned by Archbishop Fonseca, whose remains are located here in an ornate sepulchre. The museum itself is very small, but note the ornate ceiling. There is also one of those strange revolving wooden doors that allow the nuns to take the entrance fee without being seen.

Palacio de Anaya (Anaya Palace), Plaza de Anaya — directly across from the new cathedral. The original building on this site was the Colegio Mayor, a university residence hall established in 1411. In 1762 the present neoclassical edifice replaced it and the façade and large, rather severe, patio are worth a visit. Next to it is the *hospedería* (hospice) with a patio that is of entirely different proportions. Note the brand type marks around the walls; these also appear elsewhere in the city. This is a right each student wins when they graduate.

Torre de Clavero (Clavero Tower), Plaza de Colón. This is a very unusual 15th century fort. It is octagonally shaped and each side has a tall, narrow, protruding battlement at the top.

Sightseeing train Trips between 1030-1430, 1600-2000 in the summer months. Fare: adults 350 ptas, children 250 ptas. Trips start in the Plaza Anaya, just in front of the new cathedral, and take 30 minutes.

Museums

Casa-Museo de Unamuno (House and Museum of Miguel de Unamuno), Libreros. To the side of the main entrance to the university; tel: 29 44 00 ext 1196. Open Tuesday to Friday 1130-1330, 1630-1830; Saturday and Sunday 1000-1400. Closed Monday and holidays. Research: Monday to Friday (except holidays) 0830-1430. Entrance: free. Miguel de Unamuno lived in this 18th century house when he was rector of the university and this museum, besides exhibiting his personal belongings, is also a research centre dedicated to his life and works.

Museo de Historia de la Ciudad (City History Museum), Plaza de Juan XXIII — across from the tower of the new Cathedral; tel: 21 30 67. Open July, August and September Tuesday to Saturday 0900-1300, 1730-1930. Closed Monday, Sunday and holidays. Entrance: free. Just a few rooms here and, really, the exhibits are not that interesting.

Station/location/transport to city centre
RENFE, Paseo de la Estación; tel: 23 22 73. This is a modern station, at an elevation of 808m, and is located about 1km from the city centre.

Layout

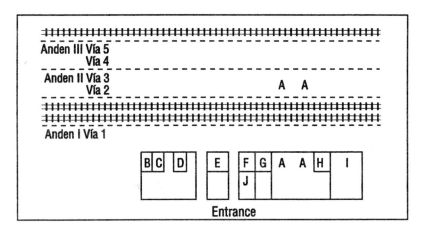

Key
A: Underpass to other platforms
B: *Servicios* — women
C: *Servicios* — men
D: *Circulación*
E: *Jefe de Estación*
F: *Consigna Automática*, 200 ptas per 24 hours, two sizes
G: *Información*
H: *Combination Librería/Estanco*
I: Bar/cafeteria, open daily 0600-0200
J: Ticket office

From station to city centre
By bus No 1, Estación/Buenos Aires. The fare is 55 ptas and the journey should take less than 10 minutes, but longer in the rush hour.

On foot Turn left out of the station forecourt and the Plaza Mayor is more or less straight ahead about 15-20 minutes away.

By taxi Depending upon traffic conditions between 5-10 minutes and 300/400 ptas.

Train services
To Madrid by
Regional: via Ávila 1½; Madrid 3¼.

To Barcelona by
Estrella: via Burgos 2¼; Zaragoza 7½; Barcelona 9½.

To Irún/France by
Diurno: via Valladolid 1¾; Burgos 3¼; Irún 7.

Accommodation
Close to the station
These hotels are located directly opposite the railway station and there are many shops, banks, bars, restaurants, drugstores and a post office and *telefónica* close by.

** **HR Los Infantes** Paseo de la Estación, 125; tel: 25 28 44. Single: 2,000 ptas; double 4,000 ptas. Small clean rooms with bath/shower. Right across from station.

* **Pensión Virginia** Paseo de la Estación, 109-115; tel: 24 10 16. Single: 2,200 ptas; double 3,500 (smaller) or 4,000 ptas (larger). Located on the first floor using the right side staircase. Two singles and two doubles. Completely remodelled in 1986 and furnished in Castilian style. Price includes one shower a day and arrangements can be made for clothes to be washed.

* **Pensión Isabel** Plaza de Barcelona, 24-25; tel: 24 92 54. Doubles: 3,400 ptas, triples 5,100 ptas (smaller) or 6,000 ptas (larger). The Plaza de Barcelona is located to the side of the Pensión Virginia. A new *pensión* located on 5/6th floor. Three doubles and two triples, none with private bath. TV room. Extra beds can be supplied in the rooms for an additional cost.

Close to the Plaza Mayor
** **HA Zoboso** Clavel, 7; tel: 27 14 62. Single: 4,200 ptas; double 7,975 ptas; Treble 7,500 ptas. Lovely reception area. Rooms with bath/shower and TV. Larger sizes have kitchenettes. Side street 50m from Plaza Mayor.

** **HR Amefa** Pozo Amarillo, 18-20; tel: 21 81 89. Single: 5,500 ptas;

double 7,975 ptas. Rooms with bath/shower and TV. Largish with modern style; two hundred metres from Plaza Mayor.
** **HR Orly** Pozo Amarillo, 7; tel: 21 61 25. Single 3,000 ptas; double 4,500 ptas. Second floor with lift, TV lounge, clean and modern. Twenty metres from Plaza Mayor.
** **Pensión Dahos** Plaza Mercado, 15; tel: 21 48 32. Single 1,400 ptas; double 1,800 ptas. No bath/shower in rooms. First floor; old-fashioned. Other side of *mercado* from Plaza Mayor.
* **Pensión Robles** Plaza Mayor, 20; tel: 21 31 97. Single 1,500 ptas; double 2,500 ptas. No bath/showers in rooms. Second floor and small rooms.
CH San Antonio Plaza del Peso, 6; tel: 21 40 65. Single 1,000 ptas; double 1,500 ptas. Deceptively large but rather run down. No bath/shower in rooms.
Fonda Las Rías Pozo Amarillo, 17-19; tel: 21 33 39. Single 1,10 ptas; double 1,800 ptas. Second floor; small and plain.

General information
Car hire
Avis, Paseo Canalejas, 49; tel: 26 97 53.

Fiestas
Easter week (*Semana Santa*) variable dates; annual fair middle/end of September.

Hospital
National Health Hospital, Paseo de San Vicente; tel: 26 40 00.

Police
Comisaría, Ronda de Sancti Spiritus, 2; tel: 24 53 11. Emergency 911.

Radio taxi
Tel: 25 00 00.

RENFE city office
RENFE, Plaza Libertad, 11; tel: 21 24 54. Open: Monday to Friday 0900-1400, 1700-1900. Closed Saturday, Sunday and holidays.

Telefónica
Junction of Pena I/Iscar Peyra, close to Plaza de los Bandos. Open: Monday to Saturday 0900-1500, 1600-2300.

Telephone code
for Salamanca province is (923).

Tourist offices
Oficina de Turismo de Castile — León, España, 39; tel: 26 85 71.
Open Monday to Friday 0930-1400, 1600-1900; Saturday 1130-
1400. Closed Sunday and holidays. This is located about 300m from
the other tourist office in the Plaza Mayor.
Oficina Municipal de Turismo, Plaza Mayor. Open Monday to
Friday 1000-1330, 1600-1800; Saturday 1000-1400. Closed Sunday
and holidays. A small office located right on this beautiful plaza.

SAN SEBASTIÁN/DONOSTIA
The city

San Sebastián, or Donostia — its Basque (Euskara language) name — is a city with about 200,000 inhabitants which has been the capital of the province of Guipúzcoa since 1854. It is located just 20km from the French border at Irún/Hendaye, on the Cantabrian coast between the mountains and the sea, and this combination gives the city the spectacular bay for which it is world famous. La Concha, the shell, well deserves its name. It is surrounded by beautiful green mountains — the result of the temperate climate — two of which, Monte Igeldo to the west and Monte Urgull to the east, guard either side of the entrance, while the Isla de Santa Clara protects the centre. Its spectacular natural setting is enhanced by the solid, Victorian style buildings and the promenade all around the bay that, themselves, contrast delightfully with the old harbour and town at the foot of Monte Urgull. The latter and the monument of the Sacred Heart are attractively illuminated at night.

Although San Sebastián has an interesting history very little remains to be seen today; in fact it has a very modern façade which is due to devastation incurred during the Wars of Independence. The city was completely destroyed by a great fire on August 31 1813 as a result of a blockade by Spanish, Portuguese and British forces relieving the city from five years of French occupation.

Culturally, besides being Basque, the city is very different to most others in Spain and this, again, is due to a war. But this time the results were far more beneficial to the city. During the first World War Spain was neutral and, due to its proximity to France, the city attracted many very wealthy people who wanted to escape the hostilities. As a consequence there developed a social life, and style, that gave — and still gives — the city a unique character.

As with all of this northern coastline, San Sebastián is a very popular resort for the Spanish, particularly during July and August, and as a consequence it is difficult to find a room then. This is compounded during the week of August 15, when the local *feria* is held. There are not that many places to stay anyway, especially at the lower end of the market, so the law of supply and demand makes accommodation slightly more expensive here than in many other places in Spain.

Likewise, the beaches around La Concha are very crowded so, if you fancy a swim, walk over the river to the much less popular

Playa de Gros. This is more open to the sea and, as a consequence, the waves are much stronger.

Places of interest
Must see
La Concha, the harbour and the 'old town' It is immediately obvious why this beautiful natural bay is called La Concha (The Shell). The hills guarding the entrance — Monte Igeldo to the west, Monte Urgull to the east — and Isla de Santa Clara in the centre make it one of the most picturesque bays in Spain, some say the world. To walk around the promenade is a delight, especially at night when most of the buildings are illuminated. There is a totally different atmosphere here from other Spanish resorts — especially those on the Mediterranean coast. The small harbour is on the eastern side of the bay directly under Monte Urgull and next to the old town. Boat trips can be taken from there — they are detailed below — and it is lined by small outdoor seafood restaurants, each with mouthwatering menus. Beware, they are not cheap; expect to pay at least 1,500 ptas a person for a set meal and much more à la carte.

The 'old town', an area of narrow lanes and passageways, is famous for its men-only gastronomic clubs ('popular societies'), restaurants and bars and is best visited at night. If you do not want a full meal just wander into any bar and there will be an array of snacks from one end of the bar to the other. Each place tries to outdo the other with its selection and variety; there are even competitions between the bars. The snacks are called, amongst other things, *pinchos* or *banderillos* and usually cost between 100 and 150 ptas each, they are not to be confused with *bocadillos* (sandwiches) which are also on display. Even the beer glasses are different; in most of Spain they are narrow and tall, here they are very wide and shallow. As this area is a popular meeting place for the young people of the city expect it to be on the noisy side, especially at weekends.

By choice
Aquarium At the end of the harbour. Open Tuesday to Sunday 1000-1330, 1530-2000 (1930 outside of summer months). Closed Monday and from September 15 to May 15. Entrance: adults 250 ptas, children (1-9) 100 ptas. Opened in 1928 this is the headquarters of the Guipúzcoa Oceanographic Society. There are

exhibits of relevance to the local seafaring traditions, a selection of live fish of the kind that are found in local waters and the skeleton of a whale captured in 1878, a reminder of the days when the city was a pioneer in the whaling industry that took sailors as far away as Newfoundland.

Boat trip to Isla de Santa Clara Price: adults 205 ptas, children 55 ptas, old-age pensioners 110 ptas. The boats leave from the southeast corner of the innermost harbour and the last departure is 2030 in summer.

Castillo de la Mota The castle and citadel are located at the summit of Monte Urgull surrounded by an attractive park. The figure of the Sacred Heart was erected in 1950 and measures 28.8m. There are wonderful views of the city and surrounding areas but there is one major drawback — the only way up is on foot.

Sea trips Price: adults 350 ptas, children (3-8) 150 ptas. Trips last 30 minutes and depart from the inner harbour, north side.

Sightseeing trip Departure point — Town Hall; tel: 48 11 80. Hours 1100-1400, 1600-2100. Price: adults 300 ptas, children (under 10) 200 ptas; groups of over ten people 200 ptas each. This unusual 'train', Txu-Txu, takes you on a 30-minute tour of the city; there is a multilingual commentary.

Museums
Museo de San Telmo (St Telmo Museum), Plaza I. Zuloaga. Open Tuesday to Saturday 0930-1300, 1530-1930; Sunday and holidays 1015-1400. Closed Monday. Built during 1530-59 as a Dominican convent it was converted into an army barracks in 1836 and finally bought by the San Sebastián authorities to be restored and converted into a museum in 1932. The Renaissance-style cloister is particularly attractive and there are 16 murals, covering 590m², which depict typical Basque stories and legends. There are also natural science exhibits as well as an art gallery.

Station/location/left luggage office/transport to city centre
RENFE, Estación del Norte, Avenida de Francia; tel: 28 30 89. The station is on the east bank of the River Urumea close to the María

Cristina bridge. It is fairly close to the centre of town but just far enough way to make it difficult to carry heavy luggage. Unfortunately there is no left luggage office at the station: this is about a ten minute walk away on the Calle de Easo. The signs at the station are a little confusing because they are in both Spanish and Basque, the latter being particularly difficult to understand.

The **Key** shows the Spanish first and then the Basque.

Layout

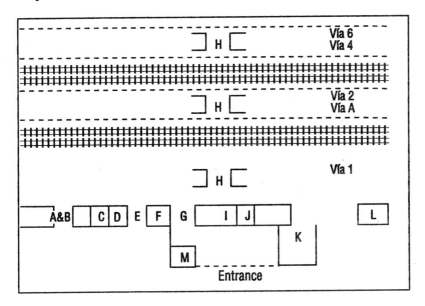

Key

A: *Restaurante, Jatetxea*, open 1300-1530, 2000-2230.

B: *Cafeteria, Kafetegia*, open 0700-0200

C: *Sala Espera, Itxatongela*

D: *Circulación, Zirkulazioa*

E: *Jefe Estación, Trengeltoki Burua*

F: *Salida, Irteera*

G: *Kiosco* for newspapers, magazines, etc, open 0730-2230.

H: Subway to other platforms, *Paso Inferior, Pasqunea Azpitik*

I: *Tábacos* for tobacco, stamps, etc, open 0800-1345, 1500-1945

J: *Bombonería*, shop for chocolates, etc, open 0800-1400, 1500-2030

K: Ticket office

L: *Servicios, Komunak*

M: Train *Información* office, open 0700-2300

Left luggage office (*Consigna*)

Plaza Easo. Open daily 0830-2100. Price: 1 day 150 ptas; 1 night

250 ptas; 2 nights 375 ptas. Surfboards and bicycles 250 ptas. This is nowhere near the station; about ten minutes' walk or about 250 ptas by taxi. Its 'remoteness' is presumably because of terrorist campaigns by ETA, the Basque nationalist movement.

Train station to city centre
By taxi Apart from walking this is by far the most convenient method. It takes just a few minutes and costs about 250 ptas.

Train services
To Madrid by
	InterCity	Talgo	Estrella
Burgos	3	3	4
Valladolid	4		5½
Ávila	5		7
Madrid	6½	6¼	9

To Barcelona by
	Diurno	Estrella
Pamplona	1¾	2¼
Zaragoza	4	5¼
Lerida	6	7½
Barcelona	8¼	10¼

To Valencia by
Estrella: via Burgos 4½; Madrid 8; Albacete 11½; Valencia 15.

Accommodation
Close to the station
** Hotel Terminus Avenida de Francia; tel: 29 19 00. Single 3,500 ptas; double 6,000 ptas. Actually part of the station complex — the cafeteria and restaurant open on to platform 1. Bound to be noisy and also somewhat expensive.

In the new town (west bank of the River Urumea)
**** Hotel Aranzazu Donostia Vitoria-Gasteiz, 1; tel: 21 90 77; fax: 21 86 95. Part of the Aranzazu chain, this is a new, well-appointed hotel, just 250m from the bay. Single 11,000 ptas; double 17,000; double for single use, 13,600 ptas. Each room has air-conditioning, soundproofing, private bath, telephone, fax connection, satellite TV with 22 channels, safe box and minibar. There is also a restaurant, cafeteria, money change, hairdresser and dry cleaner and fax/photocopy service.

**** Hotel San Sebastián Avenida Zumalacárregui, 20; tel: 21 44 00; fax: 21 72 99. This beautiful Aranzazu chain hotel is located just a short walk from La Concha bay. Single 10,000 ptas; double 15,500 ptas; double for single use, 12,400 ptas. The rooms all have private bath, telephone, music, TV with Canal + and a safe box. There are also extensive facilities including a swimming pool, cafeteria, restaurant, bars, money change and medical assistance.

*** Hotel Europa San Martín, 52; tel: 47 08 80; fax: 47 17 30. This Best Western hotel has two seasons: low, January 1 to April 10, April 19 to June 30, October 1 to December 31; high, April 11 to April 18 (Easter week, variable dates), July 1 to September 30. Single low, 10,865 ptas, high 14,500 ptas; double low, 16,430 ptas, high 20,405 ptas. These rates include breakfast. Located in the town centre, close to La Concha, this has 60 rooms all with bath/shower, hairdryer, direct dial telephone, satellite colour TV, video, in-house movies, radio and piped music, safe, minibar and balcony. There is also a solarium, coffee shop, bar and restaurant.

** HR Bahía San Martín, 54; tel: 46 92 11; fax: 46 39 14. double 7,300 ptas; no singles. Close to La Concha but expensive.

** Hostal Comercio Urdaneta, 24; tel: 46 44 14. Single 3,300 ptas; double 3,900 ptas. Old-fashioned style. Close to the cathedral and the left luggage office.

In the 'old town'

** HR La Estrella Plaza Sarriegui, 1; tel: 42 09 97. Single 2,300 ptas; double 4,400 ptas, with shower 5,200 ptas; treble 5,900 ptas, with shower 7,000 ptas; quadruple 8,100 ptas with shower. More distinguished than most places and in a quieter part of the *barrio*; 30 large rooms and a TV lounge.

** Hostal Eder Alameda de Boulevard, 16; tel: 42 64 49. High season: single 3,500 ptas; double 4,500 ptas; low season: single 3,000 ptas; double 3,800 ptas. On second floor pleasant and stylish; 16 rooms.

* Pensión Amaiur 31 de Agosto, 44; tel: 42 96 54. High season: Single 2,500 ptas; double 4,500 ptas; low season: single 1,500 ptas; double 2,500 ptas. Next door to the Iglesia de Santa María. On second floor; clean and comfortable.

* Pensión Lizaso San Vicente, 7; tel: 42 29 77. High season: double 4,000 ptas; low season: double 2,500 ptas. Doubles only. Small and basic; on third floor.

* Pensión San Lorenzo San Lorenzo, 2; tel: 42 55 16. High season: double 4,000 ptas; treble 6,000 ptas. Low season: double 2,000 ptas; treble 3,000 ptas. Only four small rooms, each with three beds; very basic.

General information
Car hire
Avis, Triunfo, 2; tel: 46 15 56.

Fiestas
Semana Grande: this coincides with the week of August 15.

Telephone code
for Guipúzcoa province is (943).

Tourist office
Centro de Atracción y Turismo, Calle Reina Regente; tel: 48 11 66.

SANTIAGO DE COMPOSTELA
The city
Located in the far northwest corner of Spain at an altitude of 260m
Santiago de Compostela is 678km (424 miles) from Madrid and has
a population of nearly 110,000. Its claim to fame is twofold. The
tomb of the Apostle Saint James (Santiago in Spanish, and the
Patron Saint of Spain) was discovered here and, ever since, the city
has been an attraction for millions of pilgrims who have followed *El
Camino de Santiago* (the pilgrim's way to Santiago). This, in turn,
has led to the construction of so many elegant and beautiful
buildings that the city was declared a World Heritage Site by
UNESCO in 1985. It is also a Holy City as Pope Calixus II granted
the Church of Santiago the *Jubileo pleno del Año Santo* and this was
later made an everlasting honour. The Holy Year (*Año Santo*)
festival of Saint James the Apostle is held every year that July 25
falls on a Sunday, and on December 31 of the previous year the
Holy Door of the Cathedral is opened to start the celebrations.

In fact there are not that many places that are open to the public,
but do not let that put you off — the city is stunning. This
particularly applies to the Praza do Obradoiro, one of my favourite
plazas in Spain. My everlasting memory of it is when, one night at
sundown, a busker was playing a haunting tune on a pipe. With no
one else around this echoed around the plaza and the surrounding
narrow *rúas* creating a very unusual sound effect.

The only problem for most prospective visitors is the city's
isolated position; indeed at one time it was the western limit of the
known world. To save going to and from Madrid, thus duplicating
the route and wasting precious time, the following alternative might
be considered. Take in Burgos, Valladolid, León, Santiago,
Salamanca and Ávila in a loop. This can be done in either direction
and it minimises the time needed to visit these interesting cities.

Whichever way you do it Santiago de Compostela should not be
overlooked.

Places of interest
Santiago de Compostela is rather different from other cities as all of
the places of interest, with the exception of one museum, are located
in the area known as the *Zona Monumental*. The main places to visit
are listed below but there are many, many other things to see,
although most of these are convents and churches that are not open
to the public. The only way to explore this area is on foot and you

are sure to come across surprises around every corner. Even the small streets (*rúas*) are a delight; often the lower levels are colonnaded and they are frequently connected by small plazas (*prazas*). These *rúas* also have many bars and restaurants selling typical regional food.

Catedral y Museo (Cathedral and Museum), Praza do Obradoiro. Museum open Monday to Saturday 1000-1330, 1600-1830; Sunday 1000-1330. Closed Sunday afternoon. Entrance: 250 ptas. Alfonso II ordered the construction of a simple church on the site of Santiago's tomb and in 899 Alfonso III built a much larger Basilica in pre Romanesque style. The Muslims, under Almanzor, burnt the city to the ground in 997 and construction of the present day cathedral started in 1075 under the auspices of Bishop Diego Peláez. Although some of the altars were consecrated earlier in the century by Bishop Gelmirez, work was not completed until 1128. There have been additions in varying styles over the centuries and the most notable was the *Obradoiro* façade in the 18th century. This is truly spectacular, and when viewed in context with the other memorable buildings in the Praza do Obradoiro, especially at night, it is a sight one will always remember. There are also other notable façades that can be viewed from the squares surrounding the cathedral.

The inside of the cathedral is no less dramatic. It is very large and the craftsmanship is outstanding, especially the *Pórtico de la Gloria* which is considered the best example of Romanesque sculpture in the world. The *botafumeiro* (swinging incense burner) is also of interest. This is huge and hangs by rope from a mechanical device and it takes several men to swing it, pendulum like, during important ceremonies.

The museum is no less interesting; there are many rooms and varying exhibits including archaeological remains taken from the site and a very important collection of tapestries.

There is a strange custom when entering the cathedral from the Praza do Obradoiro; the right palm is put on one of the marble columns — there is now an ingrained palm print — and the forehead is brought down to touch another column three times.

Hostal de los Reyes Católicos   (Hostelry of the Catholic Monarchs), Praza do Obradoiro. This building, just to the right of the cathedral, was commissioned by the Catholic Monarchs to provide accommodation for pilgrims and the sick. Work was begun in the early 15th century and completed a decade later but other additions date from the 17th and 18th centuries. The façade is comparatively plain with the exception of the archway over the main door that has statues of the Monarchs, the Twelve Apostles and a figure of Christ. To either side are the coats of arms of the Monarchs. Today it is a very handsome addition to the Parador Nacional hotel chain.

Palacio de Gelmirez (Gelmirez Palace), Praza do Obradoiro. Open May to September 1000-1400, 1700-2000; October to April 1100-1400 1600-1800. Entrance: 150 ptas. A fine example of civil Romanesque architecture, this was commissioned by Bishop Gelmirez in 1120. It is right next to the cathedral and the façade dates from the 18th century. Inside it is plain and austere but very elegant. The most notable room is the banqueting hall, the Synodal Hall. This is supported by elegantly carved ribvaults and only one central arch — the Palace Arch.

Palacio de Ranjoy (Ranjoy Palace) Praza do Obradoiro. Directly opposite the cathedral this palace, built in the mid 18th century, offers an interesting contrast of style compared with the other buildings in this elegant square. Its original use was as a Confessor's Seminary but today it doubles as the headquarters of the Council of Galicia and Town Hall of Santiago de Compostela.

Praza da Quintana (Quintana Plaza) This plaza, on the opposite side of the cathedral from the Praza de Obradoiro, is not as grand but nevertheless the contrasting architectural styles are very pleasing. It is pleasant to sit on the steps and look at the rear of the cathedral, to your right, the 18th century Casa de Conga, with shops and cafeterias on the lower level, directly ahead; the San Payo Monastery, dating from the 17th and 18th centuries, with its long austere walls and high metal grilled windows stretching the length of the plaza, to the left, and, behind, the much smaller, but equally attractive, Casa de la Parra.

Museums
Museo do Pobo Galego (Poblo Galego Museum), Monasterio de San Domingos; tel: 59 79 10. Open Monday to Saturday 1000-1300, 1600-1900. Closed Sunday and holidays. Entrance: 100 ptas (includes a comprehensive guide in English). Located just outside

the *Zona Monumental* in what was the Santo Domingo de Bonaval monastery. Originally founded in 1219 the present building dates from the 17th and 18th centuries and it was donated by the city as a home for this museum, which first opened in 1977. The museum has seven rooms, each of which is dedicated to subjects such as the sea, crafts, countryside and popular architecture, with the exhibits showing the evolutionary changes over the centuries.

Although the museum's exhibits may be of peripheral interest one thing should not be missed. In one corner there are triple helicoidal (spiral) staircases; they have different ramps, no supports and besides being most unusual make a strange sight when viewed from above. They are designed to connect all levels of the monastery.

The adjoining church was built between the 14th and 16th centuries and houses the Pantheon of Illustrious Galicians.

A museum of contemporary art is being built in an adjacent building.

Station/location/transport to city centre

RENFE, Estación del Ferrocarril; tel: 59 18 59. A small, modern station located fairly close — but a difficult uphill walk — from the *Zona Monumental* at an altitude of 220m.

Layout

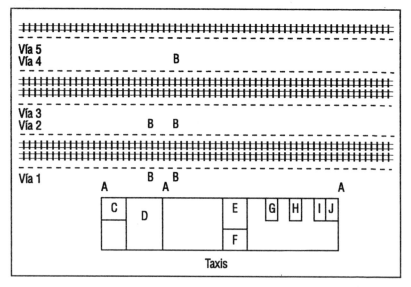

Key

A: *Carritos Portaequipajes*
B: *Paseo Inferior*
C: *Consigna Automática*, open 0730-2300, cost 200 ptas for each 24 hours and tokens can be bought from the *Información* office
D: Bar/cafeteria, open 0600-2300
E: Ticket office

F: *Información* office, open 0730-2300
G: *Jefe de Estación*
H: *Circulación*
I: *Librería*, newspapers, magazines, open 0700-2300
J: *Aseos*

Train station to city centre

On foot This is not very far but it is uphill all the way. Cross the station forecourt, go up either side of the concrete staircase and follow the main road up and to the left. The entrance to the *Zona Monumental* is about 10-15 minutes away.

By taxi A journey of about 5 minutes and about 350 ptas.

Train services

To Madrid by

Talgo Pendular: via Zamora 4½; Ávila 6; Madrid 8.
Estrella: via Zamora 6; Ávila 8; Madrid 10.

To Irún/France by

Diurno: via León 6; Burgos 8; Irún 11½.

Accommodation

Close to the station

*** **Hotel Gelmirez** Horreo, 92; tel: 56 11 00. Single 5,700 ptas; double 8,000 ptas. On the hill up to the *Zona Monumental*. Modern facilities but rather plain.

Outside the *Zona Monumental*

*** **Hotel Santiago Apostol** Carretera del Aeropuerto; tel: 58 71 99; fax: 58 64 99. This modern hotel, part of the Husa chain, is located 2km outside the town on the way towards the airport. There are 100 rooms all with private bath, telephone, colour TV, background music and a minibar. There is also a restaurant, coffee shop, disco and children's playground. Single 6,600 ptas; double 9,500 ptas; double for single use, 7,600 ptas; treble 13,540 ptas.
** **HR La Senra** Senra, 2; tel: 58 04 48. Single 2,000 ptas; double 2,500 ptas. Rooms without bath/shower. Close to Praza de Galicia and facing the *Zona Monumental*; plain and rather dark.

** **HR Mino** Montero Ríos, 31; tel: 58 03 18. Single 2,000 ptas; double 3,500 ptas. Rooms without bath/shower. Second floor no lift; quite nice and close to Praza Galicia.

** **Hostal Maycar** Doctor Teijeiro, 15; tel: 56 34 44. Single 3,900 ptas; double 5,500 ptas. Modern and pleasant.

* **Hostal Europa** Montero Ríos, 31; tel: 56 44 37. Single without bath 2,000 ptas; double with bath 3,500 ptas. First floor of modern building; rather plain rooms.

CH El Ferrol Calvo Sotelo, 30; tel: 58 59 75. Single 1,000 ptas; double 2,000 ptas. Close to Praza Galicia; over a bar.

CH Giadás Plazuela del Matadero, 2; tel: 58 70 71. Single 1,200 ptas; double 2,400 ptas. No bath/shower in rooms. Close to Santo Domingo museum; away from centre.

CH Hospedaje Recarey Patio de Madres, 15; tel: 58 81 94. Single 1,200 ptas; double 2,000 ptas. Deceptively large. Two/three hundred yards to the right of Praza Galicia; small clean rooms with no bath/shower.

CH Villa de Cruces Patio de Madres, 16; tel: 58 08 04. Single 500 ptas; double 1,000 ptas. Next door to Recarey. Small basic rooms without bath/shower; the cheapest I have seen in Spain.

Inside the *Zona Monumental*

*** **Hostal Hogar San Francisco** Campillo de San Francisco, 3; tel: 57 25 64; fax: 57 19 16. High season (June to October and Easter week): single 5,650 ptas, double 7,500 ptas; all other times single 4,900 ptas, double 6,200 ptas. This is located in a historic building just 200m from the cathedral; 71 rooms with baths and telephone. An interesting place to stay.

Note: Many of the rooms in the following places are quite small.

** **Hostal El Rápido** Franco, 22; tel: 58 49 83. Single 2,200 ptas; double 3,500 ptas. Plain large rooms; in a typical *rúa*.

** **Hostal Suso** Rúa Do Villar, 65; tel: 58 11 59. Single without bath 1,800 ptas; double with bath 3,800 ptas. In one of the nicest *rúas*; very pleasant but call ahead.

* **Hostal Cabalo Blanco** Pescadería Vieja, 5; tel: 56 40 98. Single 1,500 ptas; double 3,000 ptas. Rooms without baths. In a corner above a pleasant bar/restaurant.

* **Hostal Girasol** Puerta de la Peña, 4; tel: 56 62 87. Single without bath 1,500 ptas; double without bath 2,700 ptas, with bath 3,500 ptas. On the other side of the cathedral from the new town in a quiet street.

CH La Carrileña Franco, 48; tel: 58 24 13. Single 1,00 ptas; double 2,000 ptas. Rooms without bath. Typically old-fashioned; above bar/restaurant.

CH La Tita Rúa Nueva, 46; tel: 58 39 84. Singles only without bath 1,500 ptas. Small modern rooms; over a bar/restaurant.

CH Santa Cruz Rúa Do Villar, 42; tel: 58 28 15. Single 1,000 ptas; double 1,800 ptas. Rooms without bath; nice location but typically small.

General information
Car hire
Avis, República del Salvador, 10; tel: 57 39 08.

Fiestas
Easter week (*Semana Santa*); week of July 25th.

Police
Comisaría, Rodrigo del Padrón; tel: 58 11 10. Emergency: 091.

Telephone code
for La Coruña province is (981)

Tourist offices
Oficina de Turismo, Rúa de Vilar, 43; tel: 58 40 81. Open Monday to Friday 0900-1400, 1600-1800; Saturday 1000-1300, 1630-199; Sunday 1030-1300. Closed holidays. This is the central government tourist office.
Oficina Municipal de Turismo, Esquina (corner) Toral/Huerfanas; tel: 57 39 90. Open Monday to Friday 1000-1400, 1700-2000; Saturday 1100-1400, 1700-2000; Sunday (July/August/September) 1000-1400, 1700-2000. This is the city tourist office.

SEGOVIA
The city
Located 87km (54 miles) northwest of Madrid, at an altitude of
1,005m (3,296ft), Segovia has a population of about 70,000. It was
a Roman military base and when Alfonso VI reconquered the city
from the Moors in 1088 he resettled and fortified it, taking
advantage of its natural topography. Most of the defensive walls and
three of the five gates can be seen today.

The 12th and 13th centuries saw many Romanesque churches built
and 18 are to be seen today. During the 15th century, under the
court of Trastamara, the city became a centre of culture. In 1474
Isabella was proclaimed queen here and in 1480 it became the
headquarters of the Inquisitor Torquemada. During these periods of
affluence noblemen built fortified houses in the city and many were
later converted into palaces. These are famous for the coats of arms
above the doorways and Segovia can boast more such houses than
most other Spanish cities.

The city was also a centre of the Communidades Revolt against
Carlos I as he tried to implement absolute rule and raise new taxes.
The leaders, Juan de Padilla of Toledo and Juan Bravo of Segovia,
were finally defeated at Villalar in 1521 and executed in Segovia.

Approaching from Madrid the geography does not allow you to
see Segovia at its best. However the view from the north is truly
dramatic: the city stands in the middle of a plain in isolated
splendour.

Segovia, declared a 'World Heritage City' by UNESCO in 1986,
really should not be missed but it is a shame that the authorities
have not taken more effort to signpost more clearly the places of
interest. There are many more places to see, from the outside only,
than are listed under *Places of interest*. If you allow yourself the
time just to wander through the town you will have many pleasant
surprises.

Places of interest
Must see
Acueducto Romano (Roman Aqueduct) This is one of the finest
aqueducts still in existence and also one of the largest Roman
structures left in Spain. Dating from the 1st or 2nd century it is
728m (2,392ft) long with 165 arches and, at its maximum in the
Plaza del Azoguejo, it has a height of 28m (92ft). None of the
granite stones are held together by cement, or any thing else, and

this imposing structure is symmetrically pleasing to look at. A different perspective can be gained from the ramparts of the city walls where it is possible to get very close to the top levels.

Alcázar (Fortress), tel: 43 01 76. Open daily summer (May-September) 1000-1900; winter (October-April) 1000-1800. Entrance: 300 ptas, children (8-14) 150 ptas, no reduction for students. This must be everyone's idea of a fairytale castle. Approached from the cathedral, as it usually is, the Alcázar is not seen best in context with its dramatic surroundings. It is located at the end of a wedge shaped promontory above the confluence of the Eresma and Clamores rivers. This makes it both highly defensible and dramatically beautiful. Although there have been defensive fortifications here since Roman times the earliest parts of the existing structure date from the 12th and 13th centuries. However, the main construction dates from the 14th century, and it was also remodelled in the 15th. It was a favourite for many monarchs — Isabella left from here to be proclaimed queen — and in 1762 the Royal Artillery School, founded by Carlos III, was established here until the roofs were destroyed by fire on March 6 1862. This damage was restored and in 1898 the General Military Archives were moved here.

Today the Alcázar houses a museum that has ten rooms of very interesting exhibits and an informative brochure detailing these is included in the admission price. For those with the energy, the view from the top of the tower of St John — both of the city and of the surrounding countryside — is spectacular. Be warned, there are 152 steps (*peldaños*) from ground level (but only 140 from the very good gift shop).

Catedral y Museo Catedralicio (Cathedral and Cathedral Museum), tel: 43 53 25. Open summer (May-September) 0900-1900; winter (October-April) Monday to Friday 0930-1300, 1500-1800, Saturday, Sunday and holidays 0930-1800. Entrance: 150 ptas. This is considered to be the last Gothic church built in Spain. The original cathedral of Santa María, located close to the Alcázar, was destroyed during the Communidades War and work began on this new cathedral in 1525, after a royal decree was obtained from Carlos V. Juan Gil de Hontanon, also involved with the cathedral in Salamanca, initiated the work and on his death his son continued the work. However, for one reason or another work continued through the 16th and 17th centuries. Although located at the highest point of the city it is seen at its best from the tower of the Alcázar.

The cloister was moved piece by piece from the old cathedral and the museum is located in several rooms off it. Perhaps the most intriguing exhibit is the 18th century carriage that is used to carry the silver monstrance during the Corpus Christi celebrations.

By choice

Churches There are numerous churches, many Romanesque, in and around the city that have their own points of interest. **San Esteban**, close to the cathedral, has an unusual six storey tower and spire. **San Millán**, just outside the walls, is considered one of the most beautiful of the Romanesque churches. Isabella was proclaimed Queen of Castile on the steps of the original **San Miguel** in 1474, although the present building dates from 1558. **Corpus Christi** was consecrated in 1410 and is on the site of what was the largest synagogue in the city.

Convento de los Carmelitas (Convent of the Carmelites), tel: 43 13 49. Open daily 1000-1330, 1600-1900. Entrance: free. This is located outside the city walls almost underneath the Alcázar and, as a consequence, is difficult to get to especially as there is no public transport. Founded by St John of the Cross who actually worked on its construction between 1588 and 1591, the church was built early the next century and a plaque indicates where St John was buried prior to being transferred to an ornate sepulchre after his beatification in 1675.

Convento de San Antonio el Real (Royal San Antonio Convent), tel: 42 02 28. Open daily 1600-1800. Entrance: 200 ptas. This is located well away from the 'old town' close to Plaza de Toros and not that far from the station. Before he became king, Enrique IV had this built on what was then the outskirts of Segovia. In 1455 he gave it to the Franciscans but in 1488 it came into the hands of the Santa Clara monks, to whom it still belongs. The church is particularly ornate and has an elaborate wooden Mudejar ceiling similar to those that used to exist in the Alcázar, before the fire.

Iglesia de la Vera Cruz (Vera Cruz church), tel: 43 14 75. Open Tuesday to Sunday (May-September) 1030-1330, 1530-1900; Tuesday to Sunday (October-April) 1030-1330, 1530-1800. Closed Monday.

Entrance: 100 ptas. This is located very close to the Convento de
Carmelitas Descalzos and is equally difficult to get to. The church
dates from early in the 13th century and, with its 12-sided shape, is
unique in Spain. Some think that it was founded by the Knights Templar
as the style is similar to their other churches in Portugal and Italy.
Very small and unostentatious, this is particularly charming and its
shape can best be seen from the ramparts of the Alcázar.

Monasterio del Parral (Parral Monastery), tel: 43 12 98. Open
Monday to Saturday 0900-1300, 1500-1830; Sunday and holidays
1100-1300, 1600-1800. Another monument that is located outside
the walls and, therefore, a little more difficult to reach. It was
founded in 1445 by Enrique IV but sponsored by the Marqués de
Villena. It passed to the Jerónimos Brotherhood but fell into
disrepair after the monasteries were sacked in 1835 and it was not
until 1914 that it was declared a national monument. There is an
interesting mix of styles here and a particularly ornate sepulchre
containing the remains of the Marqués de Villena.

Plazas and Casas/Palacios (Squares and Houses/Palaces) There
are many squares, houses and palaces throughout the city and some
of the more prominent are: **Plaza del Conde de Cheste** Knights and
noblemen lived in this area and this can be seen by the surrounding
buildings; the **Casas de los Marqueses de Moya, del Marqués de
Lozoya, de los Marqueses de Castellanos** and **de los Uceda-
Peralta**. The **Casa del Conde de Cheste** is notable for its size,
occupying the whole southern side of the plaza, and the **Casa del
Marqués de Quintanar** has an ornate doorway with an arch of 11
helmets topped by the coat of arms of the Heredia-Peraltas. The
Casa de los Picos, close to the Plaza de San Martín, dates from the
15th century and has a most unusual exterior decorated with
diamond-shaped stones. And the **Torre de Arias Dávila**, on the
other side of the Plaza de San Martín, is an interesting example of
a 15th century fortified house that has ramparts towards the top of
the tower.

Plaza de San Martín/Plaza de las Sirenas (San Martín/Mermaids
Square) Located just a few minutes walk away from the Plaza
Mayor, these two plazas are joined by steps and surrounded by
interesting buildings, and are home to two statues. One of the
statues is of Juan Bravo, the leader of the Communidades revolt,

and the most dominant building is the **Iglesia de San Martín**. This is particularly attractive, has fine examples of paintings and sculpture and dates from the 12th century. The **Torreón de Lozoya** dates from the 14th century and the coat of arms belongs to one of its previous owners, the Aguila family. Other notable buildings are the **Casa del Siglo** from the 15th century and the **Casas de los Condes de Bornos, de Soller** and **de los Mexia-Tovar**. Behind the Iglesia de San Martín is the **Carcel Vieja**, the old prison. This stands alone and was used as such until well into this century, but today it houses the library and city archives.

Museums
Casa-Museo de Antonio Machado (House/museum of Antonio Machado), Desamparados, 5; tel: 43 66 49. Open summer (May-September) 1600-1900; winter (October-April) 1600-1800. Closed Monday and holidays. Antonio Machado was a poet who resided in Segovia between 1919 and 1932. This is a small museum and the furniture and other exhibits shows how modestly he lived.

Station/location/transport to city centre
RENFE, Obispo Quesada, 1; tel: 42 07 74. At an altitude of 1,008m this is a long way from the city centre and, as it was being completely remodelled when I visited, no layout is shown here. The *consigna automática* is supposed to be open from 0600-2300.

Train station to city centre
By bus Línea 3, Hierro via Camino Nuevo or José Zorrilla. Monday to Friday 0730-2245; Sunday and holidays 0930-2245; Saturday has a reduced service. Frequency: Monday to Friday, Sunday and holidays every 15 minutes between 0730-1445; every 30 minutes between 1445-2245. The buses, green with an orange stripe, run between the station and Plaza Mayor and the fare is 70 ptas.

On foot This is a long walk. Turn right out of the station, bear left at the junction and continue straight ahead. After about a mile it becomes rather complicated and the last part is all up hill.

By taxi This takes about 10 minutes and costs around 400 ptas.

Train services
To Madrid by
Regional: Between 1¾ and 2.

To Valladolid by
Regional: via Medina de Campo 1¾; Valladolid 2¼.

Note: There is only a very limited service on this route.

Accommodation
Close to the station
* **Hostal Sol Cristina** Obispo Quesada, 40-42; tel: 42 75 13. Single 2,000 ptas; double 3,000 ptas. Clean and comfortable. Opposite station.

Out of the old town near the Aqueduct
**** **Hotel Los Arcos** Paseo Ezequiel González, 24; tel: 43 74 62; fax: 42 81 61. This Best Western hotel has the following two seasons; low, January 1-March 31, November 1-December 31; high, April 1-October 31. Single low, 8,612 ptas, high, 10,388 ptas; double low, 11,501 ptas, high, 13,727 ptas. These rates include breakfast. There is also a special offer for Friday and Sunday nights that includes a half bottle of *cava brut* (dry sparkling wine); the rates are, per person: single low 5,167 ptas, high 7,051 ptas; double low 3,578 ptas, high 4,390 ptas. It has a restaurant specialising in Segovian cuisine and a *taberna* and cocktail bar. Each of the rooms has bath/shower, satellite colour TV, air-conditioning, telephone and minibar. It is located outside the old town fairly close to the aqueduct.

In the old town
* **HR Las Sirenas** Juan Bravo, 30; tel: 43 40 11. Single 4,500 ptas; double 7,000 ptas. No TVs, a little expensive. Not far from Plaza Mayor.
* **HR Plaza** Croniate Lecea, 11; tel: 44 02 44. Single without bath 2,900 ptas, with bath 3,900 ptas; double without bath 3,600 ptas, with bath 4,600 ptas. 350 ptas for bath/shower; nice rooms. Next to Plaza Mayor.
* **Hostal Juan Bravo** Juan Bravo, 12; tel: 43 55 21. Single 2,500 ptas; double 3,800 ptas. Rooms without baths; 200 ptas for bath/shower. Plain; in pedestrian area.
* **CH Casa Cubo** Plaza de Franco, 4; tel: 43 63 86. Single 900 ptas; double 1,800 ptas. Rooms without baths; very central and very basic.

General information
Car hire
Avis, José Zorrilla, 123; tel: 42 25 84.

Hospital
Social Security Hospital, Carretera de Soria; tel: 43 63 63.

Police
Comisaría, Perucho, 2; tel: 42 51 61.

Telephone code
for Segovia province is (911).

Tourist office
Tourist Information Office, Plaza Mayor, 12; tel: 43 03 28. Open Monday to Friday 0900-1400, 1600-1800; Saturday 0900-1400. Closed Sunday and holidays. (This was closed for renovation when I visited.)

SEVILLA
The city
History
The area around Sevilla has been settled for millennia. Carmona was settled in 3000 BC. These are the important dates since the Roman invasion:

206BC   The Romans defeat the Carthaginians at Alcala del Río. Two Roman emperors, Hadrian and Trajan, are born in Italica.

45BC   Caesar founds a colony called Hispalis.

5thC AD   After a series of invasions by Vandals and Swabians, the city becomes the Visigoth capital.

711   The Moors invade Spain and take over the city. The city remains under the control of the Caliphs in Córdoba until the empire begins to break up in the early 11th century.

1069   Reign of poet King Al Motamid brings a period of prosperity.

12thC   The Almohades take over and build a mosque, the Giralda and the Torre de Oro.

1248   The city is reconquered by the Castilian/Leonese King Ferdinand III 'The Saint' and resettled.

1401   Construction of the Gothic cathedral begins.

1503   The Casa de Contrataciín in Sevilla is awarded the monopoly for Spanish trade with the Americas; the beginning of another period of prosperity for the city.

1519   Magellan leaves Sevilla to sail around the world.

17thC   Early this century the trade monopoly ends and prosperity begins to wane.

Overview
Sevilla is located in the western part of Andalucía and, at an altitude of only 7.8m above sea level, it lives up to the name early settlers gave it: Hispalis — flatlands. Directly to the west, 94kms (58 miles) away, is the Atlantic port of Huelva, from where Columbus set sail for the Americas. The busy port and resort of Cádiz lies 149kms (92 miles) due south. The River Guadalquivir, upon which much of the city's prosperity has been based since Sevilla is the country's only river port, flows southwards through flat, marshy land and the Parque Nacional de Doñana to the Atlantic at Sanlucar de Barrameda.

Sevilla is a large city both in area and population, about 700,000, and as such it does not escape the social problems that beset such cities everywhere. Unemployment is very high in Andalucia, and the city has a reputation for a high crime rate and drug problem. Always be cautious, especially with bags being carried by hand or on shoulders, and also with camera equipment, as a popular crime is to ride by on a moped and whisk them away. Also beware of leaving any valuables openly visible in the car, whether you are in it or not. Many of the problems originate in the apartment blocks that ring the city.

Most visitors will spend the majority of their time in the centre of the city as this is where almost all the tourist sights are, as well as most of the hotels, hostels, *pensións*, etc. Of all the *Places of interest* listed, no less than 16 are in this area. Wherever you go in this part of the city you are in for a pleasant surprise: at every turn there are beautiful old churches, palaces, large and small houses, plazas, narrow lanes and Roman ruins, and even the city's pedestrian shopping district, around the famous Sierpes, is an architectural delight. The people bring the scene to life. Sevillianos have a special flair, vitality, style and pride in their unique city.

Other areas, outside the centre, have more subtle charms. See the main tourist sights first but after that it is worth taking a little time simply to wander around. Certainly, do not miss the flea market on Sunday mornings in the Alameda de Hercules, and the nearby area of La Macarena is particularly interesting. The old building, just outside the walls, is very impressive and has been restored to house the Andalusian parliament building.

The northwest of the River Guadalquivir is the Expo '92 site and, to the south of that, still on the west side of the river, is an area generally known as Triana. The oldest area lies between the river bank and the street Pages del Corro, and is interesting to walk around. The rest of the district is much more modern, a mixture of apartments and commercial areas that become more upmarket the further south you go. Avenida de República Argentina is the largest and busiest street on this side of the river. The fairgrounds for the *Feria de Abril* are located in the very south of this district. Although there is really not very much of touristic interest on this side of the river it is a good place to see how people live in modern, inner city Spain. Do not, though, waste any time looking for accommodation here; there are very few places.

Places of interest
Must see

Catedral y Giralda (Cathedral and the Giralda (weathervane)),
Avenida de la Constitución; tel: 421 4971. Open Monday to Friday
1100-1700; Saturday 1100-1600; Sunday 1200-1400. Entrance 200
ptas. In 1184 a minaret was built on a Roman base and this is now
known as the Giralda (literally, weathervane) after the revolving
bronze statue of Faith at its summit. It is a very attractive building
on the outside with typically intricate design work, and it contrasts
starkly with the much more austere brickwork of the cathedral. On
the inside, though, it is extremely bland indeed, just a series of 34
gently elevated ramps leading up to the observation platform at a
height of 70m (230ft). This is the best vantage point in Sevilla:
besides the long-distance views it is the only place where you can
look down on the old town and get a bird's-eye view of the patios.
The bells all around were added, with the statue of Faith, by Hernán
Ruiz between 1565 and 1568; they raised the height of the
monument to 98m (322ft).

The Patio de los Naranjos, the 'Orange Tree Patio', was the patio
(Sahn) of the original mosque which was demolished in the early
15th century, when the cathedral was built in its place. It is one of
the last to be built in the Gothic style and, at 116m long and 76m
wide, it is not only the largest in Spain but the third largest in the
Christian world after St Peter's in Rome and St Paul's in London.
It is a very ornate church whose many points of interest include a
Capilla Real (Royal Chapel), the tomb of Alfonso X, a treasury of
cathedral valuables and the tomb of Christopher Columbus (*Cristobal
Colón*), perhaps the most popular with visitors. The dress code is
very strict here for both men and women — no shorts are allowed.

Real Alcázar y Jardínes (Royal Palace and Gardens), Plaza del
Triunfo; tel: 422 71 63. Open Tuesday to Saturday 1030-1800;
Sunday 1000-1400. Closed Monday. Do not be put off by the
automatic entrance ticket machines here: they are a modern
invention that, once passed, allow you back through the centuries
into one of Spain's most delightful places.

The first fortress was built on this site in 712 by the Arab invaders
and a palace was added by the Emir Abdel-Rahman II in the 9th
century. Some of the walls still exist today and stretch around the
Barrio de Santa Cruz to the Plaza del Triunfo. More palaces and
gardens were added during the 11th and 12th centuries.

After the reconquest in 1248, the Christian monarchs established
a court in the Alcázar, and in 1364 King Rey Don Pedro ordered a
luxury palace, as distinct from a fortress, to be constructed. Later,
in the 16th century, Carlos V made more major changes to this, the
oldest royal seat in Spain.

The juxtaposition of different styles and cultures makes it
particularly interesting to visit. Some of the Moorish buildings are
only surpassed in the Alhambra, Granada. And this does not take
into account the magnificent gardens which are worth a visit on their
own account: an oasis from the busy, noisy city.

Barrio de Santa Cruz   This is the old Jewish quarter, full of
charming little streets of houses with magnificent patios. Typical of
these are the Callejon del Agua, one side of which is the wall of the
Real Alcázar, and the Calles Pimienta and Nieve. There are also
pretty plazas such as those of Don Elvira and Santa Cruz. Take time
to wander through this area which has not been spoilt too much by
the tourist industry; there are many restaurants, bars and interesting
small shops.

Museo de Bellas Artes   (Museum of Fine Art), Plaza del Museo;
tel: 422 07 90. Open Tuesday to Friday 1000-1400, 1600-1900;
Saturday and Sunday 1000-1400. Closed holidays. Entrance: Spanish
nationals and citizens of the EC (on presentation of passport) free;
others 250 ptas. The Museum of Fine Art is located in a 17th
century building that was the Convento de la Merced. It was opened
in 1835 and is considered to be the second most important in Spain,
after the Prado in Madrid. In these very attractive surroundings
there are paintings by El Greco, Velázquez and Valdés Leal,
amongst others. After extensive restoration many rooms were
reopened in 1993.

The square outside is a pleasant place to rest for a while and, if
you fancy a drink in a most unusual bar, go across the plaza and
walk up Monsalves to the corner of Fernán Caballero. Here is a tiny
grocery store that doubles as a bar; there is no place to sit but the
atmosphere is worth experiencing.

By choice
Animal Market Plaza de la Alfalfa, Open Sunday mornings 0800-
1300. This is a street market where people bring birds, hamsters,
mice, rabbits and even kittens and puppies.

Archivo General de Indias (General Archives of the Indies), Avenida de la Constitución; tel: 421 12 31. Open Monday to Friday 1000-1300. Closed Saturday and Sunday. Entrance free. The archive is open for research purposes between 0800 and 1300.

Boat hire Calle Betis. Entrance between Río Grande/El Puerto restaurants. Pedalo: 300 ptas per hour for two people; rowing boat: 400 ptas per hour for two people; rowing boat (large): 500 ptas per hour for five people; motorboat: 6,000 ptas per hour for 20 people. Although difficult to find this place offers a variety of options for spending a delightful hour or so on the river.

Casa de Murillo (Murillo's House), Santa Teresa, 8; tel: 421 75 35. Open Tuesday to Friday 1000-1400, 1600-1900; Saturday and Sunday 1000-1400. Closed Monday. This museum, opened in 1982, is a typical Sevillian house. Murillo lived here as well as in other places in the city.

Casa de Pilatos (Pilatos' House), Plaza de Pilatos, 1; tel: 422 52 98. Open daily 0900-1900. Entrance 400 ptas. Construction of this typical Andalusian palace was begun towards the end of the 15th century and completed early in the 16th century by the first Marquis of Tarifa. The patio is considered a classic piece of Spanish Renaissance art. There is also a collection of 24 busts of Roman emperors.

Rastro (Flea Market), Almedade de Hercules. Open Sunday morning. This is well worth a visit and usually has everything including the proverbial kitchen sink. Even if you have no intention of buying anything the atmosphere is absolutely delightful.

Plaza de España This is an amazingly intricate building in the shape of a semicircle, with two huge towers at either end and a large block in the middle that houses the offices of the Capitán General. Around the base there are ceramic coats of arms and pictures of every Spanish province. Following the curve of the building, and protruding from each end towards the middle, is a waterway crossed via ornate bridges. Boats can be hired here too. In the middle of the semicircle there is a fountain and during the *Feria de Abril* this area is sometimes utilised as a private open air restaurant.

Stamp and Coin Market   Plaza Cabildo. Open Sunday morning. Here you can buy stamps, coins, keyrings and other small items of memorabilia such as old banknotes. If you go look out for the old 1 and 5 peseta notes.

Torre de Oro   (Golden Tower), Paseo de Cristobal Colón; tel: 422 24 19. Open Tuesday to Friday 1000-1400; Saturday and Sunday 1000-1300. Closed Monday. Entrance 25 ptas. The Golden Tower was constructed in 1220 at the end of a wall protecting the port, and the upper additions were made in the 18th century. Today it houses a small nautical museum containing many illustrations of the old docks and quays.

Museums

Museo Arqueológico   (Archaeological Museum),   Pabellón Renaissance, Plaza de América; tel: 423 24 01. Open Tuesday to Sunday 1000-1400. Closed Monday. Entrance Spanish nationals and citizens of the EC (on presentation of passport) free; others 250 ptas. Housed in one of the pavilions built for the 1929 Iboamerican Exhibition, located in the Parque María Luisa. Its Roman exhibits are particularly interesting with many objects from the ruins of Italica.

Museo Arte Contemporaneo (Contemporary Art Museum), Santo Tomás, 5; tel: 421 58 30. Open Tuesday to Friday 1000-1400, 1700-2000; Saturday and Sunday 1000-1400; Closed Monday and holidays. Entrance: Spanish nationals and citizens of the EC (on presentation of passport) free; others 250 ptas. Located in an 18th century house the museum contains paintings from the 20th century.

Museo de Arte y Costumbres Populares   (Popular Art and Costumes Museum), Pabellón Mudejar, Plaza de América; tel: 423 25 76. Open Tuesday to Sunday 1000-1400. Closed Monday. Entrance: Spanish nationals and citizens of the EC (on presentation of passport) free; others 250 ptas. Another museum located in a pavilion (*pabellón*) built for the Iboamerican Exhibition of 1929, this has ceramics, clothes, furniture and other typically Sevillian objects.

Museo de la Real Maestranza y Plaza de Toros   (Bullfighting Museum and Bullring), Paseo de Cristobal Colón; tel: 422 45 77. Open Monday to Saturday 1000-1400. Price 200 ptas. The property

CARMONA

The short bus trip from Sevilla to Carmona, just 30kms away to the east, will not disappoint anybody. Even the first sighting is intriguing; the city sits on top of a hill that seems to rise from nowhere out of the surrounding fertile plain. Designated as a 'Historical and Artistic Entity', it has been inhabited for over 5,000 years and survived the rise and fall of successive empires: Tartessans in the 8th century BC; Carthaginians in the 4th century BC; Romans, under whom Carmona was the largest and strongest city in the region; the Visigoths; the Moors, under whom it became an independent kingdom in 1029 AD; it was the site of battles between Pedro I of Castile and his half-brother Enrique of Trastamara, and Ferdinand and Isabella made it their last base before launching the reconquest of Granada in 1492.

Carmona never had a feudal lord as it was a 'Crown' city and, as a consequence, there is an extraordinary number of important homes, palaces, convents and churches here. Pay particular attention to the Roman/Arabic walls and the *Puertas de Córdoba and Sevilla* (gates of Córdoba and Sevilla); the latter is one of the most important Roman gates in Spain; the two *Alcázars*, and the Santa María church. Just outside the city is the *Museo y Necropolis de Carmona*, Avenida de Jorge Bonsor. Tel: 414 08 11. Open Tuesday to Saturday 1000-1400, 1600-1800; Sunday 1000-1400. This is the largest necropolis outside of Rome and there are over 800 tombs, of which about a quarter have been excavated.

Besides all this it is worth visiting Carmona just to stay in what is, quite simply, the most beautiful and charming hotel I have seen in all Spain, the *****Hotel Casa Palacio Casa de Carmona*, Plaza de Lasso, 1; tel: (95) 414 33 00, fax: (95) 414 3/ 52. It is housed in the Lasso de la Vega palace, basically 16th century but with parts from the 15th and 17th centuries, that has been painstakingly restored to incorporate the most modern technology in a completely unobtrusive manner. All of the 30 double rooms, 12 of them deluxe, and two apartments have been furnished with their own combination of antique furniture and appropriate fabrics. The same applies to the public rooms, which even have free bars, and the Loggia terrace and swimming pool. Besides the normal services one would expect, there is a mini-gymnasium, sauna, hairdresser, antique shop, currency exchange, travel service and, in deluxe rooms, even compact disc and cassette players. The level of service matches the surroundings, discreet and exquisite; you can even leave your shoes out overnight to be cleaned! And the prices are more than reasonable: single 12,000 ptas; double 15,000 ptas; deluxe double and apartments 19,000 ptas.

of the Real Maestranza of Knighthood, construction of this bullring was begun in 1761 but not completed in its present form until 1881. As well as being an active *plaza de toros*, considered one of the most beautiful in Spain, it is an important architectural monument. Also of interest is the covered bridge from the plaza to the 'social house' for members of the Real Maestranza. The museum itself is not particularly good (those in Barcelona, Córdoba, Madrid and Ronda are better) but the admission price also entitles you to wander a little inside the plaza. If you take the opportunity to walk in the ring itself you will be surprised by how much bigger it seems when you are out there alone. Imagine what it must feel like to be confronted by a *toro bravo*! Also, take a look at the *burladeros* — the places where the *toreros* enter and exit from the ring. These heavy wooden barriers are deeply scarred by the bulls' horns when they charge into them, which gives an insight into the strength and power of these animals.

Station/location/transport to city centre

RENFE, Estación Santa Justa; tel: 441 41 11. This is a large new station that was partially opened on May 2 1991 and completed in April 1992 when the new high speed line, AVE — *Alta Velocidad Española* — was inaugurated. The station is some distance from the centre. The concourse is air-conditioned and there are both lifts and escalators down to the platforms below.

Key

A: Cafeteria/restaurant, open 0700-0030

B: *Telefónica*, open 0345-2345

C: Shop for food, drinks, souvenirs, newspapers, etc, open 0700-2330

D: Automatic cash dispenser, Cajero Telebanco system (all major cards)

E: *Servicios/Aseos*

F: Train *Información*

G: Ticket office

H: *Consigna/consigna automática*, open 0500-0030. Price: small 200 ptas, medium 300 ptas, large 400 ptas. The entrance is outside the station and below the concourse level

Train station to town centre

By bus Route 70 — to the Prado de San Sebastián which is close to the old bus station and Plaza España.

Layout

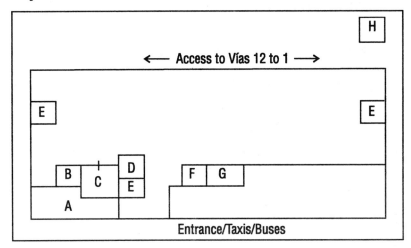

By taxi The station is some distance from the centre of town and the fare can be as high as 450 to 500 ptas.

Train services
To Madrid by

	Regional	Talgo	Talgo Camas	Estrella	AVE
Córdoba		¾	1½	¾	¾
Ciudad Real		2¼		2	
Alcázar de San Juan				6¼	
Zafra		2¾			
Mérida	3¾				
Cáceres	5¼				
Madrid	10¾	3½	9¼	3	2¾

To Barcelona by

	Diurno	Talgo Camas	Estrella
Córdoba	1¼	1¼	1½
Alcázar de San Juan	5	4½	6
Valencia	8		9¾
Tarragona		10¼	13¾
Barcelona	12¾	12	15

To Almería by
Estrella: Almería 9.

To Cáceres by
Regional: via Zafra 2¾; Mérida ¾; Cáceres 5.

To Cádiz by

	Regional Expres	Diurno	Inter City	Talgo Pen	Estrella
Jerez de la Frontera	1¼	1	1	1	1¼
Cádiz	2¼	1¾	1¾	1¾	2½

To Granada by
Regional Expres: Direct 4; with a change at Bobadilla 5 or more.

To Huelva by
Regional: 1; *InterCity*: 1½; *Talgo Pendular*: 1½; *Estrella*: 2.

To Málaga by
Regional: 3; *Regional Expres*: 3¼; *Talgo*: 2½.

Accommodation
Close to Santa Justa station
There are very few places to stay close to this new station.

Close to San Bernado station
** **HR Del Prado** Avenida de Málaga, 6 and Manuel Bermudo, 3; tel: 441
00 11. Single 1,713 ptas; double 3,726 ptas. Located in an old building
between the train and bus stations, this can be entered from both sides,
hence the two addresses. It is a little old-fashioned.
* **Pensión Jerez** Rastro, 2; tel: 423 45 22. Single 1,000 ptas; double 2,000
ptas. Very small. Close to the Avenida Menéndez y Pelayo.

In the city
**** **Husa Sevilla** Pagés del Corro, 90; tel: 434 24 12; fax: 434 27 07.
This modern Husa hotel is located in the heart of the famous gypsy quarter
of Triana, just ten minutes' walk from the historical area of the city. There
are 128 rooms all with private bath, air-conditioning, telephone, satellite
TV, radio, background music and minibar. Single 12,400 ptas; double
19,000 ptas; double, for single use, 15,200 ptas; treble 25,000 ptas.
*** **HR Zaída** San Roque, 26; tel: 421 11 38. Single 2,500 ptas; double
4,000 ptas. Very attractive Moorish columns in the lobby with an open

patio behind.

** HR Avenida Marqués de Paradas, 28; tel: 422 05 85. Single 2,000 ptas; double 3,500 ptas. Located on first floor of a modern block. Clean, friendly, but possibly noisy.

** HR Capitol Zaragoza, 66; tel: 421 24 41. Single 1,800 ptas; double 3,700 ptas. An old-fashioned place with similar decor and a small TV lounge.

** HR Central Zaragoza, 18; tel: 421 76 60. Single 2,200 ptas; double 3,800 ptas. Old-fashioned style and decor.

** HR Goya Mateos Gago, 31; tel: 421 11 70. Single 2,225 ptas; double 3,655 ptas, with shower 3,340 ptas. Clean and pleasant. Situated directly opposite a church.

** HR Nuevo Suiza Azofaifo, 7; tel: 422 91 47. Single 2,500 ptas. double 4,000 ptas. Located in a narrow passageway, just off Sierpes, the outside is a strange red and mustard colour. Inside it is very dignified and has three floors of beautiful wooden balconies.

** HR Paris San Pedro Martír. tel: 422 98 61. Single 3,000 ptas; double 4,500 ptas. A nice old-style place that has been tastefully modernised.

** HR Regente Amor de Dios, 30; tel: 437 73 49. Single 2,000 ptas; double 3,500 ptas. Small and clean.

* HR Córdoba Farnesio, 12; tel: 422 74 98. (Between San José and Fabiola) Single 1,500 ptas; double 2,400 ptas. In the same passageway, and in the same style, as Pensión Buen Dormir (see below).

* HR Monreal Rodrigo Cano, 6; tel: 421 41 66. Single 1,590 ptas; double 4,770 ptas, without bath 2,650 ptas. A lovely old building with flowers hanging down from the balconies. Located in a very quiet street close to the Real Alcázar.

* Hostal Aguilas Aguilas, 15; tel: 421 31 77. Single 2,200 ptas; double 3,500 ptas. With only six rooms this is very attractive; the rooms overlook a strangely shaped high lobby.

* Hostal la Gloria San Eloy, 58; tel: 422 26 73. Single 1,500 ptas; double 3,500 ptas. Small. Much character.

** Pensión Duque Trajano, 15; tel: 438 70 11. Single 2,120 ptas, without bath 1,375 ptas; double 3,815 ptas, without bath 2,670 ptas; treble 5,300 ptas; quadruple 6,300 ptas. Lovely and old-fashioned in style, with rooms set around a patio with roof. Trajano is a busy, noisy, street.

* Pensión Arenal Pastor y Landero, 21; tel: 422 61 77. Single 1,000 ptas; double 1,750 ptas; showers are 200 ptas extra. Close to the *mercado* and Plaza de Toros.

* Pensión Arguelles Alhóndiga; tel: 421 44 56. Single 1,300 ptas; double 2,700 ptas. There is an extra 300 ptas charge for a bath if you have a single room. Eleven rooms only; small and clean.

* Pensión Buen Dormir Farnesio, 8; tel: 421 74 92. (Between San José and Fabiola); Single 1,250 ptas, without bath 1,000; double 2,500 ptas, without bath 2,000 ptas. Located in a small passageway; it has a small patio and caged birds on the wall.

* **Pensión Cruces** Plaza de la Cruces, 10; tel: 441 34 04. Single 1,000 ptas; double 2,000 ptas. This pension, over 500 years old, has two patios and much character. The owner tells me it has even featured in television programmes.

* **Pensión Monsalves** Monsalves, 29; tel: 421 68 53. Single 1,500 ptas; double 2,500 ptas. A very small pension with only three rooms, but it is clean and the people are friendly.

* **Pensión San Pancracio** Plaza de las Cruces, 9; tel: 441 31 04. Single 1,000 ptas; double 2,000 ptas. A very neat, small pension typical of the area.

* **Pensión San Pedro** Doña María Coronel, 12; tel: 422 11 68. Single 1,250 ptas; double 2,500 ptas. Small, with only six rooms. Located on second floor and reached through an attractive patio.

CH Pedro Vergara León Ximénez de Enciso, 11; tel: 422 47 38. Single 1,500 ptas; double 2,500 ptas. A small guesthouse above a bar in an area of passageways. Very much part of a private house.

General information
Car hire
Avis, Estación RENFE Santa Justa, Terminal AVE; tel: 453 78 61.

Fiestas
Easter week (*Semana Santa*) variable dates, and *Feria de Abril* which usually starts around the middle of April. These are world famous fiestas and accommodation needs to be booked many months in advance.

Hospital
Hospital Universitario, Avenida Dr Fredriani; tel: 437 84 00.

Laundromat
Self-Service Laundromat, Castelar, 2; tel: 421 05 35.

Police
Comisaría, Plaza de la Gavidia; tel: 422 88 40.

RENFE city office
RENFE, Zaragoza, 29; tel: 421 79 98.

Telephone code
for Sevilla province is (95).

Tourist office
Oficina de Información de Turismo, Avenida de la Constitución, 21 B; tel: 422 14 04. Open Monday to Friday 1000-1300, 1500-1930. Saturday 1000-1300.

TOLEDO
The city
History
These are some of the most important dates:

193BC	Romans conquer the city, name it Toletum, and establish a strategic stronghold.
414-466AD	First Vandals, and then Visigoths overrun Spain. The Visigoth kings establish Toledo as their political and religious capital.
711	Moors conquer Spain and Toledo is incorporated into the Córdoba Emirate. After the fall of Córdoba in 1012 the city becomes the capital of an independent kingdom.
1085	King Alfonso VI, of León, reconquers the city for the Christians and makes it the capital.
Early C13th	The Jews, whose position often fluctuated, become very powerful.
Mid C14th	During the reign of Pedro I 'The Cruel' there is much internal strife and finally his half-brother to late Henry of Trastamara leads a revolt and succeeds in killing the king and massacring the Jews.
15th cent	Trastamara dynasty rules Spain. During this period Toledo becomes a major cultural centre and Moors, Jews and Christians coexisted peacefully.
1469	Isabella of Castile and León, of the Trastamara dynasty, marries Ferdinand of Aragón, Catalonia, Sicily and Naples, thus uniting all these areas under one kingdom. Ferdinand and Isabella are later known as the 'Catholic Monarchs'.
1476	Ferdinand and Isabella defeat La Beltraneja's and the Portuguese forces at the battle of Toro. This assures Isabella's succession and marks the beginning of Spain's 'Golden Era'.
1492	A very important year. Ferdinand and Isabella defeat the last Moorish kingdom in Granada; Columbus discovers the Americas and, more ominously, the Moors and Jews are expelled from Spain.
1504	Isabella's daughter Joanna 'The Mad' and her husband Felipe 'The Handsome', son of the Hapsburg Emperor, Maximilian, are proclaimed sovereigns of Spain and the Netherlands under the regency of

Ferdinand.

1506   Felipe dies at an early age and the insane Joanna is
        locked away. Ferdinand, her father, is Regent until
        1516 when his grandson Carlos I becomes of age and
        is proclaimed king.
1519   Carlos I becomes the Holy Roman Emperor Carlos V.
1556   Carlos I abdicates and his son, Felipe II, succeeds him.
1561   Felipe II decides to move his court to Madrid and this
        small provincial town becomes the new capital. It
        marks the decline of Toledo even though it remains the
        seat of the Primate of Spain.

Overview

Beautiful, dramatic, charming, these and many more adjectives can
be used to describe this imperial city, but perhaps the most
important is historic. For the history of Toledo is, in many respects,
the history of Spain. Located just 71km from Madrid, at an altitude
of 529m, it is also a natural stronghold as the River Tajo has looped
around and cut a deep ravine through the hills, effectively making
the city a promontory. No matter how much one has read, or how
many photographs one has seen, the first sighting of Toledo will
take your breath away. The city itself, designated a National
Monument, is a maze of narrow streets, lanes and plazas —
protected by fortified gates — that wind up and down the steep hills
and are all bordered by old medieval buildings, many churches and,
now and again, some of the most important monuments in Spain.
The latter are all detailed under *Places of interest* and some are well
signposted, in red, by the local authority. Amazingly the old town
has been preserved almost intact and there are few instances where
modernisation has intruded upon this intriguing place. There are,
though, numerous tourist shops and as Toledo is famous for its steel
these sell everything from small knives up to, and including, suits
of armour. One of the more famous products is Damascene — black
steel inlaid with gold, silver and copper wire.

There are not many places to stay in Toledo; really only a handful
at the lower end of the scale and some of those are quite basic. As
the city is one of the most visited in Spain this can cause many
difficulties at Easter and in the summer months and particularly on,
and the week after, August 15 — a major national holiday that starts
a local fiesta. There is nothing more frustrating than wandering up
and down, literally, these beautiful streets looking for a place to

stay. I know from experience; add in a temperature of 108F and it is nearly enough to put you off Toledo for life. The only possible alternatives to taking pot luck are: (a) Make a reservation in advance, but even this can be difficult; (b) Stay in Madrid and take the train to and from Toledo; (c) If you are heading south or east make Toledo a day trip — leaving the luggage in the *consigna* — and plan to catch your connection in Aranjuez late in the evening. This saves making a return journey all the way to Madrid. Which ever way you plan it do not miss going to Toledo.

Places of interest

Note 1: Many of the places detailed here are rather difficult to locate due to the geography of the city and the maze of very small and narrow streets. As they are not always that well signposted either, I would highly recommend that the first stop is at one of the tourist offices to obtain a free copy of the excellent plan of the city that is available in different languages.

Note 2: It is very difficult to differentiate between *Must see*, *By choice* and *Museums* in Toledo. In reality almost everything is a *Must see* but most visitors will have a time constraint. Therefore see the cathedral and Alcázar first and then as many of the others as time, and taste, allow. There are also many churches of note, the most important of which are the Santiago de Arrabal, El Cristo de la Vega and the San Roman.

Must see

Alcázar y Museo de Ejercito (Alcázar and Army Museum), Open Tuesday to Saturday 0930-1330, 1600-1730 (summer 1600-1830); Sunday 1000-1330, 1600-1730 (summer 1600-1830). Closed Monday and holidays. Entrance: 125 ptas. There have been fortifications on this site dating back as far as the 3rd century and the present building, the most imposing in Toledo, has been completely rebuilt since it was destroyed during the Spanish Civil War. It really has been renovated beautifully and, given its immense proportions, the patio is especially elegant. Although army museums are not to everyone's taste this is particularly good. There are eight rooms around the main patio with exhibits ranging from swords, guns of all types, uniforms and documents. On the upper level are three more rooms with scale models of battles, thousands of model soldiers and more exhibits from past African campaigns.

During the Spanish Civil War forces loyal to Franco, and many civilians, were kept under siege in the Alcázar and the exhibits and rooms on the lower level show how they lived during this period.

Probably the most famous event related to the Alcázar took place in July 1936 when the commander, Colonel Moscardó, had a telephone conversation with the leader of the forces besieging the Alcázar. Moscardó was told that his son was being held captive and that if he did not surrender his son would be executed. Moscardó then talked to his son who was subsequently shot when the colonel refused to surrender. Colonel Moscardó's office has been left exactly as it was; ceiling hanging down, bullet holes in the walls and torn furniture, etc; there are also plaques and photographs commemorating these events. Kept as a shrine, this room has a greater impact because it is in total contrast to the rest of the carefully renovated Alcázar.

Catedral y Museo Catedral (Cathedral and Cathedral Museum), open Monday to Saturday 1030-1300, 1530-1900; Sunday 1600-1900 (winter open to 1800). Entrance: cathedral free; cathedral museum 350 ptas. This, the seat of the Primate of Spain, is the most important monument in the city. A cathedral was first built on this site in the 6th century by the Visigoth King Recaredo I and San Eugenio, Toledo's first bishop. However it was converted into a mosque by the Moors and it was not until 1227 that King Ferdinand III 'The Saint' began construction of the present building. There is some ambiguity as to when it was finished — some guides say 1497, others as late as 1593 — but because of the many different architectural styles involved it is sometimes called the 'Museum Cathedral'. It really is a magnificent example of its kind and has over 20 side chapels. There is also a curious tradition here. If you look up you will see strange looking hats hanging precariously from the ceiling and, underneath, a plaque indicating the tomb of a primate. The hats belong to the respective primates and when they fall from the ceiling the tomb is removed to the vaults. The cloisters are also unusual in that part of them is blocked off as there are painted murals on the walls.

The 'museum' actually consists of five separate entities and these are varied indeed. Some are small while others consist of many different rooms, and there are some beautiful works of art by some of the most renowned artists of their time, in the form of sculpture, paintings, wrought iron and stained glass. One of its greatest treasures is Enrique de Arfe's Monstrance: made of solid gold, silver and precious stones it weighs 195 kg and has some 5,600 individual parts. Other monstrances by the same artist and his brother are on display in, amongst other places, La Mezquita in Córdoba, and the cathedrals in Ávila and Valladolid.

By choice
El Cristo de la Luz (Christ of the Light)   There are no official opening hours here. According to the tourist office it is open as and when a caretaker decides. For such an important monument this is very strange indeed! This 10th century building was copied from La Mezquita in Córdoba and used to be a mosque until the reconquest. Today it is the only building in its original condition still existing from that period.

El Tránsito Sinagoga (Transito Synagogue), open Tuesday to Saturday 1000-1345, 1600-1745; Sunday 1000-1345. Closed Monday. Entrance: 200 ptas. Built in 1365 during the reign of Pedro I 'The Cruel' by his treasurer and Minister of Finance Samuel Halevi — after whom it was originally named. The main room is 23m long, 9.5m wide, 17m high and has a beamed wooden ceiling. The cornice all around the ceiling has Hebrew inscriptions with verses from the Psalms. The eastern wall, where the Torah's sacred rolls were located, is decorated with beautiful hand-carved stucco and the south wall houses the galleries where the women used to sit.
   When the building was taken over for Christian worship it was first used by the Monks of St Benedict (San Benito) and later by the Knights of Calatrava. Today a Sephardic museum is being created here to document the history of the Jewish community in Spain.

Monasterio Cisterciense de Santo Domingo de Silos (Antiguo) (Cistercian Convent of Santo Domingo de Silos — The Ancient), open Monday to Saturday 1100-1330, 1600-1900; Sunday 1600-1900. November to March open only at weekends. Weekday visits can be requested at the nunnery porter's office. Entrance: 150 ptas. This is the oldest convent in the city, having been founded by King Alfonso VI in 1085. El Greco's first commission in Spain was to paint the reredos here and the original contract is on display. He and his family are also buried here. The first part one sees is the Renaissance style church and this is very much in contrast to the other part of the building, behind a metal grille. Here you will find many rather unusual exhibits, an interesting carved wooden choir and, of course, paintings by El Greco.

Plaza de Zocodover (Zocodover Square) Irregularly shaped and not of much note architecturally this, nevertheless, has been the most important meeting place for the people of Toledo through the centuries. The Moors held a market here — a tradition which was continued until recently — and feasts, tournaments as well as executions have also taken place here. It is even said that King Ferdinand 'The Saint' listened to his citizens complaints, and dispensed justice where necessary, whilst seated on his throne in this square. Today, as ever, it is the central gathering place for the citizens of this amazing city.

Puentes y Puertas (Bridges and Gates) There are only two bridges and the **Puente de Alcántara** is the most important. The first of the gates guarding this bridge dates from the 18th century and, carved on the front, is the city's coat of arms. Further across is a much older — it originates from the early 13th century — double-doored tower with a portcullis. The **Puente de San Martín** is less important and, because of its location, is unlikely to be of much interest. The **Puerta del Sol** dating from the 14th century is particularly elegant and the archway is unusual. The **Puertas Nueva de Bisagra, Antigua de Bisagra** and **de Alfonso VI** are all close to each other and worth seeing, but only after having seen everything else.

San Juan de los Reyes (Monastery of St John of the Kings), open summer Monday to Sunday 1000-1345, 1530-1900; winter Monday to Sunday 1000-1345, 1530-1800. Entrance: 100 ptas. This was built by the architect Juan Guas as a combination church, cloister and monastery at the instigation of Ferdinand and Isabella. It was paid for by them, privately, to celebrate victory at the Battle of Toro — in 1476 — which confirmed Isabella as Queen of Castile. It was intended to be their burial place but they were so charmed by Granada, after they conquered it in 1492, that they had the Capilla Real built there for that purpose.

Although not nearly as large as the cathedral this is considered to be a classic of Gothic architecture and, inside, unlike many of its contemporaries, the atmosphere is one of light and openness. On both sides of the altar are the emblems of the different realms combined together by Ferdinand (Aragón, Catalonia and Naples) and

Isabella (Castile and León).

It is incongruous that this lovely place suffered much damage and was even used as a stables by Napoleon's troops in 1810. The cloister is also considered a model of its kind. Late Gothic in style, its magnificent stonework and small garden make it a place with charm and tranquillity.

The monastery is famous for its first novice, Cardinal Cisneros, who died in 1517. He has many connections with the cathedral, held many important positions and nowadays he is remembered throughout Spain as his name appears on numerous streets and hotels, etc.

Santa María la Blanca Sinagoga (St Maria the White Synagogue), open summer Monday to Sunday 1000-1345, 1545-1745; winter Monday to Sunday 1000-1345, 1545-1845. Entrance: 100 ptas. Much older than the Tránsito Synagogue, this was constructed between one and two centuries earlier and was the chief Jewish synagogue. It also has a very different character. Set in a small, secluded garden, the inside with its columns and arches is very reminiscent of a mosque. It was dedicated to Hebrew rites until 1405 when Saint Vincent Ferrer took it over for Christian worship. In the late 16th century it became a hostal for repentant fallen women and then, much later, a hermitage under the patronage of Saint Mary. She was known locally as 'the White One', after a chapel in Rome, hence its name 'St Mary the White'. Today it is rather run down and in need of some repairs but, curiously, this adds to its charm.

Santo Tomé (St Tome Church), Open (summer) Monday to Sunday 1000-1345, 1530-1845; (winter) Monday to Sunday 1000-1345, 1530-1745. Entrance: 100 ptas. This church has a splendid Mudejar tower but the main item of interest is one of El Greco's most famous works, *The Burial of Conde de Orgaz*, painted in 1583. The Count (*Conde*) de Orgaz was a nobleman who was buried on the actual site in 1312. In his will he left large sums of money for the upkeep of the church and poor parishioners. However, this was contested by other heirs and the ensuing law suit lasted over 270 years before being decided in the church's favour. The church then commissioned El Greco, who by then had become famous, to paint a picture depicting the burial. The young boy attending the saints is reputed to be his son and, on a handkerchief hanging from the boy's pocket, El Greco signed his name — Domenico Theotokopouli — and the date.

Museums

Casa y Museo del Greco (El Greco's House and Museum), Open Tuesday to Saturday 1000-1900 (last visit 1845). Sunday 1000-1400 (last visit 1345). Closed Monday. Entrance: Spanish citizens, foreigners resident in Spain and citizens of the EC under 21 free; others 200 ptas. El Greco lived and worked here. It is a charming old house and the furnishings give one an insight into how people lived in 16th century Toledo. There is an attractive patio as well as pleasant gardens with interesting views. And, of course, many examples of El Greco's work, both in the house and the small museum.

Hospital de Santa Cruz de Mendoza (Santa Cruz Museum), Open Monday to Saturday 1000-1830; Sunday 1000-1400. Entrance: 200 ptas. The museum of Santa Cruz is housed in this old, cross-shaped building and has a wide and varied range of exhibits: 20 El Greco's and 30 Brussels tapestries along with carpets, chests, religious memorabilia, some small arms, suits of armour, other paintings and many more items, all of which are enhanced by this beautiful and elegant building.

Hospital de la Tavera (Tavera Hospital), Open Monday to Saturday 1030-1330, 1530-1800; Sunday 1030-1330. Closed Monday. Located about 400m outside the old town, past the Puerta Bisagra, this very large building was constructed by Cardinal Tavera, who is buried in the church, in 1541. The patio is large and ornate and the covered walkway dividing it in half is very unusual indeed. On the left hand side is the private residence of the Duke of Lerma and on display are some works of El Greco as well as many other exhibits of artistic value.

Museo de Arte Contemporaneo (Contemporary Art Museum), open Tuesday to Saturday 1000-1400, 1600-1830; Sunday 1000-1400. Closed Monday and holidays. Entrance: 100 ptas or 150 ptas for a combination ticket to the Museo Taller del Moro, Museo de los Concilios y Cultura Visigótica and the Museo de Arte Contemporaneo. Located in the Casa de las Cadenas which is a 16th century house with a very interesting wooden trilevel patio (*Patio de*

Mujeres). A beautiful old house that has been very tastefully restored in 1973 to exhibit contemporary paintings and sculptures.

Museo de los Concilios y Cultura Visigótica (Museum of the Councils and Visigothic Culture), Open Tuesday to Saturday 1000-1400, 1600-1830; Sunday 1000-1430. Closed Monday and holidays. Entrance: 100 ptas or 150 ptas for a combination ticket to the Museo Taller del Moro, Museo de los Concilios y Cultura Visigótica and the Museo de Arte Contemporaneo. This is located in the church of San Roman and it is a fascinating building. Half of it is like a regular church and the other half is very reminiscent of a mosque — an intriguing combination. There are not that many exhibits but the Romanesque paintings on the walls are of interest.

Museo de Taller del Moro (Moor's Workshop), Open Tuesday to Saturday 1000-1400, 1600-1815; Sunday 1000-1400. Closed Monday. Entrance: 100 ptas or 150 ptas for a combination ticket to the Museo Taller del Moro, Museo de los Concilios y Cultura Visigotica and the Museo de Arte Contemporaneo. Although rather small this is a dignified and elegant museum that is located in a 14/15th century building. It houses fine examples of Moorish ornamental plasterwork as well as ceramics and wooden items.

Station/location/transport to city centre
RENFE, Paseo de las Rosas; tel: 22 30 99. Located at an altitude of 458.3m this is quite unusual as it is designed to match the elegant architecture of this splendid city.

Key
A: Cafeteria, open 0600-2300
B: *Policía*
C: Booking hall
D: Ticket office
E: *Kiosco* for newspapers, magazines, etc, open 0700-1915

F: *Consigna Automática*, open 0600-2200. These machines are automatic but admission is controlled by the ticket office staff and the cost is 200 ptas a machine, per 24-hour period

Train station to city centre
By bus Routes 5 or 6, Estación to Plaza Zocodover. These buses are white with blue stripes, cost 70 ptas, run about every 10 minutes and, because of the rather roundabout route, the ride takes about 10-15 minutes.

Layout

```
┌────────────────────────────────────────────────────────────┐
│                 Entrance, Car Park and Taxis                 │
│  ┌───┐       ┌───┐           ┌──────C──────┐                 │
│  │ A │       │ B │           │   ┌───┐ ┌─┐ ┌───┐             │
│  └───┘       └───┘           │   │ D │ │E│ │ F │             │
│                              └───┘   └─────┘   └───┘         │
│  Vía                                                         │
└────────────────────────────────────────────────────────────┘
```

On foot Turn right out of the station and, after a short distance, follow the Paseo de la Rosa around to the left. Before very long you will see this magnificent city, and the formidably large Alcázar, towering above you on the opposite bank of the River Tajo. Unfortunately this is where the journey becomes difficult as the remaining walk is all uphill, some of it very steep indeed. It is only advisable for the fittest and even they might find it uncomfortable in the heat of summer; temperatures of well above 100F are not uncommon. To get across the river walk up to the Puente de Alcántara, the most important of the two old bridges crossing the Tajo. Once on the other bank there is a choice: the long route that climbs slowly around following the river to the left or the much more interesting, but very steep, direct way that will bring you out at the Plaza de Zocodover.

By taxi Because of the layout of the city, and the unusual geographical location, traffic to and from the station is forced to take rather a roundabout route. This raises the fare to between 400 and 450 ptas to and from the Plaza de Zocodover.

Train services
To Madrid by
Regional: 1¼.

Cuenca by
Regional: 3½.

To León by
Regional: via Madrid 1¼; Ávila 3¼; Valladolid 4½; León 6½.

To Segovia by
Regional: via Madrid 1¼; Segovia 3.

Accommodation
Close to the station
* **Hostal Santa Barbara** Avenida de Santa Barbara, 8; tel: 22 02 98. Single 2,750 ptas; double 3,500 ptas. About 100 metres to the left of the station. Rooms with bath/shower; pleasant and clean.

In the city
*** **Hotel Real** Real del Arrabel, 4; tel: 22 93 00; fax: 22 87 67. Single 6,784 ptas; double 9,540 ptas. These rates include breakfast. In a quiet location this hotel has a 19th century façade. There is a cafeteria, restaurant and 56 rooms that have bath/shower, satellite colour TV, video, telephone, air-conditioning and piped music.

** **HR Labrador** Juan Labrador, 16; tel: 22 26 20. Single without bath 1,375 ptas, with bath 1,640 ptas; double with bath 2,435 ptas. A plain building close to the Alcázar.

* **HR Imperio** Calle de las Cadenas, 5; tel: 22 76 50. Single 2,400 ptas; double 3,800 ptas. Named the 'Empire'; modern and medium sized. Recognisable by the various national flags flown on the outside.

* **HR Las Armas** Armas, 7; tel: 22 16 68. Single 1,900 ptas; double 3,135 ptas. Very old fashioned; beautiful plants in the patio. Doors close at 0100 hours. Located just off the Plaza de Zocodover.

* **HR Posada del Estudiante** Callejon de San Pedro, 2; tel: 21 47 34. Single 1,500 ptas; double 2,000 ptas. *Menu del día* only 600 ptas. Named the 'Students Inn' this is very close to the cathedral. Small and basic.

* **Hostal Nuncio Viejo** Nuncio Viejo, 19; tel: 22 81 78. double 1,900 ptas. Old-fashioned; on third floor, no lift. Pleasant aroma from the flower shop on the ground floor.

* **Pensión Lumbreras** Juan Labrador, 9; tel: 22 15 71. Single 1,200 ptas; double 2,000 ptas. Old and with a traditional patio.

General information
Car hire
Avis, Galería Comercial El Miradero; tel: 21 43 35.

Fiestas
Easter week, (*Semana Santa*), variable dates; *El Sagrano* — August 15-22.

Police
Comisaría, Plaza de Zocodover, 1; tel: 21 34 00.

Telephone code
for Toledo province is (925).

Tourist office
Puerta de Bisagra; tel: 22 08 43. Open Monday to Saturday 1000-1800; Sunday 1000-1500.

Kiosco in Plaza de Zocodover. Open as above.

VALENCIA

The city

Located 404km (252 miles) from Madrid on the shores of the
Mediterranean, Valencia, the third largest city in Spain, has a
population of over 800,000. Although there had been Greek and
Carthaginian settlements here it was not until 138 BC that the
Romans founded the city, calling it Valentia. The Romans were
gradually displaced by the Visigoths and they, in turn, were
succeeded by the Moors who ruled until Rodrigo Diaz de Vivar (El
Cid) conquered the city in 1094. However in 1102, a few years after
his death, the city was reclaimed by the Moors who retained power
until 1238 when James I, El Conquistador, reconquered the city and
proclaimed the Kingdom of Valencia.

During the 15th century the city became very prosperous and the
population grew from around 4,000 to about 80,000 and this period
of prosperity lasted through the next century as well. When the
Moors and Jews were expelled from Spain very early in the 17th
century, the city lost nearly a third of its population and a period of
decline began. This continued with the repression after the War of
Succession was lost at Almansa in 1707. In 1808 there was an
independent city government against the French and Valencia
remained a walled town until 1865.

The advent of new forms of transport combined with new
industries and its traditional citrus fruit products enabled the city to
begin to grow again during the late 9th and early 10th centuries. For
a short period during the Civil War, November 1936 to October
1937, the city was the headquarters of the Republican Government.
In 1982 Valencia became the capital of the Autonomous Region
consisting of the provinces of Valencia, Alicante and Castellón.

Although the city is very large the vast majority of the *Places of
interest* are located in the old area of town bordered by the railway
station and the dried up bed of the River Turia. This area is large
enough that one can wander around and explore it, coming across
all kinds of surprises such as the numerous churches and palaces not
detailed below, yet small enough that all the important places can be
reached easily. In fact Valencia has a really pleasant atmosphere,
full of Mediterranean charm but without the modern, trendy, image
that spoils Barcelona. And unlike Barcelona, almost all the museums
and other places of interest are free, or very inexpensive.

One thing that should be mentioned is the *Las Fallas* fiesta held
every March. This unusual and interesting fiesta in honour of Saint

Joseph, the patron saint of carpenters, dates from the Middle Ages when carpenters burnt their accumulated wood shavings in bonfires (*fallas*). Today there are very elaborate and colourful papier-mâché and cardboard figures that depict local customs, current events, etc, on every street corner. All, except the one judged to be the best, are put to the torch on the night of March 19 and this is combined with fantastic fireworks displays. If you go, beware of the loud firecrackers thrown everywhere, especially behind the unsuspecting.

Places of interest
Must see
Catedral, Museo de la Catedral y El Miguelete (Cathedral, Cathedral Museum and El Miguelete Tower), Plaza de la Reina; tel: 391 81 27. Open March to May and October to November Monday to Saturday 1000-1330, 1630-1800, June to September 1630-1900; Sunday and holidays 1000-1330. Entrance: Museum and El Miguelete 100 ptas each. Although construction of the cathedral was begun in 1262, on the site of a Roman temple and mosque, the largest parts date from the 14th and 15th centuries. Inside it is very wide but not particularly high and there is not much stained glass. The museum is rather run of the mill, the most interesting feature being the unfinished octagonal Gothic tower, El Miguelete. For the adventurous and fit the views from the top are well worth the effort. It really is difficult though; there are 207 steps up a winding, narrow, concrete staircase that actually gets smaller as you get closer to the viewing platform — at an altitude of 70m — offering unparalleled vistas of the city.

If you are in Valencia on a Thursday there is a ceremony that you should not miss. In the area around Valencia there are over 2,300 acres of irrigated land (*huerta*) with some canals originating over 2,000 years ago. The Tribunal de Aguas (Water Council), consisting of eight men, meets at noon outside the cathedral doors of the Apostles to adjudicate over disputes. The business of this tribunal, which has met for over a thousand years, is conducted verbally in the local language, Valenciano, and all decisions are final.

La Lonja Plaza del Mercado; tel: 391 36 08. Open Tuesday to Saturday 1000-1330, 1700-2100; Sunday and holidays 1000-1400. Closed Monday. Entrance: free. Located just opposite the Mercado Central this was built during 1483-98 at the request of the silk merchants and has had a variety of uses since then. On the outside it is a rather bland and innocuous looking building, but don't be put off. Inside it is very beautiful and the main hall has the most elegant, and unusual, twisted stone columns and there is also a small garden. Quite often it is used for exhibitions of one sort or another.

Mercado Central (Central Market), Plaza del Mercado. It is not often that a food market features as a *Must see* in this guide but the Mercado Central is well worthy of its place. Built to an irregular design — seen best from the top of El Miguelete, the cathedral tower — at the beginning of this century its area of about 8,000m² makes it one of the largest in Europe. The best time to go is in the morning when the array of fresh food on display is staggering — most Spaniards prefer to see exactly what, and how fresh, it is they are buying. There is also a variety of tourist shops outside selling wineskins and paella pans, both in any size you may want.

Museo de Cerámica 'Gonzalez Marti' (National Ceramics Museum) Rinconada García Sanchís; tel: 351 63 92. Unfortunately closed for restoration work during the latter part of 1993, the museum is located in the impressive Marqués Dos Aguas palace and I have been assured that it should not be missed if open.

By choice
Academia Real de Bellas Artes de San Carlos (Fine Arts Museum), San Pío V. tel: 360 57 93. Open Monday to Saturday 0900-1500; Sunday and holidays 1000-1400. Entrance: free. Located in an old convent that is itself of interest, this is an important provincial gallery that, alongside many important international and Spanish works, has an important collection from the Valencian school. There are also contemporary art and archaeological sections.

Jardínes del Real (Jardínes Viveros) (Royal Gardens), San Pío V; tel: 362 35 12. Open daily 0800 to dusk. Entrance: free. Located just outside the Turia riverbed these once surrounded the Royal Palace. Today, besides flower gardens, there is a children's recreation area and zoo here.

Jardín Botánico (Botanical Gardens), Beato Gaspar Bono. tel: 391 16 57. Open Tuesday to Sunday 1000-2100. Closed Monday. Entrance: 50 ptas. Containing many thousands of species of plants, these were the first gardens of their kind in Spain.

Jardín Zoológico (Zoological Gardens), San Pío V. — In the Viveros Gardens. Open daily 1000-1900. Entrance: adults 300 ptas, children 150 ptas.

La Armoina Located just behind the cathedral this site has excavations from the following periods: Republican Roman — 173 BC to 75 BC, Imperial Roman — 1st to 3rd centuries AD, Visigothic — 6th to 8th centuries, Islamic — 8th to 13th centuries, and late medieval — 13th to 14th centuries.

Palacio de la Generalitat (Generalidad Palace), Caballeros, 2; tel: 386 34 61. Open, by previous arrangement only, 0900-1400. This is a very attractive 15th century Gothic building that has a small garden at one end. It was originally the assembly hall of the *Cortes* (parliament) but this was disbanded by Felipe V in 1707. It now houses the Diputación (city council) and, if you don't want to visit all of it just have a quick look through the main door.

Plaza de la Redonda (Round Plaza) Although not a 'classic' tourist spot I still think this should be seen, if you have time, as it is rather unusual. The format, a circular plaza with shops on the outside and another inner ring of shops, is something I have not seen anywhere else. On Sundays and holidays open-air markets are held here.

Torres de Cuart (Quart Towers) These, providing access to the city from the west, were built in the 15th century. They are very imposing if slightly less decorative than the Serrano Towers.

Torres de Serranos (Serrano Towers) Built in the 14th century these are very elegant: twin, octagonal-shaped crenellated towers with very unusual fortifications attached to the outside two-thirds of the way up. These are joined by a central fortification with a fairly small gateway at its base. The towers also house the Museo Marítimo.

Museums

Casa-Museo Jose Benlliure (House/Museum of Jose Benlliure), Blanquerías, 23; tel: 319 16 62. Open Tuesday to Friday 0900-1330, 1600-1800; Saturday 0900-1330. Closed Sunday, Monday and holidays. Entrance: free. Only the ground floor of this artist's house can be visited; interspersed between the paintings there are fine examples of period furniture.

Centro de Artesanía Comunidad Valenciana   (Centre for Valencian Arts),   Hospital, 7; tel: 351 30 90. Open Tuesday to Saturday 1000-1400, 1700-2000; Sunday and holidays 1000-1400. Closed Monday. Entrance: free. There are typical dresses, fine silks, fans and other such handmade objects here.

Instituto Valenciano Arte Moderno - IVAM   (Valencian Institute of Modern Art), [Centre Julio González], Guillem de Castro, 118; tel: 386 30 00. Open Tuesday to Sunday 1100-2000. Closed Monday and holidays. Entrance: 250 ptas, Sunday — free.

Centro del Carme, Museo, 2. Open Tuesday to Sunday 1200-1430, 1630-2000. Closed Monday. Entrance: free. The purpose of this institute, operated under the auspices of the Regional Government of Valencia, is to act as a research and education centre for modern art in Valencia. It was inaugurated in 1989 and the modern Julio González Centre has, on permanent exhibition, collections of works by González and Pinazo as well as temporary exhibitions dedicated to the development of modern art from the classical avant-garde period to the 1970s.

The Centro del Carme is an important monument in its own right. Originally constructed as a Carmelite convent in the 13th century, important parts still exist today, and these, together with a newer wing added at the beginning of this century, are used for international exhibitions of modern art.

Museo Ciudad - Palacio Marqués de Campo   (City Museum) Plaza del Arzobispo, 3; tel: 391 02 19. Open Monday to Friday 1030-1400, 1800-2030; Saturday, Sunday and holidays 1030-1400. Entrance: free. This museum has pictures, paintings and photographs depicting how the city has changed throughout the ages. There are also exhibits that have been excavated from sites within the city.

Museos Etnológico y de Prehistoria   (Museums of Ethnology and Prehistory),   Corona, 36. tel: 391 71 66 and 391 71 64, respectively. Both are open Tuesday to Saturday 1000-1400, 1630-1830; Sunday and holidays 1000-1400. Closed Monday. Entrance:

free, for both. These two museums are both located in the same building, rather drab on the outside but more than compensated for by the unusual patios and fountains inside. The Prehistory Museum was in the process of being installed late in 1992 whilst the exhibits in the Ethnology Museum are likely to be of interest only to those specialising in the subject.

Museo del Artistas Fallero (*Fallas* festival Museum), del Ninot, 24; tel: 347 65 85. Open Monday to Friday 1000-1400, 1600-2000; Saturday and Sunday 1000-1400. Closed holidays. Entrance: adults 250 ptas, children 100 ptas. This modern museum is some way from the city centre and it is best to take bus number 13 for 65 ptas. The museum is dedicated to the world famous *Fallas* festivals that take place every March in Valencia and, to a lesser extent, in nearby towns. At this time you will see fantastically elaborate effigies on every street corner all of which, with the exception of the one designated the best, are burnt on the evening of March 19. This museum has photographs, paintings, sketches, scale models, full size models and other exhibits relating to this festival.

Museo Histórico Municipal (Municipal History Museum), Plaza Ayuntamiento, 1; tel: 352 54 78. Open Monday to Friday 0900-1400. Closed Saturday, Sunday and holidays. Entrance: free. Located on the first floor of the very elaborate town hall this small museum has many fascinating exhibits. Besides paintings, manuscripts and books there is the *Senyera*, the reconquest banner, the sword of the conqueror, James I, and a 1704 map of the city.

Museo Marítimo 'Joaquin Saludes' (Joaquin Saludes Maritime Museum), Plaza Fueros — Torres Serrano; tel: 391 90 70. Open Tuesday to Friday 0930-1330, 1600-1800; Saturday 0900-1330. Closed Sunday, Monday and holidays. Entrance: free. The location for this museum could not be more dramatic, the Torre de Serranos (Serranos Tower) — see *By choice*. The exhibits, mainly model ships and maritime related objects recovered from the harbour, are housed in two identically sized small rooms at the base of each tower.

Museo Paleontológico Municipal (Municipal Palaeontology Museum), Arzobispo Mayoral, 1; tel: 352 54 78. Open Monday to Friday 0900-1330, 1600-1830; Saturday 0900-1330. Closed Sunday and holidays. Entrance: free. This is located on the ground floor of the town hall but the entrance is at the rear. There are only five rooms but the exhibits, ranging from small fossils to dinosaurs, are quite interesting. There is also a fine view through the ceiling into the very elaborate town hall.

Museo Taurino (Bullfighting Museum), Pasaje Doctor Serra, 18; tel: 351 18 50. Open Monday to Friday 1030-1330. Closed Saturday, Sunday and holidays. Entrance: free. This museum, located in a covered passageway/shopping centre immediately behind the ticket offices (*taquillas*) of the Plaza de Toros, has only two floors and will be of interest mainly to the bullfighting *aficionado*.

Station/location/transport to city centre
RENFE, Término, Jativa, 24; tel: 352 93 62. A traditional style station, with a very ornate and attractive façade, that is located in the centre of the city.

Layout

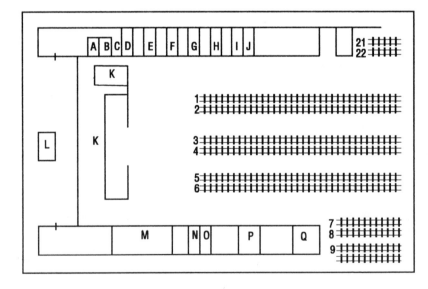

Key
A: *Télefono fax público*, open daily 0800-2200; payment can be made by Visa/Eurocard/ Mastercard

B: Librería Prodesa Rail Press, open daily 0600-2200

C: *Tábacos*, open daily 0730-2215

D: *Atencio al Viatger/Atención al Viajero*
E: *Informacio Turística/* TOURIST INFO, see *General information, Tourist offices*
F: *Cap d'Estacio/Jefe de Estación*
G: *Jefe de Circulación*
H: *Comisaría*
I: *Servicios —* women
J: *Servicios —* men
K: Tickets.

L: Train *Información*, open daily 0700-2300
M: Area Commercial — various shops, banks, bars, etc
N: *Aseos*, women and babies
O: *Aseos*, men
P: *Consigna Automática*, open 24 hours daily, 300 ptas per 24 hours
Q: Bar/cafeteria, open daily 0600-0130

Train station to town centre
On foot No need for anything else in this city centre location.

Train services
To Madrid by
	Regional	InterCity	Estrella
Cuenca	3¼		
Albacete		1¾	4
Madrid	5¾	4¼	8¾

To Barcelona by
Diurno: 4¾. InterCity: 4¼. Talgo: 4½. Estrella: 5.

To Irún/France
Estrella: via Albacete 2½; Madrid 6¼; Burgos 10¼; Irún 14¼.

To Almería by
Diurno: via Alcázar de San Juan 3½; Almería 9¾.

To Badajoz by
Diurno: via Alcázar de San Juan 3½; Ciudad Real 5; Mérida 8¾; Badajoz 9¾.
Estrella: via Alcázar de San Juan 4¾; Ciudad Real 5¾; Mérida 9¾; Badajoz 10¾.

To Cádiz by
Diurno: via Alcázar de San Juan 3¼; Córdoba 7; Sevilla 8½; Cádiz 10½.
Estrella: via Alcázar de San Juan 4¼; Córdoba 8¼; Sevilla 10; Cádiz 12¼.

To Granada by
Diurno: via Alcázar de San Juan 3½; Granada 9.

Accommodation
There are so many hotels, of all different classes, in the streets directly to the left of, and in front of, the station that I will only detail those belonging to the Grupo Husa.

**** Hotel Reina Victoria Barcas, 4; tel: 352 04 87; fax: 352 04 84. This very distinguished hotel was fully renovated in 1989 and is located in the centre of the city just off the Plaza Ayuntamiento, just five minutes' walk from the station. There are 97 rooms all with private bath, air-conditioning, telephone, colour TV, piped music and a safe deposit box. There are two seasons: high, March, April, May, August, September and October and low the rest of the year. Single high, 8,500 ptas, low 7,000 ptas; double high, 13,000 ptas, low 11,000 ptas; double, for single use, high 10,400 ptas, low 8,800 ptas; triple high, 15,200 ptas, low 13,000 ptas.

*** Hotel Serrano General Urrutia, 48; tel: 334 78 00; fax: 334 78 01. This hotel is located in its own grounds just a short walk away from the city centre. There are 105 rooms all with private bath, air-conditioning, telephone and colour TV. Unusually, for a city centre hotel, there are also tennis courts and a swimming pool besides a restaurant and café-bar. Single 10,164 ptas; double 12,650 ptas.

General information
Car hire
Avis, Isabel la Católica, 17; tel: 351 07 34.

Consulate telephone numbers
France — 352 41 25; USA — 351 69 73.

Fiestas
Las Fallas (San José). One week ending on March 19; Easter week (*Semana Santa*) variable dates and the July Fair in the second half of that month.

Laundromat
Lavandería Automática, Pelayo, 13. Open Monday to Friday 0900-1400, 1600-2000; Saturday 0900-1400, 1600-1800. Closed Sunday and holidays. Cost *lavado* (washing) 300 ptas; *secado* (drying) 300 ptas; *jabón* (soap) 100 ptas. Come out of the station and Pelayo is the second road on the left; the laundromat is about 300 metres down the road.

Lost property
Lost and found department; tel: 352 54 78 ext 184.

Police
Comisaría, Gran Vía de Ramón y Cajal, 40; tel: 321 45 73.

Radio taxis
Tele-Taxi, 357 13 13 or Radio Taxi 370 33 33.

Public telephones
Plaza del Ayuntamiento. Open Monday to Saturday 0900-2300. Closed Sunday and holidays. On the side of the plaza closest to the railway station.

Telephone code
for Valencia province is (96).

Tourist office
Oficina de Información Turística, Plaza de Ayuntamiento, 1; tel: 351 04 17. Open Monday to Friday 0830-1415, 1615-1815; Saturday 0915-1245. Located in the town hall just about 200m directly in front of the station.
TOURIST INFO — Informacio Turística, open Monday to Friday 0900-2200; Saturday, Sunday and holidays 1100-1900. Located in the station this offers documentation that is different from, but complements, that of the other tourist office. It also has a variety of gifts and the T-shirts are very good value at 500 ptas.

VALLADOLID
The city
Located at an altitude of 692m (2,270ft) and 192km (120 miles) from Madrid, Valladolid has a population of over 300,000 and is the capital of the province of the same name, one of nine in the autonomous region of Castilla and León. Between the 12th and 17th centuries the Castilian kings resided here, in 1469 Ferdinand from Aragón and Isabella of Castile, who united Spain, were married here, several kings were born here and Christopher Columbus died here. It was the capital of the empire during the reigns of Felipe II and Felipe III and, in 1809, Napoleon made it his headquarters. As a consequence of this illustrious history there are many beautiful buildings and several very interesting museums. These are spread around what is otherwise a pleasant, but fairly bland, modern city.

Places of interest
Must see
Catedral y Museo Diocesano (Cathedral and Museum), Plaza Universidad; tel: 30 43 62. The museum is open Tuesday to Friday 1000-1330, 1630-1900; Saturday, Sunday and holidays 1000-1400. Closed Monday. Entrance: 200 ptas. The cathedral was commissioned by Felipe II in the late 16th century but was not completed until much later. The inside is large, rather plain, and considerably less ornate than most of its kind. For 25 ptas the Chapel of San Simón de la Rojas can be illuminated. From the outside the dominant feature is the large statue of Christ that adorns the top of the tower.

The museum, on the other hand, is particularly striking both for its architecture and exhibits. There are ten rooms of these and perhaps the most interesting are the large 13th century sepulchre, the lifesize statues, and one of Juan de Arfe's masterpieces, a monstrance dating from 1587.

Museo Nacional de Escultura y Colegio de San Gregorio (National Sculpture Museum and College of St Gregory), Cadenas de San Gregorio, 1; tel: 25 03 75. Open Tuesday to Saturday 1000-1400, 1600-1800; Sunday 1000-1400. Closed Monday and holidays. Entrance: 200 ptas; citizens of EC (under 21) free. This is a must, both for the building and its contents. Fray Alonso de Burgos — the Confessor to Isabella — founded the Colegio de San Gregorio in the late 15th century and the building is simply stunning. The main points of interest are the ornately carved exterior, the unusual wooden ceilings, and the patio which is considered to be one of the most beautiful in Spain. The National Sculpture Museum was founded in 1933 and the exhibits, many of wood, are of a Spanish religious nature. Although important they could be a little monotonous for those not religiously inclined.

By choice
Note: Many of the following places are not open to the public.

Capitánia General Located in the Plaza de San Pablo, this used to be the Royal Palace.

Churches There are numerous churches of interest in Valladolid, some of which are open and some not. **San Pablo**, next to the National Sculpture Museum has a very ornate façade whilst **San Benito**, founded by Juan I of Castile in 1388, is very large and has a most unusual entrance.

Colegio de Santa Cruz (College of Holy Cross) Founded in 1479 this is another building with an elegant façade.

Palacio de los Pimentel (Pimentel Palace) Another of the elegant buildings located around the Plaza de San Pablo; Felipe II was born here in 1527.

Palaces There are several palaces spread around the city.

Plaza Mayor Although very elegant and rather large, this plaza with a statue of Count Ansurez in the centre is spoilt somewhat by all the traffic.

Museums
Casa de Cervantes (Cervantes' House), Rastro, 7; tel: 30 88 10. Open Tuesday to Saturday 1000-1530; Sunday 1000-1400. Closed Monday and holidays. Entrance: 200 ptas; citizens of EC (under 21) free. This delightful house, with an impressive small garden, is totally different from its immediate surroundings and the furniture and artefacts are typical of those of a nobleman in the very early 17th century. The old pictures show that a river used to run through the garden.

Casa de Colón (Christopher Columbus' House), Colón. tel: 29 13 53. Open Tuesday to Saturday 1000-1400, 1600-1800; Sunday 1030-1400. Closed Monday and holidays. Entrance: free. This building is on the site of a house where Columbus spent the last years of his life until his death in 1509. The exhibits are related to his travels and a large map of the world traces each journey.

Casa de Zorrilla (Zorrilla's House), Fray Luís de Granada; tel: 25 85 73. Open Tuesday to Saturday 1000-1400, 1600-1800; Sunday 1030-1400. Closed Monday and holidays. Do not be put off because this house is difficult to find and has a rather unprepossessing façade. The poet José Zorrilla was born here in 1817; the furniture and other memorabilia in the surprisingly numerous rooms show just how a man of his standing was able to live in the 19th century.

Convento San Joaquin y Santa Ana (Convent of Sts Joaquín and Ana), Plaza de Santa Ana, 4; tel: 35 76 72. Open Monday to Thursday and Saturday 1030-1300, 1600-1900; Sunday 1030-1200. Closed Friday and holidays. Entrance: 100 ptas. Pay attention to the entrance here: there is a strange wooden apparatus that revolves to allow the nuns to take your entrance money, and return the ticket, without being seen. Once inside this 18th century convent there are six rooms of important examples of religious paintings, sculptures, objects and other ornaments including a collection of Christchild figures. The church itself is also unusual: it has a large dome, wooden floor, and paintings, including Goyas, around the walls. The choir is in an entirely separate room.

Museo Arqueológico Provincial (Provincial Archaeological Museum), Plaza de Fabio Nelli. tel: 35 13 89. Open Tuesday to Friday 1000-1400, 1600-1900 (1700-2000 during July and August); Saturday and Sunday 1000-1400. Closed Monday and holidays. Entrance: 200 ptas; citizens of EC (under 21) free. Again, like other places here, this museum housed in the 16th century Palacio de Fabio Nelli is not that easy to find. There is a three-sided patio, with an elegant stairway, and the archaeological exhibits — mainly originating in this province — from prehistoric, Bronze Age, Roman, Visigoth and Moorish periods are displayed in chronological order. There are also sections for fine arts and the history of the city.

Museo Oriental (Oriental Museum), Paseo Filipinos, 7; tel: 30 68 00. Open Monday to Saturday 1600-1900; Sunday 1000-1400. Closed holidays. Entrance: 250 ptas; Students free. This museum is located away from all the other places of interest, on the side of the Campo Grande closest to the railway station, in the neoclassical 18th century Real Colegio de los Padres Agustinos Filipinos (Royal College of the Agustinian fathers).

Considered to have the best collection of its kind in Spain, the museum was inaugurated by the King and Queen of Spain on October 12 1980. The first room has an historical introduction and this is followed by nine dedicated to China and four to the Philippines.

Station/location/transport to city centre
RENFE, Campo Grande, Recondo; tel: 30 34 00. This is located away from the main places of interest, on the other side of the Campo Grande.

Layout

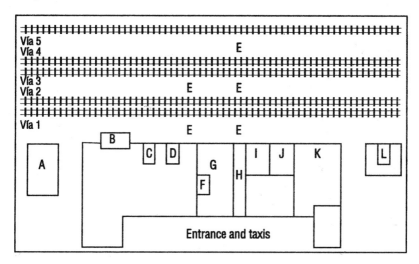

Key
A: *Consigna Automática*, open daily all day, cost 200 ptas a day and a 200 ptas a day excess charge
B: *Kiosco* for newspapers, magazines, etc, open 0600-2100

C: *Oficina de Circulación*
D: *Comisaría*
E: Underpass to other platforms
F: Train Información
G: Booking hall

H: Ticket office
I: *Sala Espera*
J: *Jefe de Estación*
K: Cafeteria, open 24 hours;

restaurant open 1400-1600, 2000-2200
L: *Servicios*

Note: This station was undergoing extensive renovation that may change some of the above.

Train station to city centre
On foot Come straight out of the station and follow, along the Campo Grande, the Acero de Recoletos to the Plaza Zorrilla then bear right, on to the Calle de Santiago, direct to the Plaza Mayor. This takes about 15 minutes.

By taxi This takes about 5 minutes, depending upon traffic conditions, and costs about 300 ptas.

Train services
To Madrid by
	Regional Express	InterCity	Regional Estrella
Ávila	1¼	1	1¾
Madrid	2¾	2½	3¾

To Irún/France by
	Diurno	InterCity	Estrella
Burgos	1½	1	1½
Irún	5½	4½	6¼

To Barcelona by
Estrella: via Burgos 1¼; Zaragoza 6; Barcelona 10.

To León by
Regional Express: León 2.

To Salamanca by
Diurno: Salamanca 1¼.

Accommodation
Close to the station
* **Hostal Avenida** Acera de Recoletos, 23; tel: 30 21 91. Single 1,500 ptas; double 2,500 ptas. No baths. Plain and old-fashioned.

* **Hostal Colón** Acera de Recoletos, 22; tel: 30 40 44. Single 1,961 ptas; double without bath 3,286 ptas, with bath 4,028 ptas.

In the city
** **Hotel Roma** Heroes del Alcázar de Toledo, 8; tel: 35 18 33. Single 4,600 ptas; double 6,000 ptas. Very nice with all facilities. In a pedestrian mall close to Plaza Mayor.
** **HR de la Torre** Alcallerres, 1; tel: 35 02 13. Single 4,00 ptas; double 5,500 ptas. Most facilities including TV; very small rooms. Very close to Galerías Preciados.
* **HR Enara** Plaza España, 5; tel: 30 02 11. Single 4,000 ptas; double 5,500 ptas. Very unusual. Antique style decor; incongruous with its surroundings.
* **HR Nueva York** Doctrinos, 8; tel: 35 42 01. Single 1,100 ptas; double 2,100 ptas. No baths in rooms; ordinary. Close to Plaza Zorrilla.
* **Hostal Miño** Plaza Mayor, 9; tel: 35 36 61. Single 1,600 ptas; double 3,200 ptas. Very clean and medium size rooms. Very central location.
* **Pensión Los Molinos** Nuñez de Arca, 5; tel: 30 98 42. Single 1,000 ptas; double 1,800 ptas. No baths and rooms basic. Close to cathedral.
CH Teyla del Correo, 7; tel: none. Single 1,100 ptas; double 2,100 ptas. Close to Plaza Mayor. Second floor and basic.

General information
Car hire
Avis, Felipe II, 3; tel: 35 60 93.

Police
Comisaría, Fray Luís Granada; tel: 26 37 04.

Telephone code
for Valladolid province is (983).

Public telephones
Plaza Mayor, 7. Open Monday to Saturday 0930-1400, 1630-2200. Closed Sunday and holidays.

Tourist office
Oficina de Información de Turismo, Plaza de Zorrilla, 3; tel: 35 18 01. Open Monday to Friday 0900-1400, 1600-1800; Saturday 0900-1400. Closed Sunday and holidays.

ZAFRA

The city

Located at an altitude of 509m in the province of Badajoz, one of
the two provinces of the autonomous region of Extremadura (the
other is Cáceres), Zafra has a population of about 15,000. The
original Moorish settlement founded during the 11th century was
known as Zafar and since 1395 it has been famous for its livestock
fairs. It became one of the most prosperous towns in Extremadura
at the end of the middle ages and during the 16th and 17th centuries.
During this period it was famous for its artisan workshops and the
tanning industry. In 1883 it was granted the status of a city by King
Alfonso XII.

Although designated in 1965 a Site of Interest to Art and
Architecture, Zafra is overlooked by most visitors as it does not
have any particularly famous places of interest. Actually this rather
adds to its charm as it has consequently remained unspoilt by
tourism. Those stopping here — one night is more than sufficient —
will see a delightful city that, despite its location in Extremadura, is
very Andalusian in style, hence its nickname *Sevilla la Chica* (Little
Seville).

Another point of interest is the lifestyle, especially in the summer
when it becomes extremely hot. During the afternoon almost
everyone takes a traditional *siesta* and very little stirs until 1730-
1800. Then late at night the plazas, particularly the Plaza de España,
become social gathering places for everyone — including very young
children — until well into the early hours.

Places of interest

This is simply a selection of the most interesting places to see, listed
in alphabetical order.

Alcázar (Fortress) Construction of the classical fortress was begun
in 1437 and completed in 1443. The coats of arms that can be seen
on the façade and throughout the building are those of Don Lorenzo
Súarez de Figueroa, the first Count of Feria, who supervised the
construction, and his wife. It was transformed into a palace during
the 16th century and today it has been restored and converted into
a luxury hotel, as part of the Parador Nacional chain. It is named
after Hernán Cortes, the Conquistador of Mexico, who was a
protégé of the one time owner, the Duke of Feria.

Arco de Jerez (Jerez Arch) Set in the old walls, on the Calle
Fernando Moreno Marquez, this small archway has an integral chapel
that has the Guild of Tanners as a patron. It is also home to a very
large stork's nest that is unusual only because of its low height.

Bodega Medina Cestería, 4. Open Monday to Friday 1000-1300,
1800-2000; Saturday 1000-1400. Closed Sunday and holidays. A
small *bodega* (wine cellar), located in a street about 400m to the
right of the Arco de Jerez.

Colegiata de la Candelaria (Candelaria Church). This Gothic/
Renaissance style church, the most dominant church in the city, was
built in the 16th century.

Convento de Santa Clara (Convent of St Clara) This convent, in
a somewhat hidden location of a pedestrian walkway, was founded
by Don Gomez Súarez de Figueroa in 1428.

Plaza Grande and Plaza Chica These two charming plazas are
located next to each other in the heart of the old city. As the name
implies Grande is rather larger, porticoed with a fountain, and the
surrounding houses date from the 18th and 19th centuries. Chica is
much smaller and has been restored: it was inaugurated by the King
and Queen on March 9 1977, but the houses are somewhat older as
they date from the 15th to 17th centuries.

    As delightful as these two plazas are they take on a somewhat
different character at night when the numerous surrounding bars are
taken over by local youths. As the noise continues late into the
night/early morning this causes conflict with the local residents.

Station/location/transport to city centre
RENFE, Estación; tel: 55 02 15. This is a small station located
some distance outside the city and very few trains stop here.

Key
A:	*Servicios*	**G:**	*Tracción*
B:	*Sala de Espera*	**H:**	Bar, open 1130-2330.
C:	Ticket office.		Restaurant; open *desayuno* (breakfast)
D:	*Circulación*		0700-1100, *comidas* (lunch) 1300-
E:	*Jefe de Estación*		1500, *cenas* (dinner) 2000-2230
F:	Material		

Layout

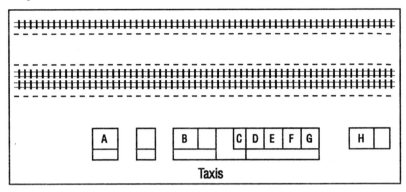

Taxis

Train station to city centre

By taxi This is the most practical way and if there are not any taxis at the station call for one on 55 10 24 or 55 10 41. Alternatively you might be met, as I was, by a man with a minibus operating his own private service.

Train services
To Sevilla by
Regional: Sevilla 2¾.

To Cáceres by
Regional: via Mérida 1; Cáceres 2¼.

To Huelva by
Regional: Huelva 4.

Accommodation
In the city
Parador Nacional Hernán Cortes Plaza de María Cristina; tel: 55 02 00. Very expensive but, in true parador style, a real historic monument; see *Places of interest*.

*** **Hotel Huerta Honda** López Asme, 30; tel: 55 41 00. Single 4,500 ptas, double 6,500 ptas. A very nice hotel. The double rooms are appreciably nicer than the singles. Pool. Air-conditioning only in doubles.

** **Hotel Don Quijote** Huelva, 3; tel: 55 47 71. Single 5,000 ptas, double 8,000 ptas. Very nice but a little expensive. All facilities except a pool. In the centre of the old town.

* **Hotel El Ancla** Plaza España, 8; tel: 55 43 82. Single 3,000 ptas, double 6,000 ptas. Pleasant hotel and restaurant. Across from a charming park.

* Pensión Rafael Virgen de Guadalupe, 7; tel: 55 20 52. Single with bath 1,750 ptas, without bath 1,100; double with bath 3,300 ptas, without bath 2,200 ptas. Charming family-run pension; very good value indeed.

General information
Fiesta
The main fiesta, the *Feria de San Miguel*/Extremadura Regional Agriculture Fair, is held in early October.

Police
Policia Municipal, Plaza Pilar Redondo; tel: 55 45 13.

Telephone code
for Badajoz province is (924).

Tourist office
Oficina de Información Turística, Plaza de España; tel: 55 10 36.

ZARAGOZA
The city
History
Before Roman times the city had been called Salduba. Some of the most important dates are:

19BC   The Romans under Emperor Caesar Augustus conquer the city, calling it Caesaraugusta and awarding it the privilege of an Immune Colony.

472   The Gothic army defeats the Romans and takes over the city.

714   The Moors, led by Musa ibn Nusayr, enter the city without resistance. It is renamed Sarakosta. After the fall of Córdoba the city is taken over by the Benihud dynasty, marking the beginning of a period of cultural splendour when, amongst other places, the Aljafería Palace is constructed.

1118   After a seven-month siege Alfonso I ('The Fighter') reconquers the city for the Christians. The city becomes the medieval capital.

14th C   In the middle of the 14th century the exterior walls are constructed.

1473   Spain's first printing press is set up.

1808   During the War of Independence Napoleon's troops besiege the city between June and August 14. The siege is lifted after the French defeat at Bailén. Another siege, led by General Lannes and nearly 20,000 troops, begins on December 21 and lasts until the city surrenders on February 20 1809. Over 55,000 citizens, half the population, are killed from a combination of battle, various epidemics and famine.

Overview
Zaragoza has a population of 600,000 and is the capital both of the autonomous region of Aragón and of Provincia de Zaragoza, one of Aragon's three provinces, the others being Huesca and Teruel. It is located at the confluence of the rivers Ebro, Gallego and Huerva in the heart of the Ebro valley, 325km (203 miles) from Madrid, 296km (185 miles) from Barcelona and at an altitude of 200m above sea level. Although it has 20 centuries of rich history much of the city is relatively modern; this is because it was rebuilt during the 19th century after the extensive damage suffered during the Wars of

Independence. In fact it is one of only five Augustan cities on the Iberian Peninsula; Lugo, Mérida, Astorga, and Braga in Portugal are the others. A stop here, but for no more than a day or day and a half, is well worthwhile, especially as most of the places you should see are very close together in the old town. The city authorities have succeeded, where many other places have failed, in the juxtaposition of modern statues and fountains with historic buildings in this area. The result is an absolute delight.

When I stayed in the city in 1965, a meal for two people was 45 ptas, a double room 80 ptas, two bottles of sparkling water 14 ptas and a half litre of wine 7 ptas. A total of 146 ptas, just over 80 pence at 1993 rates of exchange. How times change!

Places of interest
Must see
The old town Zaragoza is a little different from other towns as almost everything that there is to see is located in a fairly small rectangular area, bordered by the River Ebro and the streets of Coso and Avenida César Augusto. Since many of the places of interest are close to each other, everything is listed as *Must see*. The Basílica del Pilar and the Cathedral of La Seo are listed first and then the others are in alphabetical order.

There are numerous alleys and passageways and many fascinating old buildings, churches and shops in this area, as well as several attractive buildings surrounding La Seo, including La Maestranza and the House of Dean, but they are not open to the public. What makes it somewhat different are the modern statues and fountains that are found here, often next to old monuments; an example is the fountain and 'modern' walls next to the Roman walls. The finest example of how the old and new have been combined is the Plaza del Pilar. This long, narrow, pedestrian walkway has large, spectacular fountains at either end with smaller examples of modern art in between and historic buildings down one side and at either end. It is one of the finest mixtures of old and new that I have seen and is at its best at night when it is beautifully illuminated, preferably viewed from one of the outside bars as you enjoy a cool drink.

Basílica del Pilar (Pilar Cathedral) Open: church, 0545-2100, entrance free. Museo de Pilar; 0900-1400, 1600-1800, entrance: 100 ptas. Photography is not allowed. This is by far the largest and most dramatic building in the area. The skyline is dominated by the four thin towers at each corner which protect a series of colourful cupolas that, in turn, surround a central dome. Legend has it that in January of 40 AD the Virgin appeared to St James, and there is a very small hollow in one of the pillars dedicated to her memory. The present basilica was designed by Francisco Herrera in 1677 and is a very grand, formal church with many items of architectural and artistic interest. The museum is very small and, amongst other things, there are memorabilia of Pope John Paul's visit.

La Seo Catedral (Cathedral La Seo) Open 0730-2100. This was consecrated in 1119 and is on the site of the old mosque. It has a large, single tower and, despite being much smaller, it appears to have more interesting characteristics than the Basílica del Pilar. Unfortunately it has been closed for some time because of extensive renovations and these are planned to continue, possibly for years.

Iglesia de Magdalena (Magdalena Church) This small church, located a short distance away from the other places of interest, has a very beautiful Mudejar tower. Only the church itself is open to the public.

La Lonja This was built during 1541-51 for use as a commercial exchange and is considered to be an important example of Aragonese Renaissance architecture. In the 18th century it was used as a theatre and today, having been cleaned up so that it looks a little out of place, the town council uses it for art exhibitions, etc. Unfortunately it only seems to be open on such occasions.

Muralla Romana (Roman Walls) Originally there were over 200 fortified towers along 3,000m of the walls but what remains now was renovated in the 3rd century. They have been tastefully improved by the addition of modern sculptures and a small fountain.

Museo Pablo Gargallo (Pablo Gargallo Museum), Plaza de San Felipe, 3; tel: 39 20 58. Open Tuesday to Sunday 1000-1300, 1700-2100. Closed Monday. Entrance free. This museum, dedicated to the work of Pablo Gargallo, is small but has very interesting exhibits. There are modern sculptures and fascinating face masks; outside in the interesting plaza there are also examples of his work.

The building itself, the Argillo Palace, which originates from the 17th century, is a delight.

Museo Camón Aznar (Camón Aznar Museum), Espoz y Mina, 23; tel: 39 73 28. Open Tuesday to Friday 1000-1400; Saturday 1000-1330; Sunday 1100-1400. Closed Monday, holidays and August. This museum contains the art collection donated to Aragón by the distinguished academic Don José Camón Aznar, who lived in Zaragoza.

Torreón de Forte (Tower of Forte) Although this is considered to be the most important example of 15th century Mudejar architecture in the city it is not that impressive from the outside and cannot be visited. It is located in the charming Plaza de San Felipe that has modern statues and a fountain surrounded by charming old buildings (see *Museo Pablo Gargallo*).

Torreón de Zuda (Tower of Zuda) This is all that remains of the palace of Zuda which was the residence of the Muslim governors. There were additions in the 15th and 16th centuries but today only the ground floor is open and is used as a tourist office.

Bodegas Almau Estebanes, 10. tel: 29 98 34. Although not a recognised tourist spot this small *bodega* is typical of a dying breed. There is an impressive array of wines, spirits and liqueurs. Try a glass of Aragonese wine in the tiny bar.

Museo de Bellas Artes (Fine Arts Museum), Plaza de los Sitios, 6; tel: 22 21 81. Open Tuesday to Saturday 0900-1400; Sunday 1000-1400. Closed Monday and holidays. Entrance: Foreigners resident in Spain and citizens of the EC under 21 free. Others 200 ptas. Located in a graceful building dating from 1908 and built for the Hispano-French exhibition. The archaeology exhibits are on the ground floor and date from prehistoric times to the Muslim era. Fine arts is on the second floor and covers works from the 12th to 20th centuries. One room is dedicated to Goya's works, including his self portrait.

Palacio de la Aljaferia (Palace of Aljaferia), Avenida de Madrid. Open Tuesday to Sunday (summer) 1000-1400, 1630-2000, (winter) 1000-1400, 1630-1830. All year holidays 1000-1400. Closed

Monday. Entrance: free. This was originally built by the Moorish governor, Abu Jafar Ahamed Almoctadir, between 1047 and 1081. When Zaragoza was reconquered in 1118 it became the residence of the Christian monarchs. It has since been added to and changed on many occasions but perhaps the most important alterations, artistically, were by the Catholic Monarchs in 1492. Today the palace resembles a small castle, surrounded by a moat. Unfortunately the most interesting part, the palace of the Catholic Monarchs and, especially, the distinguished throne room, has been closed for some time because of extensive renovations, which may take years. It also houses the Aragones parliament (*Cortes de Aragón*). As the palace is some distance from the old town you might prefer to take the number 22 bus from the Plaza de España.

Station/location/transport to city centre

El Portillo, Avenida de José Anselmo Clavé; tel: 22 14 95. This modern station is located away from the 'old town' where most of the places of tourist interest are found. It is much closer to the Plaza de Toros and the Palacio de la Aljaferia. The majority of the facilities are on the concourse above the platforms but some of the latter have small cafeterias and automatic drink machines.

Layout

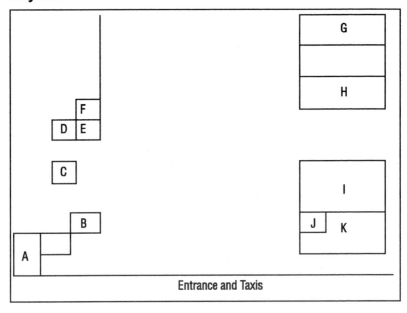

Key

A: *Consigna Automática*, 200 ptas a day. Tokens are bought from the *equipajes* attendant
B: *Equipajes*
C: *Tabacos* and general shop for food, drink, souvenirs, etc, open 0700-2300
D/E: *Servicios*
F: *Librería*, books, magazines, open 0730-2000

G: *Oficina de Atención al cliente*, open Monday to Friday 1600-2000, closed Saturday, Sunday and holidays
H: *Artículos Regalos*, a small gift shop, open 1000-1900
I: Ticket office
J: *Train Información*
K: Cafeteria/Restaurant, cafeteria open all day, restaurant open 1230-1615, 2100-2330

Train station to town centre

By bus The number 22 bus runs to and from the station and the Plaza de España in the centre of town every 10-15 minutes. The stop is outside on the Avenida Clavé and the fare is 30 ptas.

By taxi The journey, out of the rush hour, takes about five minutes and costs around 250 ptas.

Train services
To Madrid by

	Diurno	Inter City	Talgo	Talgo Pen	Talgo Camas	Estrella
Calatayud	1¼	¾	1			
Madrid	3¾	3¼	3½	3¼	4¼	4¼

To Barcelona by

	Diurno	Talgo	Talgo Pen	Talgo Camas	Estrella
Barcelona	4	4¼	3¾	4¾	5

To Irún/France by

	Diurno	Estrella
Pamplona	2	3½
Irún	4½	6½

To León/Salamanca

	Diurno	Estrella
Burgos	3½	4
León	5½	6
Valladolid	6½	
Salamanca	8	

To Valencia by
Regional: via Teruel 3½; Valencia 6¾.

Accommodation
Close to the station
** **Hostal Milmarcos** Madre Sacramento, 40; tel: 22 43 84. Single 3,500 ptas; double 4,800 ptas. In a bland building; all rooms have TV, bath and telephone. Close to the station but a little expensive.
Fonda La Ferrovía Madre Sacramento, 53. Single 1,500 ptas; double 2,000 ptas. Small and basic. No phone. Diagonally across from the station — two minutes away.

Close to the Palacio de la Aljaferia
* **Hostal Montaña** Castillo, 10; tel: 43 57 02. Single 1,300 ptas; double 2,000 ptas. In a side street next to the palacio. A little run down; no baths or showers in the 30 rooms. Quiet.

Between the old town and the Palacio de la Aljaferia
* **Hotel Posada de las Almas** San Pablo, 20-22; tel: 43 97 00. Single 2,725 ptas; double 3,825 ptas. Garage bar and restaurant. Rather unusual old-fashioned Aragonese atmosphere. In a passageway close to the Roman walls.
** **HR Conde Blanco** Predicadores, 84; tel: 44 14 11. Single 3,200 ptas; double 4,500 ptas. A large, modern, impressive building with less impressive surroundings.
* **Pensión Holgado** Conde de Aranda, 123; tel: 43 20 74. Single 1,600 ptas; double 2,900 ptas. Clean and pleasant. On third floor with 32 rooms. Close to the Aljaferia and Plaza de Toros.
CH Aragón Conde de Aragón, 45; tel: 44 03 98. Single 2,000 ptas; double 2,500 ptas. Only four rooms and on a busy street.

In the old town
*** **Hotel Vía Romana** Don Jaime I, 54-56; tel: 39 82 15. This modern hotel, with a marvellous location just off the Plaza Pilar, was opened in 1988 and is part of the Husa chain. It has 78 rooms all with private bath, air-conditioning, colour TV, telephone and some, on the corner, have views over the plaza. There are two seasons; high during the *ferias* and low the rest of the year. Single low 6,200 ptas, high 8,400 ptas; double low 9,000 ptas, high 12,500 ptas; double for single use, low 7,200 ptas, high 9,800 ptas; triple low 12,150 ptas, high 16,875 ptas.
*** **Hotel Oriente** Coso, 11-13; tel: 39 80 61. Single 4,000 ptas; double 6,000 ptas. All rooms have air-conditioning, colour TV and private bathroom. An excellent restaurant where the *menu del día*, at 1,250 ptas, is

one of the best I have had.

** **Hotel Avenida** Avenida César Augusto, 55; tel: 43 93 00. Single 3,300 ptas; double 5,000 ptas. Private bathrooms but no TV or air-conditioning. Close to the Roman walls.

** **Hotel Sauce** Espoz y Mina, 33; tel: 39 01 00; fax: 39 85 97. Single 3,900 ptas; double 6,100 ptas. Very close to the Plaza del Pilar and next to the Museo Camón Aznar.

** **HR San Jorge** Mayor, 4-6; tel: 39 74 62. Single 3,225 ptas; double 4,385 ptas. All rooms have private bath; breakfast included. Just 200m from the Pilar Basílica.

* **HR España** Estebanes, 2; tel: 29 88 46. Single (without bath) 1,800 ptas; double 3,200 ptas. Rather old-fashioned. On the second floor with 32 beds.

** **Hostal Ambos Mundos** Plaza del Pilar, 16; tel: 29 97 04. Single 1,800 ptas; double 3,200 ptas. A superb location on this beautiful modern plaza that is surrounded by ancient monuments. Some rooms have views to the Pilar, Seo and La Lonja. Named 'Both Worlds'.

** **Hostal Navarra** San Vicente de Paúl, 30; tel: 29 16 84. Single 1,400 ptas, with shower 1,700 ptas; double 2,550 ptas. Very pleasant with an agreeable style. Close to the Seo.

** **Hostal Santiago** Santiago, 3-5; tel: 39 45 50. Single 1,800 ptas; double 3,200 ptas; with meals included 2,500 ptas per person. Clean and pleasant. In a side street very close to the Plaza del Pilar.

* **Pensión Penafiel** Méndes Nuñez, 38; tel: 29 97 12. Single 1,000 ptas; double 2,000 ptas. On first floor; small and plain.

* **Pensión Rex** Méndes Nuñez, 31; tel: 39 26 33. Single without bath 1,325 ptas, with bath 1,690 ptas; double without bath 2,385 ptas, with bath 3,021 ptas. Old-fashioned but clean; 20 rooms.

Fonda Manifestación Manifestación, 36; tel: 24 57 21. Single 1,500 ptas; double 2,500 ptas. Small (five rooms) and basic. Very close to Plaza del Pilar.

General information
Car hire
Avis, Fernando el Católico, 9; tel: 55 50 94.

Fiestas
Easter week (*Semana Santa*), variable dates, El Pilar beginning October 12

Police
Comisaría, Plaza María Agustín, 34; tel: 43 67 11.

Telephone code
for Zaragoza province is (976).

Tourist office
Oficina de Turismo, Diputación General de Aragón, Plaza Pío X11; tel: 39 35 37. Open summer Monday to Friday 0830-1430, 1700-1930; Saturday and holidays 1000-1300. Winter Monday to Friday 0830-1430, 1600-1800; Saturday and holidays 0900-1330. Closed Sunday.

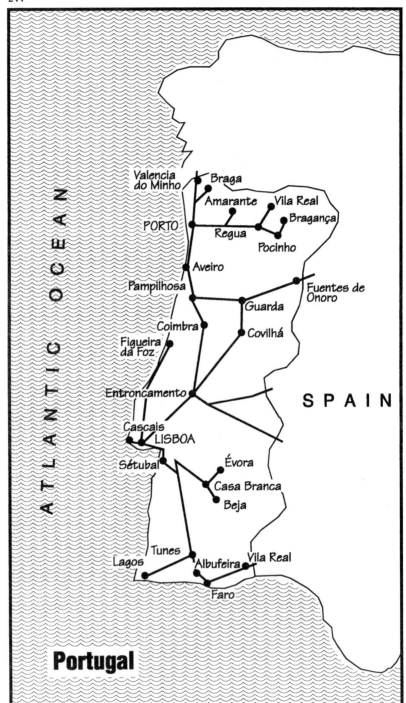

Portugal

Part Two

Portugal

CAMINHOS DE FERRO PORTUGUESES (CP)

The Network

The Portuguese railway system is run by Caminhos de Ferro Portugueses (CP), which has an extensive network throughout the country. The majority of visitors with rail passes will, however, be concerned mainly with the lines between Portugal and Spain and, internally, those lines connecting Lisbon, Porto and the Algarve, and it is on these that this section concentrates. That is not to say that other lines are not worth exploring - quite the reverse; simply, they are outside the scope of this book. An official timetable (Guia Horário Oficial) is published twice a year by CP. Timetables are also available in the UK from VOT Publications, Southern Vectis Overseas Timetables, 19 Beachfield Road, Sandown, Isle of Wight PO36 8LR, tel: (0983) 40791.

Tickets

Tickets are available from railway stations and travel agencies, and must be purchased in advance, or you may incur a substantial fine. Seats, too, must be reserved in advance on international and express trains, and certain others. Children under 4 travel free, while 4-12 year olds pay half fare. CP also has designated *dias azuis* (blue days), usually outside times of peak travel such as Fridays, national holidays, Sunday afternoons and Monday mornings, on which passengers may purchase return tickets at a reduced price. Days are altered each year, so contact CP for precise details.

In addition to those fare deals discussed in Part Three, *Getting There*, there are several categories of tickets offering savings over the individual fare, the most attractive to the visitor being the *bilhetes turisticos* (tourist tickets). Tickets are valid for seven, 14 or 21 days, and cost 15,200$00, 24,200$00 or 34,600$00 respectively.

Crossing between Portugal and Spain

There are five crossing points by train between Portugal and Spain. They are detailed below in clockwise order, starting with the most northerly:

Tui/Valença do Minho

This is the crossing point for *Inter-Regional* trains between **Vigo** and **Porto**. It is most probably the least used route between the two countries, but is convenient for those going to, or from, Santiago de Compostela.

Vilar Formoso/Fuentes d'Oñoro
This is the border crossing point for the **Lisbon/Paris/Lisbon** *Surexpreso*, an *estrella* with one service daily in each direction.The journey time is very long. The train leaves Lisbon early in the afternoon and arrives in Paris the next evening. It has single, double and four bed compartments, couchettes in second class and first and second class seating. The route takes it across northwest Spain, passing through Salamanca, Valladolid, Burgos, San Sebastián and Irún. Trains also go to **Porto** from this point.

Marvão-Beirã/Valencia de Alcántara
This is the border crossing point for both the following: The **Madrid/Lisbon/Madrid** *Luís de Camões*, which is a daytime *talgo* with one service daily in each direction and which has first and second class seats and a cafeteria; and the **Madrid/Lisbon/Madrid** *Lusitania*, which is an *estrella* with one service daily in each direction. The latter has single, double and four bed compartments, couchettes in second class and first and second class seating. There is also a restaurant and cafeteria. Both services run via Cáceres but the Inter-Rail pass (see *Getting There*) is only valid for second class travel on the *Luís de Camões*.

Elvas/Badajoz
This is not a very practical option, or even a necessary one given the proximity of the above, more direct, route between **Madrid** and **Lisbon** via Cáceres. It is slow and involves a complicated change between Elvas and Badajoz.

Vila Real de Sto António/Ayamonte
The complications of this, the most southerly crossing point between Spain and Portugal, are often underestimated by travellers. The problems start where the RENFE network ends: at Huelva. Taxi drivers wait at the station offering to take travellers on to Ayamonte, but this is an unnecessary expense of 6-7,000 ptas or more. Instead make for the Estación de Autobuses, Avenida de Portugal, from where there are frequent bus services that cost only about 425 ptas. Once at Ayamonte, ignore any taxi drivers offering to take you to Vila Real but walk straight ahead to the river, about 400m from the

bus stop. On your right is the small ferryboat that crosses the river, which operates 0800-2000, and costs 100 ptas (130$00 the other way). On arrival, the Vila Real de Sto António railway terminal, with trains to **Lisbon**, is less than 100m from the quay to your right.

The complications do not end here. After more than 6¼ hours, the train to Lisbon terminates at Barreiro, from where it is necessary to catch another ferry across the Tagus. The quay is an integral part of the station and the views on the crossing are quite dramatic, more than compensating for the troublesome journey. The ferry terminal on the other side, Terreiro do Paço, is actually on the waterfront, almost in the heart of the city by the Praça do Comércio, and offers a unique first glimpse of Lisbon.

Internal lines
Lisbon/Porto/Lisbon
This is the most important line in Portugal and, as a consequence, it has its own special service, the *Alfa*, as well as a special *Intercidades* and the *Inter-Regional* trains.

Lisbon/Vila Real de Sto António/Lisbon
This line connects Lisbon with the Algarve and southern Spain and is served by *Intercidades*(three a day, two terminate at Faro), *Inter-Regional* and *Regional* trains.

Porto/Vila Real de St António/Porto
This is a very limited service of one train each way at weekends. From Porto it runs overnight and there are beds, but from Vila Real it operates in the afternoon/evening and has only seats.

The trains
Alfa
The *Alfa* trains linking Lisbon with Porto are actually French CORAIL trains, and stop only at Coimbra. There are first and second class carriages, both air-conditioned, breakfast is served to passengers' seats and there is a bar. There are also Alfa Club facilities for frequent travellers.

Intercidades (Intercity)
The *Intercidades* between Lisbon and Porto are also French CORAIL trains, with first and second class air-conditioned carriages

and a bar or minibar. They make more stops than the Alfa.

On other routes there are non air-conditioned first and second class carriages with a bar or minibar, and trains stop only at the most important stations.

Inter-Regional

These have non air-conditioned first and second class carriages, with a bar or minibar depending upon the length of journey, and they make more frequent stops than the *Intercidades*.

Regional

These trains stop at all stations. They have non air-conditioned first and second class carriages, and no refreshment facilities.

LISBON (LISBOA)
The city

Lisbon, built on seven hills, is the largest city in Portugal and has a population of around 1,500,000 people. Its strategic location, on the wide Tagus river but protected from the Atlantic Ocean, has made it a favoured port for traders between the Mediterranean and northern Europe through the ages. These range from the Phoenicians, around 1200 BC, who called it Alis-Ubbo; the Greeks, who named it Olisipo and the Romans, beginning in 205 BC, who knew it as Felicitas Julia. After the Moors took the city, in 714, it became known as Ascbouna and was subsequently reconquered, by Alfonso I with the assistance of the northern Crusaders, on October 25 1147. In 1255 Alfonso III made Lisbon the capital, an honour previously held by Coimbra.

The 15th and 16th centuries saw Portugal, and consequently Lisbon, become the centre of the world. Vasco da Gama sailed for the Indies in 1497-99, Brazil was discovered in 1500 and the wealth that flowed into the country enabled Manuel I to, amongst other things, build the Monastery of Jerónimos and Tower of Belém in a most unusual architectural style named after him: *Manueline*.

On November 1 1755 the city was largely destroyed by a huge earthquake and was subsequently rebuilt under the auspices of the prime minister, the Marquês de Pombal. This was in a completely new style that became known as Pombaline. It can be seen today from the magnificent Praça do Comércio, next to the river, through the area known as Baixa to the Praça Dom Pedro IV, popularly known as Rossio, and along the wide Avenida da Liberdade to the Praça Marquês de Pombal and the Parque Eduardo VII. The latter offers a respite from, and views of, the city and was named after King Edward VII of England, who visited the city in 1902.

In 1933 Salazar took over as dictator until 1968, when he had a stroke and was replaced by Caetano. It was not until April 25 1974 that an armed forces coup d'état, known as the 'Carnation Revolution', ended the dictatorship.

Its favourable geographical location has made Lisbon one of the main ports in Europe. The Tagus is very wide and offers natural protection for shipping. As a consequence there are miles of docks and quays, and dry docks capable of accommodating the largest oil tankers. The best way of seeing these and the Ponte 25 de Abril, a huge suspension bridge with one of the largest central spans in

Europe, and the Christ in Majesty — a smaller version of the one in Rio de Janeiro — is from the river. There are various ferries from the Terreiro do Paço, next to the Praça do Comércio in the Baixa (shopping district) which connect with destinations the other side of the river, as well as boat trips along the Tagus. Those arriving from the south by train get a spectacular first view of the city and its environment, as they take the half-hour ferry trip across the Tagus from Barreiro to Terreiro do Paço, gaining an immediate appreciation of the city's maritime traditions.

Lisbon, with its old quarters of Alfama and Bairro Alto, the home of the Portuguese folksong *fado*, has a kind of old-fashioned charm which exists alongside a vibrant modern city and this, with the capital's historical connections and some highly attractive or even unique places of interest, make it a city that should not be missed.

Places of interest
Must see
Belém
All of the following are located in the area of Belém (Bethlehem), some distance downstream from the centre of the city. In the age of the great discoveries the sailors used to stop here on the way out and pray for safe voyages; upon returning safely they would offer prayers of thanksgiving. Today this suburb has numerous attractions and definitely should not be missed.

Getting there Number 15 or 17 tramcar, a pleasant but slow journey that costs 140$00; or train from the Estação Cais do Sodré — about five minutes from Praça do Comércio along the river — to Belém, for 90$00.

Torre de Belém (Belem Tower) Open Tuesday to Sunday 1000-1300, 1430-1700. Closed Monday. Entrance: 250$00. A brochure guide is available free. Also known as St Vincent's Tower this is a most unusual fortress indeed and is considered one of the gems of Portuguese architecture. Jutting into the Tagus it was built during the early 16th century and the exterior is a marvellously ornate example of the unique Manueline style. It was used as a prison during the Spanish occupation of Portugal and was restored in the mid 19th century. I suspect that most people will be disappointed with the rather bland, austere interior but even so it is still worth a visit.

Mosteiro dos Jerónimos (Monastery of Jerónimos) Open Tuesday to Sunday 1000-1300, 1430-1700. Closed Sunday and holidays. Entrance: 250$00. This large and very ornate construction, incorporating the monastery, the ornate church of 'Our Lady of Bethlehem' and the beautiful two level cloisters, is the finest example of Manueline style architecture in Lisbon, and is located on the site of the chapel built for sailors by Prince Henry the Navigator (Infante D Enrique). Manuel I received papal authorization for the monastery in 1496 and work began in 1500. During this period the wealth created by the discovery of new territories and trade monopolies granted by the Holy See helped pay for the construction. After the death of Manuel I in 1521, financial problems meant that the monastery was not completed until the late 16th century, and then not as originally planned.

Museu de Marinha (Maritime Museum), Praça do Império; tel: 362 00 10. Open Tuesday to Sunday 1000-1700. Closed Monday. Entrance: 250$00, free Sunday before 1200. Originally founded by King Luis I in 1863 this has had several locations before installation in the Jerónimo Monastery in 1962. Given its historical relationship with the Portuguese maritime explorers, Belém is the rightful home for such a museum. The exhibits are as interesting as one would expect.

Monumento das Descobertas (Descobertas Monument and Cultural Centre) Open Tuesday to Sunday 0930-1900. Closed Monday and holidays. Entrance: 275$00. A most unusual, leaning, modernistic monument built in 1960 on the bank of the Tagus to celebrate the 500th anniversary of Prince Henry the Navigator's death and Portuguese naval exploits. There are exhibitions and a lift up to the viewing platform.

Museu Nacional de Arqueologia (Archaeological and Ethnology Museum), Praça do Império; 362 00 00. Open Tuesday to Sunday 1000-1200, 1400-1700. Closed Monday. Entrance: 250$00, free on Sunday mornings. Located in the same building as the Monastery of Jerónimos, this has exhibits from prehistoric, Arabic and medieval periods.

Museu Nacional dos Coches (National Coach Museum), Praça Alfonso de Albuquerque. Open Tuesday to Sunday 1000-1300,

1430-1715. Closed Monday and holidays. Entrance: 250$00. Considered to be one of the best museums of its kind in the world, this has a wide variety of coaches of all shapes and sizes from the 18th and 19th centuries.

Castelo de São Jorge (St George's Castle)   There have been fortifications on this site high above the city since Roman times. The present fortifications were started by the Visigoths in the 5th century, taken over by the Moors in the 9th century and expanded by Alfonso I, the first king of Portugal, after he conquered the city in 1147. Today the castle walls loom over a strange combination of flower gardens with small ponds and even some caged animals, while one of the oldest rooms in the castle is still used for medieval banquets. It is most certainly worth a visit, if only for its panoramic views over both the city and the Tagus.

Alfama (Alfama Quarter), The oldest part of Lisbon, the Alfama is situated on the steep slopes between the castle and the river, east of the Baixa (shopping district), and not far from the Bairro Alto (old town), home of *fado*, the traditional folksong of Lisbon. Bordered by the cathedral and St Vincent church, the Alfama existed in Visigothic times and the Moors built many mansions there; later, the first churches in the city were erected in the area. Very few of these survived the earthquake and, subsequently, fishermen and seamen occupied the quarter. The area is full of narrow, steep lanes and alleys and many of the houses are decorated with elaborate tiles and flower boxes. The best times to walk through this fascinating area are either in the morning or early evening. Those who don't fancy the very steep walk up to the castle can take the number 37 bus from Rossio and then wander back down through Alfama.

Eléctricos para Turistas, Linha das Colinas (Tourist Tramcar, Hill Line), Praça do Comércio; tel: 363 93 43. Operates: last week in May and first in October 1400, 1615; June 1015, 1400, 1615; July and September 1015, 1400, 1430, 1615, 1645; August 1015, 1400, 1430, 1500, 1615, 1645, 1715. Fare adults 2,000$00, children (4-10) 1,000$00. An unforgettable, and easy way of seeing Lisbon, especially parts you would not normally get to see. These are beautifully renovated tramcars, with upholstered seats, that carry only 23 people. Arrive early, get a window seat, and sit back and enjoy this unique guided tour. (Or take tram 28 from Baixa and for around 140$00 you can follow the same route, without the frills.)

By choice

Casa dos Bicos (Bicos House) Rua dos Bacalhoeiros. The unusual exterior of this house is decorated with diamond-shaped stones, similar to the Casa de los Picos in Segovia. Originally a 16th century mansion, it was destroyed in the earthquake of 1755 and was subsequently used as a codfish warehouse. Rebuilt in 1982, it is currently the seat of the National Commission for the Celebrations of Portuguese Discoveries, but is not open to the public.

Sé (Cathedral) Known as the 'old Cathedral', this dates from the 12th century and was built in a fortress style. Renovated extensively after the earthquake, it really is not of that much interest.

Museums outside Belem

Museu Arqueológico (Archaeological Museum), tel: 346 04 73. Open Monday to Saturday 1000-1300, 1400-1700. Closed Sunday and holidays. Entrance: 300$00. Tram 24. The dramatic ruins of the Senhora do Monte do Carmo church in the Bairro Alto overlooking Lisbon now house this small museum, famous for its tombs and for some macabre skeletons. Other parts of the church are used for open air classical concerts. Originally dedicated in 1423, the church was largely destroyed in the earthquake of 1755 and the museum is housed in one of the restored parts.

Museu Calouste Gulbenkian (Calouste Gulbenkian Museum), Avenida de Berna, 45; tel: 795 02 36. Tuesday, Thursday, Friday and Sunday 1000-1700; Wednesday and Saturday 1400-1930. Closed Monday and national holidays. Entrance: 200$00, students and Sundays free. Metro Palhavã and S Sebastião. Tram 24, 27. Located in private gardens, this museum houses Gulbenkian's unique private collection of international art and artefacts and other items donated by his foundation. Try not to miss it.

Museu de Centro de Arte Moderna (Central Museum of Modern Art), Fundação Calouste Gulbenkian, Rua Dr Nicolau Bettencourt; tel: 795 02 41. Open Tuesday, Thursday, Friday and Sunday 1000-1700; Wednesday and Saturday 1400-1930. Closed Monday. Entrance: 200$00. Metro Palhavã and S Sebastião. Tram 24, 27.

Located in the same gardens as the Gulbenkian museum, this houses works by Portuguese artists of this century.

Museu da Cidade (City Museum), Campo Grande, 245; tel: 759 16 17. Open Tuesday to Sunday 1000-1300, 1400-1800. Closed Monday. Entrance: 270$00, free on Sunday. Bus 3, 7, 17-B, 36, 47. Located in the Palácio Pimenta, the Museu da Cidade has exhibits tracing the development of Lisbon through the ages.

Museu da Marioneta (Puppet Museum), Largo Rodrigues de Freitas, 19; tel: 87 83 96. Open Tuesday to Sunday 1000-1300, 1500-1800. Closed Monday. Entrance: 300$00. Tram 26, bus 37. Puppet exhibits and a puppet theatre run by the São Lourenço Puppet Theatre Company.

Museu Militar (Military Museum), across from Santa Apolónia railway station; tel: 888 21 31. Open Tuesday to Saturday 1000-1600; Sunday 1100-1700. Closed Monday and national holidays. Entrance: 150$00; free on Wednesday. Bus 9, 28, 39, 46. Originally founded by King Manuel I in the 16th century, the Military Museum is now situated in an elegant building dating from the late 18th century. Alongside the wide-ranging collection of military exhibits, the rooms themselves are worth seeing.

Museu Nacional de Arte Contemporanea (National Museum of Contemporary Art), Rua de Serpa Pinto, 6. Open daily 1000-1700. The exhibits here are all forms of contemporary art from the mid 20th century to date.

Museu Nacional de Arte Antiga (National Museum of Ancient Art), Rua das Janelas Verdes, 9; tel: 397 60 01. Open Tuesday to Sunday 1000-1700. Closed Monday. Entrance: 250$00, free on Sunday morning. Important collections of European paintings, ceramics, sculpture, etc, from the 15th to 19th centuries.

Museu Nacional do Azulejo (National Tile Museum), Rua da Madre de Deus, 4; tel: 814 77 47. Open Tuesday to Sunday 1000-1230, 1400-1700. Closed Monday. Entrance 200$00; students free. Bus 18, 24, 104, 105. A unique museum housing an extensive collection of *azulejos* (ceramic tiles), and showing how this artistic form has developed in Portugal. Don't miss the impressive panorama showing the Lisbon waterfront before the earthquake.

Station/location/transport to city centre

Santa Apolónia; a traditional-style railway station located a short distance to the east of the city centre. Trains from Paris, Madrid and northern Portugal, including Porto.

Layout

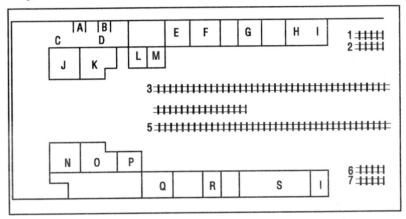

Key

A/B: *Consigna Auto*, left luggage lockers, cost 390$00 for 24 hours
C: *Informaçoes*, train information
D: *Consigna*, left luggage office, open 0830-2330, cost 180$00 for 4 hours and 300$00 for 24 hours
E: *Sala de Espera*, waiting room
F: Bar
G: *Homens*, men's toilets
H: *Chefe da Estação*, station master's office
I: Waiting room
J: Ticket office

K: Newspapers, magazines, etc
L: Ice cream, chocolates, etc
M: Europcar, Car hire
N: Ticket office
O: Newspapers, magazines, etc
P: Avis Car-hire
Q: Snack bar
R: *Senhoras*, ladies' toilets
S: International travel office; this includes a ticket office, train information office, bar, bank, automatic cash machine and toilets

Train station to city centre

By bus Number 39 or 46 to Rossio; the fare is 140$00.

On foot It is about a 15-minute walk to the Praça do Comércio, although it is probably too far if you have luggage to carry.

By taxi Certainly the quickest, and relatively cheap, too, as taxis are subsidised: a five-minute taxi ride to Rossio costs around 400$00/450$00.

Train services
To Porto by
Alfa: 3. *Intercidades*: Coimbra 1; Porto 3½. *Inter-Regional*: Coimbra 1½; Porto 4¼.

To Vila Real de Sto António by
Intercidades: Faro 4½; 5¾.

Accommodation
There are no places close to the station but there are numerous *pensões* in and around the Praças D Pedro IV and da Figueira, an area also known as Rossio. As most of these are of the same standard, don't expect a private bath/shower and toilet, with prices between 2,500$00 and 4,000$00 for a double. I only list those I have stayed in.

***Pensão Norte** Rua dos Douradores, 159; tel: 87 89 41. Single 2,500$00; double 4,000$00; doubles with bath/shower. Four floors and a lift. Quiet side street just off Praça da Figueira.

Pensão Ibérica Praça da Figueira, 10; tel: 886 57 81. Single 2,500$00; double 4,000$00; prices include Continental breakfast. No lifts; old-fashioned but comfortable; no bath/shower in rooms. Rooms on fourth floor overlook the Praça and have good views of Bairro Alto part of city.

Note: For those wanting a higher standard try:

***Hotel Eduardo VII** Avenida Fontes Pereira de Melo, 5; tel: 53 01 41; fax: 53 38 79. Metro Rotunda. A Best Western hotel with three seasons: low January 1 to March 31; high April 1 to October 31; medium November 1 to December 31. Single low 12,500$00, high 15,300$00, medium 13,500$00; double low 15,000$00, high 17,500$00, medium 16,200$00.

The Metro
Open daily 0630-0100. Tickets for one and ten trips can be purchased either from the cashier or from an automatic machine, which is slightly cheaper. For one trip they cost 65$00 from the cashier and 55$00 from the machine, for ten trips they cost 475$00 from the cashier and 450$00 from the machine. For four days the cost is 1,350$00 and for seven days 1,900$00, both purchased from the cashier.

Tickets must be punched in the machines provided before entering the platforms.

It is a relatively simple network with a loop line and one other. Care needs to be taken because the destination on the loop line is the same both ways: Campo Grande. Metro stations are indicated by the letter 'M'.

General information
Post office
Correio, Praça dos Restauradores (opposite tourist office), open daily 0800-2200, tel: 346 36 24/346 91 13.

Public telephones
Praça D Pedro IV (Rossio). Open daily 0800-2300.

Telephone code
for Lisbon is (1).

Tourist office
Palácio Foz, Praça dos Restauradores, Balcão CML, tel: 346 2866/346 6307. Open daily, except Christmas Day, 0900-2000.

PORTO
The city

Porto has a population of around 400,000 and is the second largest city in Portugal. There are ancient links with Celtic societies but it was the Romans who set up twin towns here: Cale, the city on the left bank and Portus, the port on the right bank.

The Moors invaded the region but the Christians did not allow them to settle and the region, known as Portucale, formed the dowry of Princesa Dona Teresa, daughter of King Alfonso VI of Castile and León, when she married Henry of Burgundy in 1095. Later their son, Alfonso Henriques, proclaimed himself King of Portugal. Porto is also the birthplace of Prince Henry the Navigator who equipped the fleet that took Ceuta from the Moors in 1415 and led the famous explorations founding the Portuguese overseas empire in the first half of that century.

In 1703 the Metheun Treaty between England and Portugal was signed, facilitating an exchange of goods procedure which enabled the sale of English merchandise in return for port wine. Subsequent to this the English began to take over all phases of port wine production.

Visitors will find a most dramatic location; the city is on the steep right bank of the Douro and is connected to the left bank by some unusual metal bridges. The oldest, completed in 1877, is the María Pia railway bridge that was designed by Eiffel, but the one closest to the city is the Dom Luis I. This is built on the same lines as the María Pia but is a double decker and most visitors will walk across the lower level to the port lodges on the right bank. Just down river, and easily visible from the highest points in the city, is the Atlantic Ocean. For those with time to spare, trains run down the beautiful Douro valley with branches up to Vila Real and Mirandela.

The city itself is rather unusual, and not just geographically. To walk down from the cathedral through the narrow cobbled lanes, where some bars have the strange half-size wooden swing doors more familiar in westerns, towards the picturesque old *Ribeira* (riverside) area is like going back in time. The people, too, are different, with a fierce reputation for independence and hard work. Porto may have no really unforgettable places of interest, but it has a unique character and few people will regret their visit.

Places of interest
Must see
The Port Lodges No trip to Porto would be complete without visiting the *caves* (lodges) of one of the producers of the product that has made this city famous throughout the world. In Gaia, across the river by way of the lower section of the elegant D Luis I Bridge, you will see numerous signs directing you to one or another of these lodges, many of whose names will already be familiar. Which one to visit is a matter of personal choice but all offer guided tours and, of course, free samples. One of the oldest, and most interesting, is Taylor, Fladgate and Yeatman, situated towards the top of the hill. Although further away from the river down which the wine was traditionally brought to Porto, this is a more favourable position as it is not vulnerable to flooding.

A Sé (Cathedral), tel: 31 48 37. Open Monday to Saturday 0900-1215, 1430-1730. Entrance: free. Entrance to Cloisters, Chapel of St Vicente, Casa Capitular and a Panoramic View 150$00. Originally built as a fortress church in the 12th and 13th centuries but with many baroque changes dating from the 17th and 18th centuries. This is not one of the most interesting cathedrals but its location gives it fantastic views over the old town, Douro river and the port houses on the southern bank.

Casa do Infante (House of the Infante) Located in the old riverside area this is reputed to be the site where Henry the Navigator (Infante de Sagres) was born in 1394. There are other historical connections, with disagreements earlier in the century between the king, Alfonso IV, and the church over who should receive customs duty payments on goods unloaded on the left bank of the river.
   Today the house is a small museum, but it was closed for extensive restoration in 1993.

Palacio da Bolsa (Bolsa Palace), tel: 200 44 97. Open October to May Monday to Friday 0900-1200, 1400-1700. Closed Saturday, Sunday and holidays; June to September Monday to Friday 1000-1730, Saturday, Sunday and holidays 1000-1200, 1400-1700. Guided tours only in Portuguese, English and French. Entrance: 400$00. This Stock Exchange dates from the 19th century and the main feature is the trading hall with its painting of the Alhambra in Granada.

Torre dos Clérigos (Clerigos Tower), tel: 200 17 29. Open Monday to Saturday 1000-1200, 1400-1700; Sunday (winter) 1000-1200, 1400-1730, (summer) 1000-1200, 1430-1800. Entrance: 75$00. Built in the mid 18th century the church boasts, at over 70m, the highest bell tower in the country. For those sturdy enough the view from the top, up 225 steps, is the best in Porto.

Igreja de S Francisco (San Francisco Church), tel: 200 64 93. Open Monday to Saturday 0920-1730. Entrance: 350$00. A Gothic-style Franciscan convent that was started in the late 13th century but with reconstructions in both the 14th and 15th centuries. Sections of it were destroyed during the 1833 siege and some of the renovations are in the baroque style. There is a small museum but it is the church itself which is of most interest; it is particularly ornate with some magnificent altar pieces.

Tramcar Trip Number 18 from Carmo to Boavista; 80$00. These tramcars are a delight in themselves: wooden seats with reversible dividers, sash windows, leather straps, etc. The journey takes you down to the river and then out to the Atlantic and up as far as the Castelo do Queijo. By way of contrast it returns along the Avenida da Boavista, passing through one of the city's most affluent areas, to the Praça de Mousinho de Albuquerque. From there it is a short walk to the Solar do Vinho do Porto and Museu Romantico.

By choice
River Cruises Vinho do Porto offer one-hour cruises under the four bridges that cost 1,000$00, and leave at 1130, 1600, 1700, 1800. Endouro Turismo offer a fifty-minute trip down river leaving at 1000, 1100, 1500, 1700 and 1800, costing 1,500$00.

Solar do Vinho do Porto (Institute of Port Wine), Quinta de Macieirinhe, Rua de Entre Quintas, 220; tel: 69 77 93. Open Monday to Friday 1000-2345, Saturday 1100-2245. Closed Sunday. Located under the Museu Romantico, and run by the Ministry of Agriculture, this is a port lover's paradise. The menu, pages and pages of it, consists simply of every kind of port that is produced. Most can be bought by the glass but the most expensive, and these are expensive, have to purchased by the bottle. An added bonus is the charming garden high over the Douro that has views out to the Atlantic.

Museums

Casa Museu de Guerra Junqueiro (House and Museum of Guerra Junqueiro), C/ D. Hugo, 32; tel: 31 36 44. Open Tuesday to Sunday 0900-1200, 1400-1700. Closed Monday and holidays. This 18th century baroque house is located directly behind the cathedral and has furniture, works of art, etc, collected by the famous Portuguese poet Guerra Junqueiro (1850-1923). This was closed for restoration during 1993 and no reopening date had been scheduled.

Museu Nacional de Soares dos Reis (National Museum of Soares dos Reis), C/ D. Manuel II; tel: 200 71 10. This is located in the 18th century Palace of the Carrancas, which was a residence of the royal family. There are collections of Portuguese jewellery and porcelain from the 16th to 19th centuries, Portuguese paintings from the 19th century and sculptures of Soares dos Reis. The museum was closed for restoration during 1993 and no other information was available.

Museu Romantico (Romantic Museum), C/ de Entre Quintas, 220; tel: 609 11 31. Open Tuesday to Thursday 1000-1230, 1400-1730; Friday and Saturday 1000-1230, 1400-1800; Sunday 1400-1800. Entrance: 100$00; Saturday and Sunday Free. This delightful house shows how elegantly the rich of the 19th century were able to live. Of particular interest is the room where the exiled Italian king, Carlos Alberto of Sardinia, died.

Station/location/transport to city centre

Campanha, telephone information (0800-2300) 56 41 41. The majority of long-distance trains use this station on the outskirts of Porto, to the east, with trains approaching from the south offering fantastic views of the city.

Key

A: Underpass to other platforms
B: Men's toilets
C: *Caixas Automaticas*, left luggage lockers, open 0500-0100, cost 350$00 for 48 hours
D: *Chefe da Estação*, station master's office

E: Ticket offices
F: *Informacões*, train information, open 0830-2000
G: Bar/restaurant, open 0630-0100
H: Women's toilets
J: Waiting room

Layout

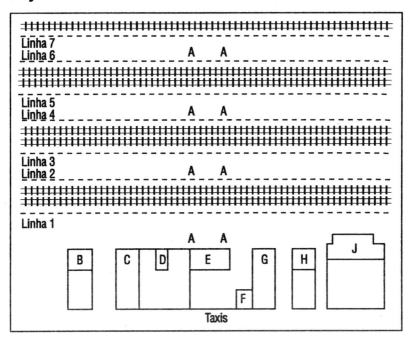

Train station to town centre

By bus Take the 35 from the bus stop directly in front of the station, on the same side of the road. The fare is 140$00 and the journey time varies according to the time of day but allow at least 15 minutes.

On foot This is not a viable option.

By taxi This can take a long time during rush hours and cost up to 600$00.

By train The best option if there is not too long a wait is to take the next train to the Estação São Bento, just a few minutes away from Campanha in the city centre. This offers the added advantage of the chance to see the baroque station building with its magnificent entrance of glazed tiles depicting scenes from Portugal's history.

Train services
To Lisbon by
Alfa: 3. *Intercidades*: Coimbra 1¼; Lisbon 3½. *Inter-Regional*: Coimbra 1¾; Lisbon 4½.

To Vila Real de St António by
Comboio Azul: Coimbra 1½; Faro 8¾; Vila Real 10½.

To Vigo by
Inter-Regional: Tui 3¼; Vigo 4¼.

Accommodation
Close to the station
*** **Pensão Poveira** Rua da Estação, 56; tel: 57 98 44. Single with shower but no toilet 2,400$00, with shower and toilet 2,900$00; double with shower but no toilet 3,700$00, with shower and toilet 4,300$00. TV room with bar and restaurant; 28 rooms. Directly across from the station.
** **Pensão Residencial** Ribadouro Rua da Estação, 28; tel: 57 12 28. Single 2,500$00, double 3,500$00. All rooms with bath and telephone. Next to the Poveira but smaller.

In the city
*** **Grande Hotel do Porto** Rua de Santa Catarina, 197; tel: 200 81 76; fax: 31 10 61. This Best Western hotel has two seasons: low from November 1 to March 31 and high from April 1 to October 31. The rates include an American buffet breakfast in the restaurant or Continental breakfast served in the room. Single, low 10,500$00, high 11,600$00; double low 11,600$00, high 13,200$00. Each room has air-conditioning, direct dial telephone, radio, satellite TV and a minibar. The public rooms, bar and very elegant restaurant are on the ground floor. This charming hotel is located in the shopping district just a short walk from the tourist area.
*** **Pensão Residencial dos Aliados** Avenida dos Aliados (Entrance in Rua Elísio de Melo, 27); tel: 200 48 53. Single 5,500$00, double 6,500$00. All rooms with private bath, TV and telephone. Pleasant atmosphere and lift.
*** **Pensão Monumental** Avenida dos Aliados, 151; tel: 200 39 64. Single with shower 2,500$00, with bath and toilet 2,700$00; double with bath and toilet 3,700$00. Fourth/fifth floor with lift. TV lounge; pleasant atmosphere.
* **Residencial Avenida** Avenida dos Aliados, 141; tel: 200 95 51. Fax: 31.49.07. Single 2,500$00; double 3,500$00. Rooms with bath but no toilet. Fourth/fifth floor with lift. Interesting mix of old-fashioned and new rooms.
** **Pensão Residencial Douro** Praça Parada Leitão, 41; tel: 208 12 01.

Single 3,000$00; double 3,500$00. Small and interesting. TV lounge. Just away from centre, 100m from the Torre dos Clérigos.
** **Pensão Franca**   Praça Gomes Teixeira, 7; tel: 200 27 91. Single 4,000$00; double 5,000$00. All rooms with private bath. TV lounge and restaurant. Across from the Pensão Douro.

General information
Post office/Public telephones
Correios, 62 Batalha. Open Monday to Friday 0900-1800.

Telephone code
for Porto is (2).

Tourist office
ICEP, Praça de D Joao I, tel: 317514. Open Monday to Friday 0900-1900; Saturday 0900-1400; Sunday 1000-1400.

Part Three

Getting there

THOMAS COOK EUROPEAN TIMETABLE
The most complete current
European rail schedule available!

The famous Thomas Cook European Timetable gives passenger rail service timings for nearly 50,000 daily trains over almost every European and British rail route, including International EuroCity trains, High Speed TGV, ICE, X-2000, AVE services, plus narrow gauge and tourist trains, holiday special trains, sleeping car and couchette services, etc.

Quick reference index maps show the routes covered for easy timetable finding. Many simple European city maps show railway station locations. Also includes ferry services throughout Europe and all cross-Channel modes.

New EuroStar and LeShuttle services included showing new English Channel Tunnel schedules, plus airport links, winter sports coach services, expanded Eastern European schedules, etc. Averages 500+ pages but lightweight and easy to carry with you. (All English language.) Most current timetable available.
Only $24.95.

THOMAS COOK
NEW RAIL MAP OF EUROPE

Detailed map of European passenger railways as far east as Moscow and the Black Sea. Includes insets of densest networks plus city rail maps. Newly drawn for 1994. Scale 1:3, 750,000. Folded, with protective cover. Ideal companion to the Thomas Cook European Timetable.
Only $10.95.

EUROPEAN RAIL
TRAVELLER'S PHRASEBOOK

By Thomas Cook. Over 350 useful phrases in nine European languages with hints and tips on rail travel. • French • German • Italian • Czech • Polish • Bulgarian • Spanish • Greek • Turkish. 288 pages. Paperback *Only $6.95*

Special offers:
Current Timetable and Rail Map of Europe.
Only $34.95 + $4 priority shipping.

BEST BUY: Timetable, Rail Map & Rail Traveler's Phrasebook
Only $39.95 + $4 priority shipping.

For Travelers from North America

To order, call or write to:
Forsyth Travel Library, Inc.
9154 W. 57th St., P.O. Box 2975
Shawnee Mission, KS 66201-1375

1-800-367-7984 (Charge to Visa, Discover or MasterCard)
Fax – (913) 384-3553

Important notice: All prices and offers are subject to change, availability and revision and the reader should expect that prices will increase in 1995.

BONUS: Free pamphlet on "Defeating Jet-lag from North America to Europe" with every order!

RAIL PASSES

British Rail International

British Rail International issues two kinds of passes: one that can be used throughout Europe and another that can only be used in individual countries. Full details of these are shown below.

The following applies to both passes. All information is as of 1993. The 1994 prices and details were not available at the time of going to press.

Available in the United Kingdom from British Rail International, International Rail Centre, Victoria Station, London SW1 1JY, tel: 071-834 2345, and from other selected railway stations and British Rail International appointed travel agents.

Other benefits 34% discount on rail travel in Great Britain and Northern Ireland; 50% on the rail portion of tickets between London and the Continental ports; 30% or 50% (depending upon the company and route) on most services to the European mainland and Ireland operated by Stena Sealink Line, Hoverspeed, Dover-Ostend Line, P&O European Ferries, Olau Line, Scandinavian Seaways, B&I Line and Irish Ferries; various discounts on other shipping services, eg: in the Mediterranean and around Scandinavia, and discounts on many private railways in Switzerland and other countries.

Passes valid throughout Europe

There are two types of these but only one, the Inter-Rail Europe is detailed here. The other, Inter-Rail 26+, is available only to those over 26 years of age but is not appropriate to this guide as it is not valid in France, Spain or Portugal.

Qualifications Age under 26, a resident in Great Britain or Northern Ireland for at least six months and holder of a valid passport, which must be shown when booking the pass

Available for travel in Austria, Belgium, Bulgaria, Croatia, Czechoslovakia, Denmark, Finland, France, Germany, Greece, Hungary, Republic of Ireland, Italy, Luxembourg, Morocco, Netherlands, Norway, Poland, Portugal, Romania, Slovenia, Spain, Sweden, Switzerland, Turkey and Yugoslavia

Class Second class

Period of validity One month

Price £249

Passes valid only in specific countries

British Rail International issues Euro-Domino Freedom Passes that are valid for travel on either 3, 5 or 10 days within a one month period in any of the following countries: Austria, Belgium, Croatia, Czechoslovakia, Denmark, Finland, France, Germany, Greece, Hungary, Republic of Ireland, Italy, Luxembourg, Morocco, Netherlands, Norway, Poland, Portugal, Slovenia, Spain, Sweden, Switzerland, Turkey and Yugoslavia.

Only the details for France, Spain and Portugal are shown below.

France — general * *3 days* 2nd class £103, 1st class not available; *5 days* 2nd class £141, 1st class £231; *10 days* 2nd class £221, 1st class £345.

France — under 26 years old and second class only *3 days* £84; *5 days* £124; *10 days* £195.

Spain — general * *3 days* 2nd class £92, 1st class £134; *5 days* 2nd class £143, 1st class £196; *10 days* 2nd class £228, 1st class £360.

Spain — under 26 years old and second class only *3 days* £74; *5 days* £121; *10 days* £194.

Portugal — general * *3 days* 2nd class £80, 1st class £119; *5 days* 2nd class £100, 1st class £148; *10 days* 2nd class £151, 1st class £223.

Portugal — under 26 years old and second class only *3 days* £62; *5 days* £77; *10 days* £116.

* *Children (aged 4-11 inclusive) travel at half the stated adult fare, rounded up to the nearest £; under 4 are free.*

Other benefits Reduced fares from London to the channel ports to link into the Euro-Domino Freedom Pass. *Boulogne or Calais* (2nd

class) single £28, one month return £51; (under 26 years old) single
£20, one month return £40. *Dieppe* (2nd class) single £26, one
month return £44; (under 26 years old) single £20, one month return
£39.

The Eurail Passes

There is a wide variety of passes that can be used either throughout
Europe or only in individual or pre-assigned groups of countries.
Full details of these are shown below.

The following apply to all passes and the prices stated are in
US$s. All information is valid for 1994.

Qualifications Valid passport, or residency qualifications, in
country of issue.

Available in Argentina, Australia, Bahrain, Bolivia, Brazil, Canada,
Chile, Colombia, Ecuador, Egypt, Hong Kong, India, Indonesia,
Israel, Japan, Malaysia, Mexico, New Zealand, Pakistan, Paraguay,
Peru, Philippines, Puerto Rico, Saudi Arabia, South Africa, South
Korea, Singapore, Sri Lanka, Taiwan, Thailand, Tunisia, United
Arab Emirates, United States of America, Uruguay and Venezuela.

In North America passes are available from Rail Europe on 1 800
TGV RAIL in the USA and 1 800 361 RAIL in Canada, or through
travel agents.

Other benefits There are many buses, ferries, hydrofoils, private
railways and steamers in Austria, Belgium, Denmark, France,
Germany, Greece, Hungary, Republic of Ireland, Italy, Norway,
Sweden and Switzerland that are either free or subject to a
surcharge.

For Flexipass holders the use of a transportation bonus requires
the use of a travel day.

Restrictions/special conditions In *Italy* additional fees are required
on certain IC trains named ETR 450, which offer first-class seating
only. In *Norway* there is a special supplement for the use of IC class
in ICE trains. In *Spain* use on *AVE* trains on the Madrid to Sevilla
route is excluded as are internal *Hotel* trains. External *Hotel* trains
on the Barcelona to Zurich, Barcelona to Paris and Madrid to Paris
routes are subject to a special supplement.

Passes valid throughout Europe

Travel throughout Austria, Belgium, Denmark, Finland, France, Germany, Greece, Hungary, Republic of Ireland, Italy, Luxembourg, Netherlands, Norway, Portugal, Spain, Sweden and Switzerland, is available on the following passes:

Eurail Pass *

Class First class.
Period and price 15 days for $498; 21 days for $648; one month for $798; two months for $1,098 or three months for $1,398.

Eurail Flexipass *

Class First class.
Period and price Any 5 days in two months for $348; any 10 days in two months for $560 or any 15 days in two months for $740.

Eurail Saverpass *

Class First class.
Conditions Price per person for two or more people travelling together (three people required between April 1 and September 30).
Period and price 15 days for $430; 21 days for $550 or one month for $678. Children (aged 4-11 inclusive) travel at half the adult fare and under 4 are free.

Eurail Youthpass *

Class Second class.
Period and price 15 days for $398; one month for $578 or two months for $768.

Eurail Youth Flexipass *

Class Second class.
Period and price Any 5 days in two months for $255; any 10 days in two months for $398 or any 15 days in two months for $540.

* *Available only if the passenger is under 26 years old on first day of travel.*

Passes valid only in specific countries

There is a variety of 'individual country' passes valid in Austria, the

Benelux countries (Belgium, Luxembourg and Netherlands), Czech Republic, BritFrance, European East (Austria, Hungary, Poland, Czech and Slovak Republics), France, Greece, Hungary, Poland, Portugal, Scandinavia (Denmark, Finland, Norway and Sweden) Spain and Switzerland.

The 1994 periods and prices for France, Spain and Portugal had not been determined at the time of publication.

LONDON TO PARIS — VIA THE CHANNEL TUNNEL

Introduction

The Channel Tunnel, originally due to open during the summer of 1993, is now scheduled to open in 1994. This will open up a totally new concept for direct non-stop train travel between London and Paris (and Brussels). To cater for this a new station has been purpose built at Waterloo, Gare du Nord (in Paris) has been upgraded and completely new trains have been built.

As a result the journey time will be only three hours, city centre to city centre, a saving of over 50% on current times. This will be reduced to two and a half hours when the new line, scheduled for the year 2000, is completed in the UK.

Waterloo International Station

This is a most unusual station indeed. Firstly, it has been grafted on to the existing Waterloo station, resulting in a thoroughly modern design which is user friendly and highly pleasing to the eye. Secondly, it is not like a railway station at all; much more like an airport terminal with appropriate arrival and departure areas. Indeed, entering the station, and only ticket holders are able to do so, is like passing into the departure lounge at an airport with all the attendant security — once in you can't come out again — because of immigration and customs formalities.

Within the departure lounge there are all the facilities one would expect: bars, cafeterias, bookshops, toilets, etc, as well as a special first-class area. Do not look, however, for a duty-free shop; the government has decided that these are not allowed.

There are full facilities for handicapped people both in the terminal and on the trains; this even includes tactile edges on the platforms to warn blind people.

Passengers will be kept informed of developments and directed to the platform, and even to the part of the platform where their carriage will be, by closed circuit TV screens throughout the terminal.

Although immigration and customs formalities are completed on the train passengers will find, on arrival back at Waterloo International, that they will have to pass through the Customs Hall. This will not be like the old red and green channels familiar to most travellers. The majority of people will just walk straight through as most stops will be made at random or based on intelligence regarding drugs, pornography and firearms.

The trains

Eurostar is the name given to these trains. They consist of 18 carriages plus a power plant at each end, and are capable of a top speed of 300km/h.

The layout is innovative; there are face-to-face seats, seats facing in one direction and tip-up seats. There are 210 first-class seats, all reclining, 584 standard-class seats and 52 tip-up seats. Eight of the latter are in first-class and, unlike in the TGV, these are not sold but are just for the casual use of passengers. One out of every three first-class seats is reserved for smokers and the ratio in standard class is one out of five. There are also special family compartments which consist of a bay of four seats with a table that can be folded away to leave a play area, or room for a pushchair. There are positions for two wheelchair users in the first-class non-smoking coaches which will be charged at a special rate, not the full first-class fare. Passengers will be able to remain in their wheelchair or use a tip-up seat provided; there is also one fixed seat for a travelling companion. The toilets, in this area only, are wide enough to accommodate a wheelchair.

All on-board services have been contracted out to Cross Channel Catering Company Ltd which is a consortium formed by On-Board Services (InterCity), Wagon Lits and Sabena, the Belgian airline. There are two bar-buffet coaches, one in each half of the train, and hot and cold snacks are available to be eaten in the buffet or taken back to seats. Refreshments are also available from a trolley service while first-class passengers will have an at-seat meal service which is included in the price of their ticket.

Fare structure

Fares are roughly comparable with those of the ferries, but at the time of publication information was not available regarding Eurorail and Inter Rail passes.

LONDON TO THE CHANNEL PORTS
The routes and introduction

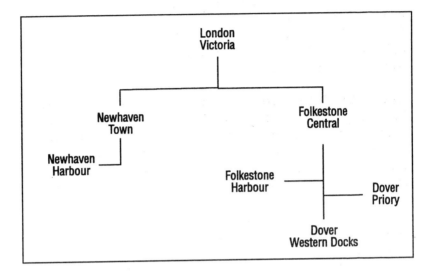

Victoria Station is the main terminus for departures for the channel ports from London and there are fast, and stopping, services to Dover Priory, Folkestone Central and Newhaven Town. As there are only limited cross-Channel services from Newhaven and Folkestone, and in any event the stations are very small, these railway stations will not be detailed in this chapter.

London/Paris/London connecting train/cross-Channel/train services

British Rail International and SNCF have combined with Hoverspeed, Stena Sealink Line and Société Nouvelle d'Armement Transmanche (SNAT) to arrange special train services timed to connect with cross-Channel sailings. Besides being faster these are also more convenient as the trains go directly to and from purpose-built stations in the respective harbours. These services are very popular and, especially during the summer months, it is wise to make a reservation for both trains and the Channel crossing. Specific details of these services are as follows:

In conjunction with Hoverspeed

This is the fastest surface journey between the two capitals. Up to three trains a day leave Victoria for Folkestone Harbour where there is direct transfer to the SeaCat catamaran for the crossing to Boulogne Gare Maritime and another direct transfer to the waiting train for Paris. The journey takes about six hours. There are three daily services in the opposite direction.

In conjunction with Stena Sealink Line and SNAT

Trains depart Victoria for Dover Western Docks where there is a direct transfer to the ferry for the sailing to Calais Maritime railway station where the train for Paris will be waiting. From Paris just reverse the procedure. There are up to three services a day (two day and one night time), and the journey time is about eight hours during the day and nine at night.

In conjunction with Stena Sealink Line

Trains leave Victoria for Newhaven Harbour where there is a direct transfer to the ferry for Dieppe Gare Maritime and another direct transfer to the waiting train for Paris. There are two services a day — one day and one night time — in each direction, and the journey time is about nine hours.

London Victoria

Victoria is a large station close to the centre of London. The fast, direct trains to the Channel ports leave from platforms 1 and 2 and the facilities close to those platforms are detailed below. There are other facilities of interest to international travellers, in different parts of the station, and these are listed separately.

Layout

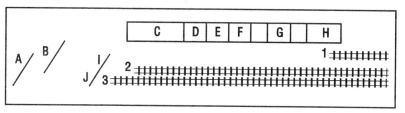

Key

A: The Belgravia public house
B: W H Smith, newspapers, magazines, etc
C: International Rail Centre: tickets and information for all continental services, open Monday to Friday 0800-1800; Saturday 0800-1600
D: Bureau de change, open daily 0700-2030
E: Dover/Ostend Jetfoil office

F: Hoverspeed SeaCat office
G: Venice-Simplon Orient Express office
H: Baggage registration office
I: Cash dispenser for Visa/ Mastercard/Eurocard and American Express cards
J: Eurotrain office. A discount office for European rail travel for people under 26 years of age

Other facilities

British Transport Police Located opposite platform 8

Bureau de Change Located close to platform 8, open daily 24 hours

Bus and Underground Information Centre Located close to platform 8, open daily 0815-2130

Hotel reservations BHRC tel: 071-828 1027, located close to platform 8, open daily 0530-2400

Hotels, bed and breakfast and youth hostels An enquiry office located on the outside of the station, at the front, open daily 0700-2300

Left luggage Located between platforms 7 and 8, open Monday to Saturday 0715-2230, Sunday 0730-2230; £2.50 or £3.00 a day, maximum 28 days, according to size. Lockers (per 24 hours): small £2.50, medium £3.50 and £5.00

Tourist Information Centre Located outside station, at front, open Monday to Saturday 0800-1900, Sunday 0800-1600

Dover Priory

Key

A: Waiting room
B: Footbridge to platforms
C: Buffet, open Monday to Saturday 0630-2100; Sunday 0730-2100
D: Kiosk for newspapers, magazines, etc
E: Ticket office, open Monday to Friday 0435-2330; Saturday 0500-

2330, Sunday 0630-2330
F: Train information
G: Men's toilets
H: Toilets for the disabled
I: Station Supervisor's office
J: Women's toilets and waiting room

Layout

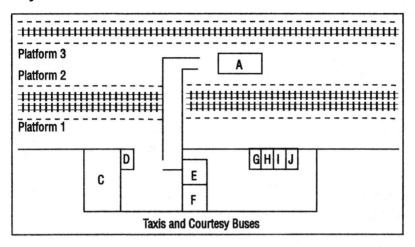

Courtesy buses

Hoverspeed Operates its own service for the SeaCat from the Eastern Docks Terminal or the hovercraft from the Western Docks Hoverport, departing about 45 minutes before each service.

P&O European Ferries Operate between 0730 and 1830, on the hour and half-hour, from the station to the Eastern Docks Terminal. Outside those hours bus leaves 2115, 2245, 2230 and 0015.

Stena Sealink Line Leaves 45 minutes before sailings, starting 0730 and ending 2215.

Besides seasonal variations in the schedules these services are run, strictly speaking, for the company's own passengers. However, I have found that, if asked politely, and there is available room, the drivers are generally flexible.

CROSSING THE CHANNEL
The companies
Hoverspeed
This company offers the following alternative, and faster forms of transportation than ferries for crossing the Channel:

Hovercraft These have been in operation since the mid 1960s and the two that operate now are the large Mark III variety. They carry 390 passengers, who must remain seated during the 'flight', and 55 cars. Drinks and duty free goods, although a smaller selection than is available in the terminal shops, are served to your seat.

SeaCat catamarans In 1991 Hoverspeed introduced SeaCat catamarans which have a capacity of 430 passengers and 80 cars. The SeaCats (3,003 tons) have the very latest technology, are the first to carry cars, and bring a new dimension to cross Channel service. Each passenger has an aircraft-style seat, with a lifejacket underneath, and there is a bar and duty-free shop at the stern. The latter, though, has a more limited stock than the shops in the terminals. There is a forward observation deck that allows you to literally look through the bridge and get the same view as the captain and, at the rear, a small promenade deck. In the cabin there is video entertainment, Vodafone facilities and a mother and baby room.

These vessels are very fast, with a cruising speed of 35 knots and a top speed of 42 knots. In fact **Hoverspeed Great Britain** holds the Hales Trophy for the Blue Riband of the Atlantic as it has made the fastest crossing of the Atlantic by a passenger vessel. Safety has not been ignored either: the catamarans meet every safety requirement and the hull is virtually unsinkable, exceeding statutory requirements for stability.

Note: The Hovercraft, and to a lesser extent the SeaCat catamarans, are subject to cancellation in the event of poor weather conditions. You will then be transferred to an alternative P&O European Ferries or Stena Sealink Line/SNAT service to Calais.

Offices Telephone reservations can be made on Monday to Friday 0800-2000 and Saturday 0800-1800 in either Dover 0304 240241 (telex: 96323), London 081 554 7061, Birmingham 021 236 2190 or Manchester 061 228 1321. Alternatively book at a travel agent or

on Viewdata; key HOV # for ISTEL and HOV for FASTRAK.
For general enquiries and information call Dover 0304 240241.

P&O European Ferries

This company operates ferries between Dover and Calais and its
vessels have a wide range of shops, bars, cafeterias, restaurants and
duty-free shops. The children's play areas and video lounges are all
decorated in the Disney theme; P&O is the first Preferred Travel
Partner of the Euro Disney Resort. There is a club class service
where, for a supplement of £5, you can travel in a special lounge
area where stewards serve complimentary tea or coffee, and free
newspapers are available.

Dover/Calais When introduced in 1987 the sister ships *Pride of
Dover* and *Pride of Calais* were the largest and fastest passenger car
ferries built for English Channel operations. At 26,433 tons these
have a capacity for 650 vehicles, and 2,290 passengers, and they
both returned to service in February 1992 after refits and
renovations costing £3 million. *Pride of Kent*, at 20,446 tons and
with a capacity for 500 cars and 1,850 passengers, has undergone,
in 1991-92, a £20 million refurbishment to raise it to the standards
required for this service. *Pride of Bruges*, a sister vessel to *Pride of
Kent* (before refurbishment), is 7,950 tons and can carry 336
vehicles and 1,326 passengers.

Offices P&O European Ferries operate a central reservations system
either through travel agents or directly from their Dover offices.
The telephone number for the latter is 0304 203388. Customer
information service: an around-the-clock service giving up-to-date
details of sailings from Dover to France is available on 0304
223603.

Stena Sealink Line/Société Nouvelle d'Armement Transmanche (SNAT)

These companies combine to operate a Dover/Calais ferry service.
Their ferries, described below, all have a variety of shops, bars,
cafeterias, restaurants and well stocked duty-free shops.

Stena Sealink Line *Stena Fantasia* (25,243 tons and with a capacity
for 723 cars and 1,800 passengers) was completely rebuilt in 1990
to a high specification especially for this service. *Stena Invicta*,

somewhat smaller at 19,763 tons and with a capacity for 330 cars and 1,800 passengers, was built in 1985 and introduced on this route in 1991 after a £6 million refit. They can be identified by the blue admiral's riband insignia.

SNAT *Fiesta* is a twin of *Stena Fantasia* and has the same specifications. *Côte d'Azur*, at 8,400 tons and with a capacity for 330 cars and 1,800 passengers, is considerably smaller and was built in 1981. These can be identified by the large, red and blue SS insignia.

Offices Stena Sealink Line operates a telephone reservations system open Monday to Friday 0730-2030, Saturday 0730-1930 and Sunday 0900-1700 on 0233 647047. Details on availability and information for all services are shown on Prestel page * 4623 #. There is also the 24-hour Sealink Ferrycheck service giving details of the exact departure time of each sailing on 0836 403200. Beware, though, these calls are charged at very high rates.

Stena Sealink Line

Operates a ferry service on the Newhaven/Dieppe route using two vessels that both have a variety of shops, bars, cafeterias, restaurants, a well stocked duty-free shop and a bureau de change. EuroLounge reclining seats are available for a small supplement but are more expensive at night.

Operating this route are *Stena Londoner* which was built in 1974, started on this route in 1987, and underwent a major refurbishment in 1991. It is 6,737 tons and has a capacity for 425 cars and 1,800 passengers. *Stena Parisien* was built in 1984, underwent a major refurbishment in May 1990, and joined this route in July 1990. It is 9,000 tons and can carry 300 cars and 1,800 passengers.

These carry the blue admiral's riband insignia and are small compared with those used on the Dover/Calais route as access to Newhaven harbour restricts the size of vessels.

The routes
Dover to and from Calais

Hoverspeed — hovercraft Operate between April and September, from Dover Hoverport/Calais Hoverport; journey time is about 35 minutes.

Hoverspeed — SeaCat catamaran Operate all year round, from Dover SeaCat Terminal/Calais Hoverport; journey time is about 45 minutes.

P&O European Ferries Ferries sail all year round, from Dover Eastern Docks/Calais; journey time is about 75 minutes.

Stena Sealink Line/SNAT Ferries sail all year round, from Dover Eastern Docks/Calais; journey time is about 90 minutes.

Folkestone to and from Boulogne
Hoverspeed — SeaCat catamaran Operate all year round, from Folkestone Harbour/Boulogne Gare Maritime; journey time is about 55 minutes.

Newhaven to and from Dieppe
Stena Sealink Operate all year round, from Newhaven Harbour/Dieppe Gare Maritime; journey time is about four hours.

The terminals
Dover Eastern Docks Terminal
P&O European Ferries and Stena Sealink Line/SNAT operate from this terminal. There is a minimum check-in time of 30 minutes for the P&O European Ferries and Stena Sealink Line/SNAT services.

The terminal is some distance from the ferries and a bus takes passengers to and from the vessels.

P&O European Ferries operate a courtesy bus to Dover Priory Station at 20 and 50 minutes past the hour between 0720 and 1820 daily and outside these hours a bus operates to coincide with vessel arrival times. Also, from Monday to Saturday, at 0420, and on Sunday at 0630, a bus leaves to connect with the first train for London. Stena Sealink Line operates a courtesy bus to Dover Priory for each of its services arriving between 0700 and 2200. Besides seasonal variations in the schedules these services are run, strictly speaking, for each company's own passengers. However, I have found that if asked politely, and there is available room, the drivers are flexible.

The telephone numbers are: Hoverspeed reservations 0304 240241; travel information 0304 240101. P&O European Ferries 0304 203388. Stena Sealink Line/SNAT latest information 0304 240028; for central reservations and guidance 0233 647047.

Dover Western Docks Hovercraft/SeaCat catamaran

Hoverspeed hovercraft and SeaCat catamaran services operate from this terminal and there is a minimum check in time of 30 minutes before departures. A courtesy bus meets every arrival to take passengers to Dover Priory Station.

The Hoverspeed telephone number is 0304 240101.

Dover Western Docks Station

This station is only used by trains connecting with specific ferry and SeaCat services and a courtesy bus takes passengers to and from the vessels.

A note of warning: these courtesy buses are not allowed to take passengers who do not have a ticket for the respective connecting services. As the station is in an isolated location, some distance from the Eastern Docks Terminal, be careful not to be stranded here.

Folkestone Harbour

Only Hoverspeed SeaCat services to Boulogne operate from this terminal and the minimum check in time is 45 minutes before departure.

Newhaven Harbour

Stena Sealink operate from here with four services daily to Dieppe. The terminal has recently been refurbished and this route is mainly used by motorists and connecting boat-train passengers. There is no bus service between Newhaven Town and the harbour but trains stop at both stations. The minimum check in time is 45 minutes before departure. The telephone number for reservations and guidance is 0233 647047, and for latest information 0273 512266.

Boulogne Gare Maritime

Hoverspeed SeaCat uses this terminal which has an integrated railway station (Gare Maritime). SeaCat has its own separate facilities and passengers are taken by a bus to the catamaran, but arriving passengers walk through passport controls to the terminal. The minimum check-in time for Hoverspeed SeaCat is 45 minutes.

Although very close to the city centre, as the crow flies, it takes about 15 minutes to walk due to the shape of the harbour itself; there are no bus services. The city railway station, Boulogne Ville, is about 30 minutes walk away and, again, there are no direct bus services.

The telephone number for Hoverspeed is 21 30 27 26.

Calais Car Ferry Terminal

Both P&O European Ferries and Stena Sealink Line/SNAT use this terminal and buses take passengers to and from the vessels. The minimum check in time is 30 minutes before departure for all ferries. Courtesy buses leave the terminal every time a ferry arrives between 0800 and 2000, for the town centre.

The telephone number for P&O European Ferries is 21 46 10 10 and for Stena Sealink Line/SNAT it is 21 96 70 70.

Calais Hoverport

Hoverspeed hovercraft and SeaCat services operate from this terminal which is located a little to the north of the port building. The minimum check in time is 45 minutes before departure for the SeaCat but only 30 minutes for the hovercraft. A bus takes SeaCat passengers to and from the terminal building whilst the hovercraft parks just outside the terminal. Courtesy buses meet every arrival to take passengers to the town centre and Calais Ville railway station.

The telephone number for Hoverspeed is 21 96 67 10.

Calais Town

The Calais Ville (Town) railway station is directly adjacent to where the courtesy buses stop in the town centre. Buses leave there every 30 minutes, between 0815 and 2015, to the port for ferry services to Dover. For Hoverspeed hovercraft and SeaCat services buses to the Hoverport leave 45 minutes before each departure.

Dieppe Gare Maritime

Stena Sealink operate from here with four sailings a day to Newhaven. There is not really a terminal at all for foot passengers. The ferry quay is in the centre of town and passengers get off the vessels directly on to the train or into the town. The minimum check in time is 45 minutes before departure.

For the city railway station, Dieppe Ville, turn left off the boat and, after a 100 yards or so, turn left again and follow the main road around the harbour; the station is about half a mile away, directly ahead of you. The telephone number is 35 06 33 03.

Duty-free goods These are not available in the terminals for P&O

European Ferries, Stena Sealink Line and SNAT services. Hoverspeed does have duty-free shops in their terminals with the exception of Dover Eastern Docks.

THROUGH FRANCE BY TRAIN
Routes and introduction

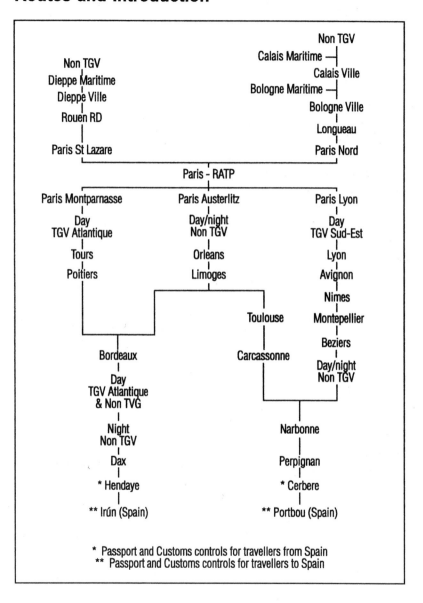

For each route there are diagrams of the key stations showing the location of all the facilities available, the types of trains and the journey times, as at December 1993, how to get between the Paris termini — on a north/south basis — and any other general information that may be of use to travellers. For details of connecting services between Paris and London see *London to the Channel Ports*.

There are three subjects that merit separate sections of their own: the *Train à Grande Vitesse* (TGV), CORAIL services and the rapid transit system in Paris, which is known as RATP. These are followed by a general information section.

The Train à Grande Vitesse (TGV)

The first section of the TGV Sud-Est was opened in September 1981. It revolutionised train travel in France and indeed Europe. As well as being capable of much higher speeds on regular track than ordinary trains, its top speed on the purpose-built sections is 270km/h (over 168mph). Apart from the technology necessary for high speeds, much design effort was put into comfort and convenience for the 108 first-class and 260 second-class passengers.

In 1989 a new TGV system was opened — the TGV Atlantique. Initially this was limited to the west branch serving Brittany and then, in 1990, the southwest line to Bordeaux and Hendaye/Irún was opened. This service has benefited from the experience gained with the TGV Sud-Est and few people would disagree with the opinion that it is not only the showpiece of SNCF but also the premier rail service in Europe. Although there have been technological changes (the top speed has been raised to 300km/h (over 186mph) on the purpose-built track), the main improvements have been commercially based. The capacity has been increased to 485 (116 first and 369 second-class) and this does not include 11 pull-down seats in first class and 26 more in the second. But the more obvious differences are the innovative new seating areas in some of the carriages, particularly in the first-class areas.

There is also a very impressive range of facilities, on both services, and the most important are

(a) meals — there is an at-seat catering service, available for first-class passengers only, provided by hostesses and stewards

(b) bar and snacks — a complete carriage on the TGV Atlantique (slightly less on the TGV Sud-Est), between the first and second-class areas, is provided for this service. Besides drinks and hot and cold snacks, which can also be taken away, cigarettes, newspapers, magazines and phone cards are also sold

(c) telephones — these are available in both the first and second-class areas as well as the bar. Calls can be made to most places using the latest radiotelephone technology and 50 or 120 unit phone cards are sold in the bar shop
(d) nursery — this is located in the second class next to the *Carre* area and, amongst other things, there is a table for changing nappies and a bottle warmer (TGV Atlantique only).

In late September 1993 the TGV Nord-Europe line was completed. The first section, Paris Gare du Nord to Lille, was opened in May 1993 and now there are services on to Calais Ville. This cuts the journey time down to 1 hour 50 minutes, a saving of over 1 hour between Paris and Calais.

It is important to remember that when travelling on the TGV you need both a ticket for your journey and also a *Résa 300* seat reservation. More information on the *Résa 300* is detailed below.

Free guides to these services, *Guide du Voyageur TGV Sud-Est*, *Atlantique* or *Nord-Europe*, current timetables, fares and *Résa 300* schedules as well as details of the service, are available from SNCF outlets as well as from stations. Some guides are multilingual.

Résa 300 Reservations

At first this system, as described in the above guides, looks rather complicated, but it is actually based on the law of supply and demand. The more popular the service the more you pay as a reservation supplement, and vice versa.

The first thing to understand is that a supplement for a seat reservation, *Résa 300*, is payable on all TGV trains and that this is variable by class, first and second, and by distance. There is a second system, *Sur Réservation*, whereby you get a *Résa 300* which does not specify which particular seat you will have. This is because when all the regular seats have been booked SNCF issue, for a cheaper supplement, extra *Résa 300* reservations equal to the number of seats that are located outside the normal carriages. Before taking a seat contact the ticket inspector; if there are vacancies in the regular seats you will be allocated one, otherwise you will be given the other sort, which are nowhere near as comfortable.

These supplements, both *Résa 300* and *Sur Réservation*, are identified by four number and colour codes. Prices, in French francs (FF), for the longest journeys — Paris to Irún on the TGV Atlantique and Paris to Béziers on the TGV Sud-Est — as at May 30 1993, are as follows:

Number code	1	2	3	4
Colour code	Yellow	Grey	Green	Orange
TGV Sud-Est:				
First class	16	32	16	56
(*Sur Resérvation*)	0	16	0	40
Second class	16	24	40	48
(*Sur Resérvation*)	0	8	24	32
TGV Atlantique:				
First class	40	120	40	120
(*Sur Réservation*)	24	104	24	104
Second class	32	32	80	80
(*Sur Réservation*)	16	16	64	64

These supplements are applied according to the following criteria:

The day you want to travel Certain days such as bank and school holidays are designated *Jours Particuliers* and their *Résa 300* code, variable for each train, takes precedence.

The day of the week On all other days the *Semaine Type Résa 300* code applies and this is variable according to the day you decide to travel and the train you take.

The *Résa 300* reservation card gives you all the information you need about the train you have chosen and where your seat is located. In the top right hand corner there is a small square box where the class, 1 or 2, is printed. Immediately below that is a long rectangular box that indicates the train and coach (*Voiture*) number on the top line and then, from the left, the number of places and the seat numbers. If you have asked for a non-smoking area it is indicated under the heading *Particularités* (remarks) as *Salle Non Fumeurs*.

Beware Before boarding your train remember to punch both the ticket and the *Résa 300* reservation. This is done automatically by one of the orange *Composteur* machines located throughout the station concourses. Failure to do so will not only render these tickets invalid but may be treated as an offence as well.

Everything about these services, from the cleanliness and variety of facilities available to the unrivalled comfort, even at the top speeds, is of the highest quality.

Note: During 1993 SNCF began an experiment using a completely new seat reservation and ticketing system named SOCRATE. This is an adaptation of SABRE, the American Airlines' computerised reservation system. It was planned to extend this to all TGV services first in late 1993 and then the spring of 1994. However, due to initial problems with the system, it is not now known when this will be implemented. SNCF were not in a position, at December 1993, to supply the new pricing information.

CORAIL services

This is the name given to the regular non-TGV express services within France. CORAIL is the French for coral, the colour of the doors, and it is also intended to combine the idea of comfort and rail. The facilities on these trains can vary according to the distance of the journey but, in any event, they are usually clean and comfortable.

On regular daytime services there are first and second-class carriages and, if there is not a restaurant or buffet, there is often a trolley service for drinks, etc. The first-class carriages are identified by a yellow horizontal stripe and the second by a green one.

On longer journeys there can be restaurant, sleeping car and couchette facilities.

The Paris Rapid Transit System (RATP)

There are four component parts to the RATP:

The Métro

The symbol for the Métro is a capital M in a circle.

The first departures, from each terminal, are at 0530 whilst the last trains arrive at their respective terminals at 0115.

This, one of the most comprehensive underground railway systems in the world, is the fastest and most popular way of getting around Paris. However, much of the time it is quite crowded and many of the connecting passageways have traders selling a wide variety of goods. There are also many down and outs who use it as a home.

It is, though, very easy to find your way around. Just select your destination on the Métro plan and follow the lines according to their number, colour and name of the terminal in the direction you need to go. If you need to use more than one line follow the signs to the platform indicated for the terminal on the first line you need to travel on. Change at the required station and follow the *Correspondance* signs — with the line number, colour and terminals

— to the correct platform for the direction in which you need to travel. If you need to change again just follow the same procedure.

The RER
The symbol for the RER is those initials within a circle.

The first departures, from each terminal, are at about 0500 whilst the last trains arrive at their respective terminals at about 0115.

This system links key points within the city to the surrounding regions outside of the Métro network. The RER and Métro systems are also interconnected so that passengers can change from one to another easily.

The Bus
The symbol is a circle enclosing the letters BUS.

The buses run to complicated schedules as follows: Monday to Saturday there is a full service on all routes between 0700 and 2030 and, after that, a much more limited evening *Soirées* service — both in the number of routes and timetables — until 0030. On Sundays and holidays there is a service, but not on all routes, between that of the day and *soirée*, from 0700 to 2030.

There are over 2,000 buses operating in Paris and they offer the traveller an ideal way of seeing the city but, given the usual traffic jams, they should only be used if you are not in a hurry. Each bus stop has information regarding the routes serving the stop, the various interchanges between routes, timetables and whether you need one or two tickets (this depends upon the route length).

Noctambus (night buses)
The symbol is a black owl superimposed over a yellow full moon in a black square.

These depart from Châtelet (near Hôtel de Ville) every hour, between 0130 and 0530 to various destinations on the outskirts of the city. From the various outskirts they leave for Châtelet hourly between 0100 and 0500.

The Noctambus stops, by request, anywhere along its route.

Fares
For an individual journey An individual ticket entitles you to travel anywhere within Paris on a combination of Métro/RER and most bus services. The only exception is on certain long bus routes where two tickets are required.

For a single day The *FORMULE 1* pass entitles you to unlimited travel on either the Metro, RER, bus (not the Noctambus) and the Ile-de France railway. It is pink, blue and yellow and comes in a plastic sleeve that has a smaller opening, on the front, where the ticket is displayed. Remember, to validate the pass, sign the *FORMULE 1* card and enter the pass number on the ticket. On the Métro and RER insert the *FORMULE 1* ticket into the automatic turnstile slot but, on the bus, only show the complete pass to the driver, do not insert the ticket into the ticket-punching machine.

There is a choice of two zones, 1-2 or 1-4 and the airports.

For between three to five days The *PARIS VISITE* pass entitles you to unlimited travel on the same systems as the *FORMULE 1* plus the Orlybus, Balabus and Noctambus. If you only plan to visit Paris and the immediate suburbs ask for a *PARIS VISITE* Zone 1-3, if you intend to go as far as Versailles, Orly or Charles de Gaulle airports ask for Zones 1-4. There are also discounts ranging from 20% to 50% for such attractions as boat rides on the Seine, the Parc Astérix, the panorama deck of the Montparnasse Tower and bicycle hire. This pass is black and works in the same way as the *FORMULE 1* pass.

General information
Finding your seat

On many stations there are *Composition des Trains* boards which show where the different carriages, first, second, buffet, sleepers, etc, are located, as well as the carriage (*voiture*) numbers. By comparing this information with your reservation it will give you an idea of where to stand on the platform.

As an additional help there are *Repère* alpha codes painted on TGV platforms which, when compared with the *Composition des Trains* board and your reservation, will indicate exactly where to stand on the platform.

Dieppe to Paris Gare St Lazare
The trains

This a journey of 171km (107 miles) and the route is served by CORAIL daytime express trains. However on most occasions, except boat trains, it will be necessary to change at Rouen. The journey time can vary from just over two hours to as long as three and a half, depending upon the time of day and the wait in Rouen.

Dieppe Ville

Tel: 35 98 50 50

A rather plain station which is a short distance away from both the centre of town and the harbour (Stena Sealink Line service). For the latter leave the station and walk straight for about 10 minutes. The ferry docks near the town centre.

Layout

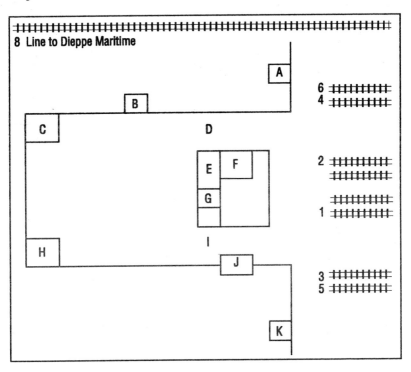

Key

A: *Chef de Service Voyageurs Accueil*

B: Information/Reservation, open Monday to Friday 0900-1900; Saturday 0900-1200, 1400-1815

C: Buffet

D: Entrance to trains, *Départ*

E: Ticket office

F: Waiting room, *Salle d'Attente*

G: Baggage office, *Bagages*

H: *Tabac Journaux*, newspapers, magazines, cigarettes, etc

I: Exit from trains, *Arrivee*

J: Left luggage lockers, *Consigne Automatique*

K: Toilets

Rouen Rive Droite (R D)
Tel: 35 98 50 50

Layout

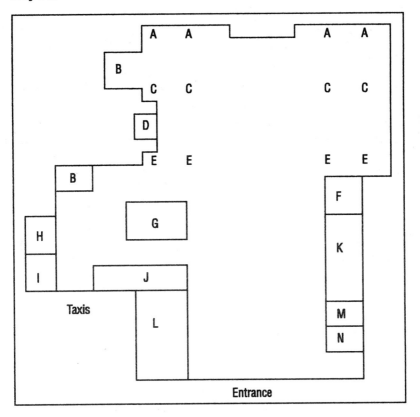

Key

A: Entrances to platforms 6 and 8
B: Left luggage lockers, *Consigne Automatique*
C: Entrances to platforms 2 and 4
D: Assistance office, *Acceuil*
E: Entrances to platforms 1 and 3
F: Frantour, a travel agency
G: Relais H, newspapers, magazines, cigarettes, etc

H: Toilets, open 0630-2000
I: Women's clothes shop
J: SOHO, gift shop
K: Ticket office
L: Brasserie, bar/restaurant
M: Information/reservation
N: Après Vente, an after sales office

Paris Gare St Lazare

Tel: (1) 45 82 50 50

This station is very close to the city centre. In fact it is just a short walk away from the Place de la Concorde, and the foot of the Champs Elysées, one of the most important shopping areas, with large department stores, is even closer. It is also a very busy commuter station and most of the platforms are used by local *banlieu* services. All the facilities detailed are on the same concourse as the platforms. However, as you go to the Métro, there are more facilities on a lower level that cannot be shown here.

Key

A: Information/reservation
B: Relais H, newspapers, magazines, etc
C: Exit to street
D: Crédit Lyonnais bank
E: Croq Voyage, croissants, drinks, hotdogs, etc
F: Joffo Coiffure, men's and women's hairdressers
G: *Tabac Cadeaux*, cigarettes, tobacco, stamps, etc
H: *Acceuil Banlieu*, assistance office for local train services
I: Frantour, a travel agency
J: Exit to Métro
K: FNAC Services, shop for films, etc
L: Police office
M: *Après Vente*, open Monday to Friday 0800-1700
N: Libraire Presse, newspapers, magazines, etc
O: *Billets Banlieu*, ticket office for local lines
P: Waiting room (second class), *Salle d'Attente*
Q: *Consigne Automatique*; left

luggage lockers
R: Thomas Cook Bureau de Change, open daily 0800-2000
S: *Bons échanger, Remboursements*, office for exchange of tickets and obtaining refunds
T: International service, information, open Monday to Friday 0715-1930, reservations and tickets open Monday to Friday 0715-2000; Saturday 0900-1800
U: *Billets Grandes Lignes*, ticket office for long distance services
V: Toilets
W: *Acceuil Grandes Lignes*, assistance office for long distance train services
X: Waiting room (first class), *Salle d'Attente*
Y: Snack/Brasserie Saint Lazare
Z: *Chef de Gare*, station master's office
AA: Brasserie l'Emnarcadère, restaurant and bar
BB: Small kiosk selling croissants, hotdogs, etc

Gare St Lazare to Gare d'Austerlitz

- **by Métro** Line 12, Pink, Direction Mairie d'Issy and change at Sèvres-Babylone; then Line 10, Brown, Direction Gare d'Austerlitz which is the end of the line.
- **by Métro and RER** Métro Line 13, Blue, Direction Châtillon-

Layout

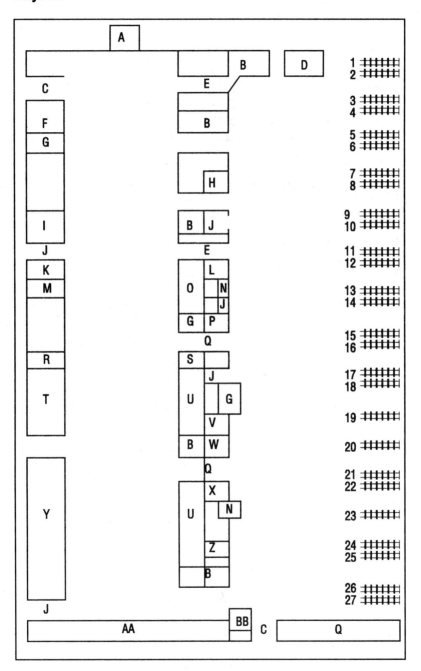

Montrouge and change at Invalides; then RER, Line C, Yellow, Direction d'Orly, Dourdan or St Martin d'Etampes to Gare d'Austerlitz.

Gare St Lazare to Gare de Lyon
- by Métro Line 12, Pink, Direction Mairie d'Issy and change at Concorde; then Line 1, Yellow/Orange, Direction Château de Vincennes to Gare de Lyon.
- by Métro and RER Métro Line 3, Olive Green, Direction Galliéni and change at Auber; then RER, Line A, Direction Boissy St Léger or Marne La Vallée to Gare de Lyon.

Gare St Lazare to Gare Montparnasse
- by Métro Line 12, Pink, Direction Mairie d'Issy to Montparnasse Bienvenue.

Calais/Boulogne to Paris Gare du Nord
The trains
This is a journey of 296km (185 miles) from Calais and 254km (158 miles) from Boulogne and the route is served by CORAIL daytime express trains. Beware, some of these services may not be direct and a change may be necessary in either Amiens or Longueau. The fastest journey time is a little over three hours but it can take over three and a half if a change is necessary.

As at September 1993 there is one daily TGV Nord-Europe service, each way, between Calais Ville and Paris Gare du Nord.

Calais Ville
(Tel: 21 80 50 50)
A rather drab station, located close to the town centre, where all the facilities are located above the tracks and the platforms are reached via stairs.

Key
A: Relais H, newspapers,   C: Train information
magazines, etc   D: Buffet and bar
B: Ticket office

Layout

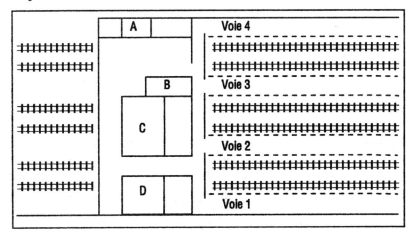

Boulogne Ville

(Tel: 21 80 50 50)

A modern, bland station located some distance from the town centre. The facilities are located below the tracks and the platforms are reached via an underpass and stairs.

Layout

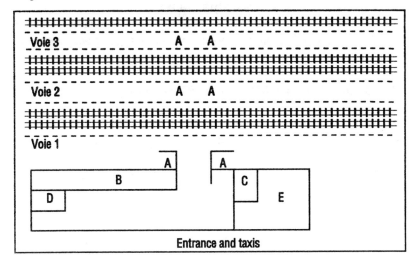

Key

A:	Entrance to platforms		magazines, etc
B:	Ticket office	**D:**	Train information
C:	Relais H, newspapers,	**E:**	Buffet and bar

Paris Gare du Nord

(Tel: (1) 45 82 50 50)

This station is located to the northeast of the centre of Paris and, as the name indicates, it serves the north of France, as well as Belgium, the Netherlands and Germany. It is a large traditional terminus and a part of it — beyond platform 19 — is dedicated to local RER services. During 1993 there was much development under way to renovate this station.

Gare du Nord to Gare d'Austerlitz

- **by Métro** Line 5, Orange, Direction Place d'Italie — direct to Gare d'Austerlitz.

Gare du Nord to Gare de Lyon

- **by Métro** Line 5, Orange, Direction Place d'Italie and change at Bastille; then Line 1, Yellow/Orange, Direction Château de Vincennes — one stop to Gare de Lyon.

Gare du Nord to Gare Montparnasse

- **by Métro** Line 4, Primrose, Direction Porte d'Orléans — direct to Montparnasse Bienvenue. *Note* There is a very long walk between the Métro and mainline station.

Paris Gare Montparnasse to Hendaye/Irún
The trains

The distances on this route are Bordeaux 581km (363 miles), Hendaye 816km (510 miles) and Irún 818km (511 miles).

The trains run at frequent intervals throughout the day and many of them terminate, and start, from Bordeaux. Some are nonstop between Paris and Bordeaux taking just under three hours, others vary their stops at intermediate stations and the journey time can take up to three and a half hours. All trains stop at the most important stations between Bordeaux and Hendaye and, overall, the fastest time between Paris and Hendaye is just over five hours. These distinctive trains are attractively painted in blue and silver and have the following colour codes: cherry red — first class, ocean blue/green — second class and yellow — bar.

To and from Bordeaux and Irún there is a choice, also, of *CORAIL* services as well as a variety of long distance trains between Spain, Portugal and Paris d'Austerlitz.

Paris Gare Montparnasse
(Tel: (1) 45 82 50 50)
This is located in the south of the city close to the Montparnasse Tower, the tallest building in France. It is a very modern station with three levels, connected by a series of open plan escalators, with the Métro on the lowest and the mainline station on the third.

Layout

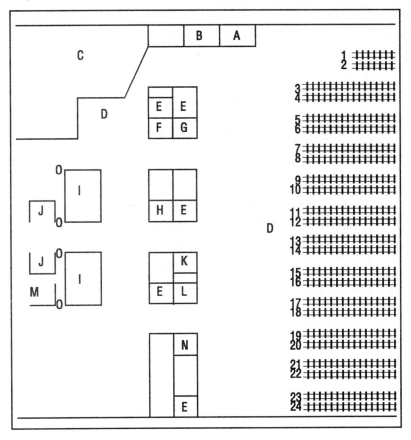

Key

A: Waiting room/toilets/ children's playroom, *Salle d'Attente*
B: Bar/Brasserie
C: Ticket office
D: Information kiosk
E: Relais H, newspapers, magazines, etc
F: *Croisière Tabac*, cigarettes, sweets, gifts, etc
G: Bar, sandwiches, hot dogs, etc
H: Thomas Cook bureau de change and cash dispenser for American Express cards
I: Open alcoves overlooking lower floor

J: Exit to Métro
K: *Acceuil Départ*; help office for departures
L: *Office de Tourisme*; tourist office, open daily 0800-2000
M: *Buffet Provisoire*
N: *Acceuil Arrivée*; help office for arrivals
O: Luggage trolleys, released by inserting a 10FF coin that is reclaimed automatically when the trolley is returned

Gare Montparnasse to Gare du Nord
- by Métro Line 4, Primrose, Direction Porte de Clignancourt direct to Gare du Nord.

Gare Montparnasse to Gare St Lazare
- by Métro Line 12, Pink, Direction Porte de la Chapelle direct to St Lazare.

Bordeaux St Jean
(Tel: 56 92 50 50)
This station is located some distance from the centre of Bordeaux close to the River Gironde. Perhaps the only unusual aspect of this station is that it has facilities for taking a shower.

Key (ground level)

A: *Aide en Gare SOS Voyageurs*, open Monday to Friday 1100-1815
B: Train information and reservations, open Monday to Friday 0900-1900; Saturday 0900-1830; Sunday 1000-1330, 1400-1900
C: Underpass to other platforms
D: Speciality wine shop
E: Relais H, Tabac, cigarettes, tobacco, gifts, etc
F: Relais H, newspapers, magazines, etc
G: Daytime waiting room, *Salle*

d'Attente
H: Small buffet opening on to *Quai 1*
I: Train information
J: Toilets and showers, *urinoirs* 1FF, WC 3FF and showers 14FF
K: Night time waiting room, *Salle d'Attente*, open 2200-0730
L: *Consigne manuel*, manual left luggage, open daily 0630-1300, 1330-2000, 2045-0400
M: *Office de Tourisme*, tourist office, open June 1 to September 30

Layout

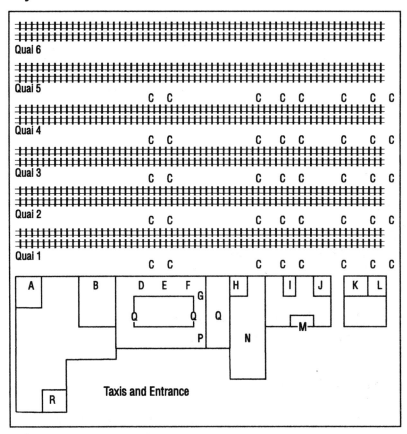

daily 0900-1900; October 1 to May
31 Monday to Saturday 0900-1900,
Sunday 1000-1900
N: Hotel Terminus

O: Brasserie, cafeteria/restaurant
P: Buffet
Q: Exit to lower level
R: Thomas Cook bureau de change

Layout (lower level)

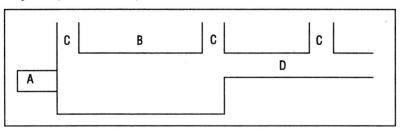

Key (lower level)

A: Relais H, newspapers, magazines, etc
B: Ticket office
C: Underpass to platforms
D: *Consigne Auto*, automatic left luggage lockers accessible only 0500-2230. (a) Find an open locker and put luggage in. (b) Close and lock the door and insert 15FF. (c) Take the automatically delivered ticket, this has a code number on the inside. (d) When ready to reclaim luggage enter the code number on the machine built into the lockers and the door will automatically open.

General There are two practical reasons why people may stop at Bordeaux St Jean. Firstly, if you leave London in the morning then Bordeaux is about as far as you can get in one day using the TGV Atlantique service. Secondly, when travelling from Spain on a regular daytime service to Paris d'Austerlitz it is quicker to change to a TGV at Bordeaux. As an example I once caught a regular train at Hendaye and changed at Bordeaux; after a leisurely lunch I caught a TGV two hours later and still arrived in Paris before the original train.

For those who stop there are several hotels and restaurants, of varying standards, just outside the station. However, if you are prepared to be a little adventurous and want to see a really typical small family hotel/restaurant, try the Hotel Bienvenu (turn right out of the station and this is about 400-500m away at 9 rue Charles Domercq, on the other side of the road.) There is certainly nothing fancy about this place, indeed it's rather basic, but apart from being interesting, it is certainly excellent value for money. A single room without shower is only 80FF while one with a shower is just 20FF more, and doubles are 120FF and 150FF respectively. The real star value though is the restaurant; a four-course meal costs only 44FF and this includes bread, wine — usually a litre of red table wine — and service. If you plan on staying here and want to make a reservation the telephone number is 56 91 77 50.

Hendaye
(Tel: 59 55 50 50)

Layout

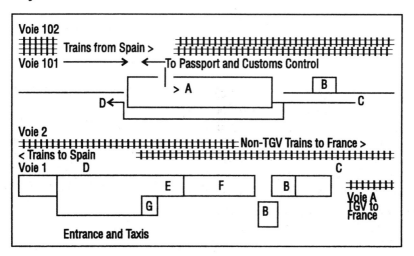

Key

A: Passport and customs control
B: Toilets
C: Underpass for TGV passengers
D: Underpass for Non-TGV passengers and exit

E: Tickets and train information
F: Cafeteria
G: *Tabac-Journaux*, cigarettes, newspapers, etc

Irún (Spain)

Layout

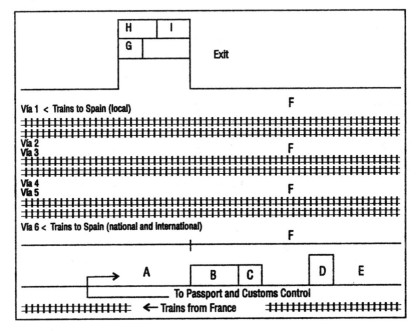

Key

A: Passport and Customs Control (from France)
B: Shop, newspapers, magazines, gifts, etc
C: Train information
D: Ticket office
E: Cafeteria
F: Underpass

G: Local ticket office
H: General shop
I: Bar/cafeteria. Upper level (above B, C and D)
J: *Aseos; Sala de Espera*; TV room (*Sala de TV*); Nursery (*Atención al Bebe*); *Tábaco*; cigarettes, tobacco, etc

General: The seats in the waiting areas are, innovatively, made of railway sleepers.

Paris Gare d'Austerlitz to Hendaye/Irún and Cerbère/Portbou
The trains

As far as the trains are concerned this is far and away the most interesting station. Besides the CORAIL expresses there are other

French, Spanish and Portuguese trains and some of these are rather unusual.

Although there are daytime services to both destinations these are very slow when compared with TGVs. Most travellers will therefore use the Gare d'Austerlitz for overnight services as these offer certain advantages. They can save money on hotels and you do not waste valuable daytime hours that can be spent sightseeing. On a more romantic note there is nothing quite as exciting as watching the sun rise to expose an unknown countryside and then to arrive at a station, perhaps in a different country, with new sounds and smells.

The selection of trains and facilities is such that it requires too much space to describe all of them here.

Bear in mind that the supplements for couchettes and sleeping cars can be rather expensive. This is certainly the case for one of the very latest services, RENFE's *Francisco de Goya* and *Joan Miró* between Paris and Madrid and Barcelona respectively. However, the facilities are second to none and if you fancy travelling in real style try the *Grande Clase* cabins. I have; besides a comfortable bed there is a toilet, washbasin and shower (towels, shampoo, etc provided) and you even get an early morning telephone reminder that you will be at your destination in about an hour. They live up to their name — Hotel Trains.

Paris Gare d'Austerlitz
(Tel: (1) 45 82 50 50)
This is a traditional style railway station and it is located on the south bank of the Seine not far west of the Notre Dame. It does, however, have a very strange design, rather like a large U turned on its side. The open inside of the U is a large car park and the closed end, facing west, fronts on to the platforms.

Key

A: *Provisions de Voyage Aramis*, buffet, bar, sandwiches, etc
B: Relais H, newspapers, magazines, etc
C: *Le Grenadier Provisions de Voyage*, buffet, bar, sandwiches, etc
D: Bar and restaurant
E: Newspapers, magazines, etc
F: *Tabac Cadeaux*; cigarettes, tobacco, stamps, etc
G: Entrance to Métro

H: Gifts, papers, etc
I: Train information
J: Tickets
K and L: *Consigne Auto*, automatic left luggage lockers cost 20FF
M: Avis carhire; *Office de Tourisme*, tourist office, open daily 0800-1500 and *Objets Trouvés*, lost property
N: Jaldry, up-market women's clothes stores

Layout

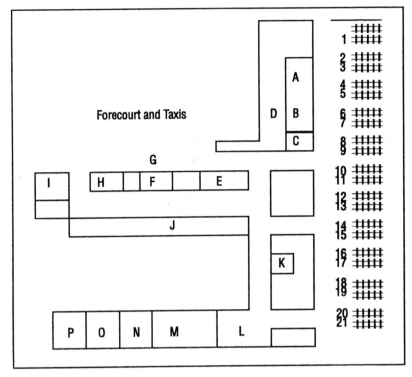

O: *Epicerie Fine*, an interesting
delicatessen
P: Left luggage, manual and

automatic lockers, manual 22FF and
auto 15/20 or 30FF

Gare d'Austerlitz to Gare du Nord
- **by Métro:** Line 5, Orange, Direction Bobigny-Pablo Picasso
direct to Gare du Nord.

Gare d'Austerlitz to Gare St Lazare
- **by Métro:** Line 10, Brown, Direction Boulogne Pont de St Cloud
and change at Sèvres Babylone; then Line 12, Pink, Direction Porte
de la Chapelle to St Lazare.
- **by Métro and RER** RER Line C, Yellow, Direction Versailles
or St Quentin-en-Yvelines and change at Invalides; then Métro Line
13, Blue, Direction Gabriel Péri or St Denis-Basilique to St Lazare.

Paris Gare de Lyon to Cerbère/Portbou
The trains
The distances on this route are Montpelier 841km (525 miles), Béziers 912km (570 miles) and Cerbère/Portbou 1043km (652 miles).

According to the schedule that expired late in 1993 there were eight TGVs each day — between 0740 and 1835 hours — from Gare de Lyon to Montpelier, with a journey time of just over four and three quarter hours. Two of these continued on to Béziers, about 40 minutes further down the line.

TGV Sud-Est is a very distinctive bright orange colour with a white stripe running below the window level, which itself is painted grey.

From Montpelier to Perpignan, and then on to Cerbère and Portbou, there are CORAIL services and the journey time can vary according to whether they are direct or it is necessary to change in Narbonne. The fastest time is just over two hours but it is safer to allow closer to three.

Paris Gare de Lyon
(Tel: (1) 45 82 50 50)
This station, architecturally traditional in style, is located very close to the north bank of the Seine, just across the river from the Gare d'Austerlitz via the bridge bearing the same name. It does, however, have two unusual features: firstly the strange numbering systems of the platforms and, secondly, a very attractive mural, almost hidden above the ticket office, depicting scenes from places along the routes served by the station.

Key
A: *Comestibles*, snack bar
B: *Relais H Tabac*, newspapers, magazines, cigarettes, etc
C: Exit
D: *SNCF Orientation*, general train information
E: Newspapers and gifts
F: *Stop Cadeaux*, a small shop
G: *Parfums Monica*, perfumes, gifts, etc
H: Snack bar
I: *Relais H*, newspapers, magazines, etc
J: Avis carhire
K: Newspapers, gifts, etc
L: *Tabac Cadeaux*, cigarettes, stamps, etc
M: Bureau de Change
N: Frantour travel agent
O: Small snack bar
P: Ticket office
Q: Train information and reservations
R: *Bagages au Départ*, baggage forwarding office
S: *Livres Journaux*, newspapers and magazines
T: Croq Voyage, snacks, drinks, etc

Layout

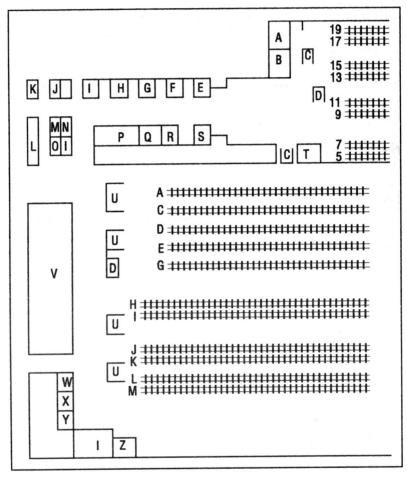

U: Exit to Métro and left luggage machines

V: (Lower level) cafeteria; (upper level) Le Train Bleu restaurant

W: *Office de Tourisme*, tourist office, open daily 0800-2000

X: *SOS Voyageurs*, help office for travellers

Y: Train information

Z: SOHO gift shop

Gare de Lyon to Gare du Nord

- by Métro: Line 1, Yellow/Orange, Direction Pont de Neuilly and change at Bastille; then Line 5, Orange, Direction Bobigny-Pablo Picasso to Gare du Nord.

Gare de Lyon to Gare St Lazare

- **by Métro:** Line 1, Yellow/Orange, Direction Pont de Neuilly and change at Concorde; then Line 12, Pink, Direction Porte de la Chapelle to St Lazare.
- **by RER and Métro:** RER Line A, Red, Direction St Germain en laye, Cergy-St Christophe or Poissy and change at Auber; then Métro Line 3, Olive Green, Direction Pont de Levallois-Bécon to St Lazare.

Narbonne

(Tel: 68 47 50 50)

Layout

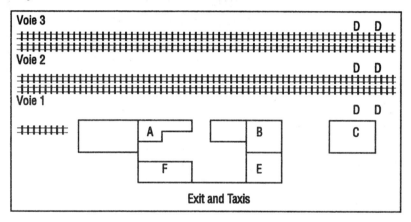

Key

A: *Consigne Auto*, automatic left luggage lockers

B: Train information and reservations

C: Cafeteria

D: Underpass to other platforms

E: Ticket office

F: *Relais H Tabac*, newspapers, magazines, cigarettes, etc

Cerbère
(Tel: 68 35 50 50)

Layout

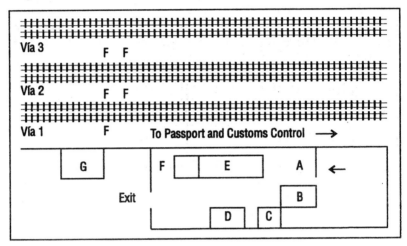

Key

A: Passport and customs control
B: *Consigne automatique*,
automatic left luggage lockers
C: Bureau de Change, open 0830-
1030, 1150-1330, 1600-1930, 2200-
2235

D: Bar
E: Tickets and information
F: Underpass to platforms
G: Bar, cafeteria and hotel

Portbou (Spain)
Key

A: *Servicios (Serveis)*
B: *Jefe de Circulación*
C: *Jefe de Estación, (cap d'estacio)*
D: *Sala d'espera*
E: Cafeteria, open daily 0530-2100
F: Exit from station
G: Train *información*
H: Ticket office
I: BBV bank, open daily 0530-
1400, 1800-2100; automatic currency
exchange machine

J: Passport and customs control
K: *Comisaría*
L: *Kiosco* for newspapers,
magazines, etc, open daily 0530-
1600, 1800-2100
M: Wagons Lits Cooks Bureau de
Change, open daily 0600-1900
N: *Consigna Automática*, cost 200
ptas a day
O: Underpass to other platforms

Layout

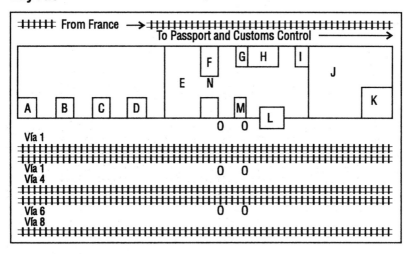

General The words in brackets are the Catalán language for that particular facility in the *Key*.

Note: If you have not stocked up on your cheap drinks — or other souvenirs — there are shops just outside the station, and more in the town, that stock a wide variety of drinks and other goods at very reasonable prices. These can be purchased in either Spanish pesetas or French francs.

NORTHERN SPAIN DIRECT
Portsmouth to Bilbao

An attractive, and relaxing, alternative way of travelling to Spain is to take the P&O European Ferries service between Portsmouth and Bilbao. There are two sailings a week, in both directions, and the ferry leaves from the Continental Ferry Port, Mile End, Portsmouth. There are frequent train connections between Waterloo station, in London, and Portsmouth where a shuttle bus connects with the port. However, if time is important, it is better to take a taxi.

Reservations can be made through travel agents, or by phone on 0304 240077.

The Vessel

At 37,500 tons *Pride of Bilbao* is the largest ferry operating from the UK, accommodating 2,500 passenger and 600 cars, and travelling on it is an absolutely marvellous experience. The journey time is 29 hours and everyone is allocated a cabin most of which, by necessity, are inside. If you want an outside cabin, at no extra cost, go immediately you get on board to the Information Desk on deck six and ask to be put on the waiting list. Within an hour of sailing you will be informed if one is available. It is also possible to upgrade to a luxury cabin or suite at £30 and £40, respectively.

Once settled it is time to explore the vessel and you will find that everything one could possibly want is available. There is a variety of bars, with shows throughout the day and night, a casino, large duty-free shop, cinemas, swimming pool, jacuzzi and sauna, games rooms, video screens and, of course, deck games if the weather permits. If none of these appeal just sit in the comfortable chairs alongside the picture windows, watch the sea go by and relax.

Food is not included in the price of a ticket and on-board you will find a cafeteria, a buffet-style restaurant that is used for breakfast, lunch and dinner and a formal restaurant. These are very good value for money.

Bilbao
From the port to the city

Pride of Bilbao docks at Santurtzi about 16km north of the city and there are really only the following two options to get to the centre of town:

By rail Just a short distance from the harbour is the *Cercanía* station of Santurtzi and trains run from here, every 10 minutes, to Bilbao la Naja. This takes about 22 minutes.

By taxi If you do not get off the ship quickly you may find there is a long wait for a taxi. When you do get one it will take about half an hour and cost in the region of 2,500 ptas.

Hotels

There is the usual array of *hostels* and *pensións*, of much the same standard, in the centre of town but for those wanting something better I recommend hotels belonging to the Aranzazu chain.

**** Hotel Villa de Bilbao Gran Vía, 87; tel: (94) 441 81 50; fax: (94) 441 65 29. Double 20,000 ptas; double for single use 15,000 ptas. This large and well appointed hotel is located at the far end, from the centre of town, of the Gran Vía. The 142 rooms are very large and have private bath, telephone, radio, minibar, satellite TV with Canal + and a safe box. The public rooms are large and gracious and there is a restaurant and bar.

**** Hotel Abando Colón de Larreátegui, 7; tel: (94) 423 62 00; fax: (94) 424 55 25. Single 10,000 ptas; double 16,500 ptas; double for single use 12,800 ptas. Located in a new building close to the centre of town and, conveniently, to the railway station of the same name. The rooms are large with private bath, telephone, radio, minibar, satellite TV and a safe box. There is also a cafeteria, restaurant, American bar, gift shop and dry cleaner and hairdresser.

The railway station

RENFE Bilbao — Abando, Plaza de España, 2; tel: (94) 423 69 54. This rather small and oddly designed station is located in the centre of Bilbao.

The concourse is at ground floor level and there are few facilities; the *consigna automática* is open from 0700-2300 and costs 400 ptas per 24 hours. The platforms, and some more facilities, are on the upper level.

The routes There is a limited number of long distance trains from Bilbao. To Barcelona there are a *Diurno* and *Estrella*, via Logroño and Zaragoza. To Madrid there are a *Diurno*, an afternoon *Talgo* and an *Estrella*, via Burgos. There are also *Estrella*s to Valencia, Alicante and Andalusian cities, all via Burgos and Madrid.

Plymouth/Portsmouth to Santander

Brittany Ferries run a ferry service up to twice a week in both directions to Santander in northern Spain. From mid-March to mid-November, services run from Plymouth, taking 24 hours, while winter services, from mid-November to mid-March, depart from Portsmouth and take up to 33 hours. Tel: Portsmouth (0705) 751833; Plymouth (0752) 263388.

There are direct rail connections from both London Paddington and Scotland to Plymouth, where the five-minute taxi ride from the station to the ferry terminal will cost £3 to £4. Alternatively, it is about a 15 minute walk. For details on Portsmouth connections, see page 312.

The Vessel

The *Val de Loire*, launched in summer 1993, is Brittany Ferries 5-star flagship. At 32,000 tons, she carries 2,200 passengers, with 1,700 berths in 550 cabins, and 160 reclining seats for those on a budget. Facilities on board will suit the most discerning, with four restaurants and two bars, a duty free and tax free shopping mall, two cinemas, beauty salon, a swimming pool, sauna and gym and a fast photo processing service. For families there are also a nursery and children's playroom.

Santander
From the port to the city

The ferry port in Santander is very close to the centre of this stylish resort, known in Spain for its casino and long sandy beaches, and is just 400m from the RENFE station:

On foot The station is a five minute walk from the ferry terminal.

By taxi If you are laden down with luggage, a taxi from the ferry terminal to the station should cost less than 1,000 ptas.

Hotels

In common with any tourist resort, Santander has a wide range of hotels and pensions. The following are within easy distance of the ferry port. Although I have visited neither, both are recommended by Brittany Ferries:

***Hotel Ciudad de Santander** C/Menendez Pelayo, 13-15; tel: (942) 227965; fax: (942) 217303. Single, high 10,000 ptas, low 9,200 ptas;

double, high 15,100 ptas, low 12,750 ptas; double for single use, high 15,100 ptas, low 12,750 ptas. This modern hotel in the city centre has 62 rooms with 2 lifts, and a restaurant.

*Hotel Romano, C/Federico Vial, 8; tel/fax: (942) 223071. Single, high 4,500 ptas, low 2,900 ptas; double, high 7,500 ptas, low 4,750 ptas. Ten minutes' walk from the ferry terminal heading for *salida de ciudad*, the Hotel Romano is in the fourth street on the left. It has 25 rooms but no restaurant.

The railway station

RENFE Santander - Estación de RENFE, Plaza de la Estaciones, tel: (942) 280202. Located in the centre of the Santander, the RENFE station is at ground floor level, with good access for the disabled.

Facilities include a cafeteria/restaurant, toilets, public telephones, advance booking facilities and a bookshop/newsagent. Automatic left luggage costs 300 ptas for 24 hours.

Almost next door is the Estación Oviedo-Bilbao, tel: (42) 211687, from where there are non-RENFE trains across the north of Spain to the Basque country, Cantabria, Galicia and Asturia.

The routes Three trains a day leave Santander for Madrid, taking 6½ hours by day and 10 hours overnight. There are also *talgo* and *estrella* services to Albacete-Alicante (one per day), Ávila (3 per day) and Valencia-Valladolid (5 trains per day, including 2 *regionales*), and a number of *cercanías*.

NOTES

NOTES

ORDER FORM

European Rail Passes
(Effective Jan. 1, 1994 - Dec. 31, 1994)

EURAIL PASS (17 Countries) 1st Class

❑ 15 Days $498   ❑ 2 Months $1,098
❑ 21 Days $648   ❑ 3 Months $1,398
❑ 1 Month $798

EURAIL FLEXIPASS – 1st Class

❑ 5 Days in 2 Months $348
❑ 10 Days in 2 Months $560
❑ 15 Days in 2 Months $740

EURAIL SAVERPASS – 1st Class

❑ 15 Days $430   ❑ 1 Month $678
❑ 21 Days $550
Price is per person / 3 people must travel together at all times. (Two people may travel between Oct. 1st and March 31st)

EURAIL YOUTHPASS* – 2nd Class

❑ 15 Days $398   ❑ 2 Months $768
❑ 1 Month $578

EURAIL YOUTH FLEXIPASS* – 2nd Class

❑ 5 Days in 2 Months $255
❑ 10 Days in 2 Months $398
❑ 15 Days in 2 Months $540
*Pass holder must be under age 26 on first day of use.

EURAIL DRIVE PASS

There is an excellent Rail/Drive program that combines a Eurail Pass with Hertz or Avis Rent-a-Car. Call us for a comprehensive brochure.

EUROPASS (5 Countries)
France / Germany / Italy /
Switzerland / Spain

3 COUNTRIES EUROPASS – 1st Class

❑ 5 Days in 2 Months $280
❑ 6 Days in 2 Months $318
❑ 7 Days in 2 Months $356

4 COUNTRIES EUROPASS – 1st Class

❑ 8 Days in 2 Months $394
❑ 9 Days in 2 Months $432
❑ 10 Days in 2 Months $470

5 COUNTRIES EUROPASS – 1st Class

❑ 11 Days in 2 Months $508
❑ 12 Days in 2 Months $546
❑ 13 Days in 2 Months $584
❑ 14 Days in 2 Months $622
❑ 15 Days in 2 Months $660
Note: You must specify the countries when ordering and the countries must border each other, e.g. Spain/France/Italy.

EUROPASS ASSOCIATE COUNTRIES

These countries may be added to any EuroPass for a flat charge per country. They expand the geographic scope of the pass, not the length.
❑ Austria $35   ❑ Portugal $22
❑ Belgium & Luxembourg $22
Youth rates – All EuroPasses are available for persons under age 26 in 2nd class at substantial discounts. Call!

(Continued on next page)

POINT-TO-POINT TICKETS, SLEEPERS, RESERVATIONS, GROUP RATES
(10 or more, 25 or more) – we can help you with all of these. Call for rates.

ORDER FORM
European Country & Regional Passes

AUSTRIA RABBIT CARD
Any 4 Days in   ❑ $153 1st Class
10 Days   ❑ $103 2nd Class

CENTRAL EUROPE PASS ■
Travel in Germany, Poland, Czech
Republic and Slovakia
Any 8 Days in 1 Month   ❑ $348 1st Class

CZECH FLEXIPASS
Any 5 Days in 15 Days   ❑ $69 1st Class

EUROPEAN EAST PASS
Travel in Austria, Hungary, Poland,
Czech Republic and Slovakia
Any 5 Days in 15 Days   ❑ $185 1st Class
Any 10 Days in 1 Month   ❑ $299 1st Class

FINNRAIL PASS
	1st Class	2nd Class
3 Days in 1 Month	❑ $125	❑ $85
5 Days in 1 Month	❑ $169	❑ $115
10 Days in 1 Month	❑ $239	❑ $159

FRANCE RAILPASS
	1st Class	2nd Class
3 Days in 1 Month	❑ $180	❑ $125
Add'l Rail Days	❑ $39	❑ $29
(6 max)		

France offers a comprehensive series of
*Rail 'n Drive, Rail 'n Fly * Fly Rail 'n Drive*
passes. Ask for our free catalog.

GERMAN RAILPASS – Adult
Validity	1st Class/Twin*	2nd Class/Twin*
5 Days in 1 Month	❑ $260/$234	❑ $178/$160
10 Days in 1 Month	❑ $410/$369	❑ $286/$257
15 Days in 1 Month	❑ $530/$477	❑ $368/$331

**Twin: Price valid when 2 people traveling
together.*

HUNGARIAN RAILPASS
Any 5 Days in 15   ❑ $55 1st Class

POLRAIL PASS
Unlimited travel in Poland
	1st Class	2nd Class
8 Days	❑ $59	❑ $40

ITALIAN RAILPASS
Please add a $10 admin. fee to the cost
of each Italian pass/non-refundable
	1st Class	2nd Class
8 Days	❑ $226	❑ $152
15 Days	❑ $284	❑ $190
21 Days	❑ $330	❑ $220
1 Month	❑ $396	❑ $264

ITALIAN FLEXI RAILCARD
	1st Class	2nd Class
Any 4 Days in 9	❑ $170	❑ $116
Any 8 Days in 21	❑ $250	❑ $164
Any 12 Days in 30	❑ $314	❑ $210

PORTUGUESE RAILPASS
Any 4 Days in 15 ❑ $99 First Class

PRAGUE EXCURSION PASS ■
From any Czech Republic border crossing
to Prague and return First Class
❑ $49 Adult   ❑ $39 Youth   ❑ $25 Child

SCANRAIL PASS
	1st Class	2nd Class
Any 4 Days in 15	❑ $199	❑ $159
Any 9 Days in 21	❑ $339	❑ $275
1 Month	❑ $499	❑ $399

Call for Youth and ScanRail 55+ Senior rates

SPAIN FLEXIPASS
	1st Class	2nd Class
Any 3 Days in 1 Month	❑ $185	❑ $145
Any 5 Days in 1 Month	❑ $265	❑ $225
Any 10 Days in 2 Months	❑ $470	❑ $345

SWISS PASS
Good on Swiss National Railroads,
most private railroads, lake steamers
city transport, buses and aerial tramways.
	1st Class	2nd Class
8 Days	❑ $266	❑ $186
15 Days	❑ $312	❑ $214
1 Month	❑ $430	❑ $296

SWISS FLEXIPASS
	1st Class	2nd Class
Any 3 Days in 15	❑ $222	❑ $148

SHIPPING There is a $7.50 minimum shipping charge for all orders. We ship by 2nd Day/AIR UPS. Rush service with overnight delivery is available at a charge of $25.
■ ADMINISTRATIVE FEE $10 for your total order (one pass or several) is assessed by the European Railroads where you see this symbol. RAIL/DRIVE Programs are available for most countries. Call for rates and free brochures.

INDEX OF PLACE NAMES

326

Other Rail Guides published by Bradt

Australia by Rail by Colin Taylor
Practical and readable information for holders of the Austrail Pass.

Eastern Europe by Rail by Rob Dodson
A practical guide to the areas of eastern Europe which are now covered by a rail pass: Poland, The Czech Republic, Slovakia, Hungary, Romania, Bulgaria and eastern Germany.

India by Rail by Royston Ellis
The second edition of this highly praised guide. 'A practical planner and fuel for the finest kind of armchair fantasy...' *The Times*

Mexico by Rail by Gary A Poole
An indispensable companion to travelling in Mexico, with itineraries, history, walking tours, and what to see in each region.

Sri Lanka by Rail by Royston Ellis
A complete guide to Sri Lanka, featuring railway journeys throughout the island, including a spectacular 12-hour trip into the hill country, and incorporating cultural information and details of how to get to places of interest not served by the railways.

Switzerland by Rail by Anthony Lambert
Due 1995.

Thailand, Malaysia & Singapore by Rail by Brian McPhee
How and where to travel by rail in these popular countries, giving the opportunity to see parts not reached by other forms of transport.

USA by Rail by John Pitt
28 long-distance train journeys, featuring outstanding sites along the route and the main towns or places of interest where the journey may be broken.

For a catalogue of these and other guides to unusual places, contact Bradt Publications, 41 Nortoft Road, Chalfont St Peter, Bucks SL9 0LA, England. Tel/fax: 0494 873478.